THE VICTORIAN SCENE

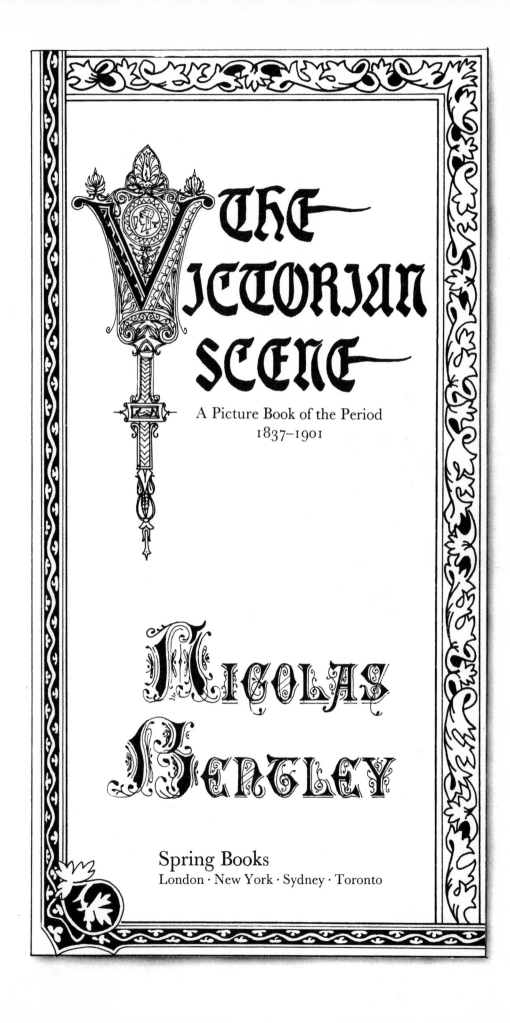

THE VICTORIAN SCENE

A Picture Book of the Period
1837–1901

NICOLAS BENTLEY

Spring Books
London · New York · Sydney · Toronto

Original edition published 1968 by
George Weidenfeld and Nicolson Ltd, London

© 1968 by Nicolas Bentley
Designed by Bruce Robertson
Decorative headings by David Gibbons
Picture research by Gay Weber and Morwenna Jones

This edition published 1971 by
The Hamlyn Publishing Group Limited
London · New York · Sydney · Toronto
Hamlyn House, Feltham, Middlesex, England

Text and illustrations printed in Great Britain by
Jarrold & Sons Ltd, Norwich

ISBN 0 600 39119 1

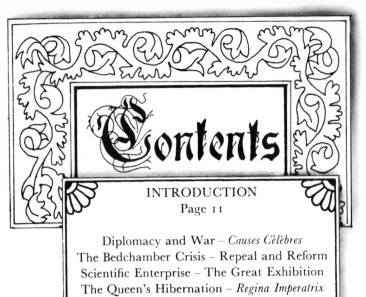

Contents

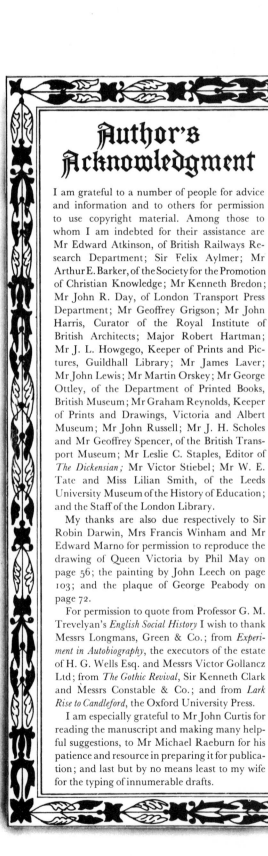

Author's Acknowledgment

I am grateful to a number of people for advice and information and to others for permission to use copyright material. Among those to whom I am indebted for their assistance are Mr Edward Atkinson, of British Railways Research Department; Sir Felix Aylmer; Mr Arthur E. Barker, of the Society for the Promotion of Christian Knowledge; Mr Kenneth Bredon; Mr John R. Day, of London Transport Press Department; Mr Geoffrey Grigson; Mr John Harris, Curator of the Royal Institute of British Architects; Major Robert Hartman; Mr J. L. Howgego, Keeper of Prints and Pictures, Guildhall Library; Mr James Laver; Mr John Lewis; Mr Martin Orskey; Mr George Ottley, of the Department of Printed Books, British Museum; Mr Graham Reynolds, Keeper of Prints and Drawings, Victoria and Albert Museum; Mr John Russell; Mr J. H. Scholes and Mr Geoffrey Spencer, of the British Transport Museum; Mr Leslie C. Staples, Editor of *The Dickensian;* Mr Victor Stiebel; Mr W. E. Tate and Miss Lilian Smith, of the Leeds University Museum of the History of Education; and the Staff of the London Library.

My thanks are also due respectively to Sir Robin Darwin, Mrs Francis Winham and Mr Edward Marno for permission to reproduce the drawing of Queen Victoria by Phil May on page 56; the painting by John Leech on page 103; and the plaque of George Peabody on page 72.

For permission to quote from Professor G. M. Trevelyan's *English Social History* I wish to thank Messrs Longmans, Green & Co.; from *Experiment in Autobiography*, the executors of the estate of H. G. Wells Esq. and Messrs Victor Gollancz Ltd; from *The Gothic Revival*, Sir Kenneth Clark and Messrs Constable & Co.; and from *Lark Rise to Candleford*, the Oxford University Press.

I am especially grateful to Mr John Curtis for reading the manuscript and making many helpful suggestions, to Mr Michael Raeburn for his patience and resource in preparing it for publication; and last but by no means least to my wife for the typing of innumerable drafts.

Introduction

It was said long ago by Augustine Birrell, an eminent though unjustly neglected Victorian, that 'history is a pageant, not a philosophy'. There are philosophies of history, of course. There are even those who read them. So it had better be said at once that this reconnaissance of the Victorian era, or rather, of its social scene, is not meant for the instruction of such earnest minds. It is meant for those who prefer history in the form of a pageant. In fact, to call it history at all would be to give it a dignity of purpose to which it does not aspire. Its aim is simply to entertain. Even so, some of the hazards of the historian remain. Professor G. M. Trevelyan in his *English Social History* remarks on the difficulties of writing about the social as distinct from the political scene. The trouble is 'the absence of determining events and positive dates by which the course of things can be charted'. Certainly this is a handicap, and it is the reason why no attempt has been made here to try and chart a course. All that has been done is to try and show the pattern of the wind upon the waters.

The reign of Queen Victoria was by far the longest of any English sovereign. It was on 20 June 1837, that the Queen came to the throne. She died on 22 January 1901, just sixty-three years and six months after her accession. The era that came to bear her name was an era of radical changes in the pattern of existence, of changes in thought and behaviour, and in moral and intellectual attitudes. There were fundamental changes, too, in the spheres of politics and diplomacy. In politics these changes meant that the corruption and nepotism of the preceding age were gradually superseded by a system which, as politics go, was relatively honest and efficient. In diplomacy it was a period of more or less constant activity, of conferences, treaties and exchanges with France, Prussia, Russia, Italy, Denmark, Turkey, Portugal and other countries. In spite of this, and even while the tide of prosperity and expansion rose, it was also an age of war. We have become so used to looking at the Victorian era through the complacent spectacles of writers like Thackeray and Trollope, or with the rational gaze of George Eliot, or the ironic glance of Dickens or Peacock, that we are inclined to forget its more belligerent aspects. Yet during almost the whole of the Queen's reign British soldiers were to be found fighting somewhere overseas.

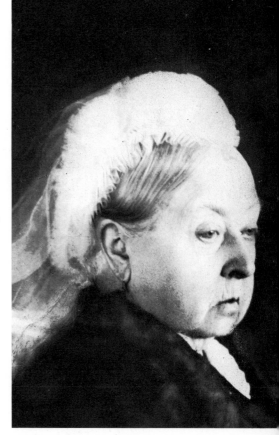

One of the last photographs to be taken of Her Majesty the Queen.

OPPOSITE: Her Royal Highness the Princess Victoria, aged eighteen; from a drawing by R. J. Lane. A month after this drawing was published the Princess had become Queen.

Within five years of her accession war broke out in Afghanistan. Six years later fighting started in the Punjab. In 1852 (and again in 1885) there was trouble in Burma. In 1854 came the Crimean War, which was followed three years later by the Indian Mutiny. In 1873 (and 1895) there was war in Ashanti, which is now part of Ghana, and in 1879 in Zululand, now within the Republic of South Africa. In 1899 came the Boer War, and two years later the Boxer rising against foreigners in China. To this grim catalogue must be added frequent skirmishes in various parts of India, Egypt and Africa.

But it is not with war, or with politics, or with diplomacy that we are concerned here. It is with the peaceable lives of the Queen's subjects at home. The doings of generals, politicians and diplomats, if they are mentioned at all, are mentioned only to throw light on those peaceable lives. Even the Queen herself takes a back seat for once; a seat suitably elevated, of course, but from which, without having to peer too closely, she should be able to get some impression of the vigour and vitality, as well as the pleasures and pains, of her subjects' day-to-day existence.

ABOVE: The Queen's Coronation in June 1838 brought with it a flood of *imagerie populaire*, crude votive offerings of an idealised sovereign.
OPPOSITE: The use of the Queen's image in advertising was not confined to the Coronation or to alcoholic beverages.

ABOVE: Salt-glazed stoneware bottles filled with wine or liquor, in innumerable shapes and ranging in capacity from a tumbler to a quart, were offered for sale by vintners, brewers and distillers, combining their humble duty with an eye to the main chance.

LEFT: A statuette in vivid Staffordshire pottery showing the Queen in her crown and robes.

Let the reader, as the Victorians were so fond of saying in their omnipotent way – let the reader imagine himself seated by the Queen's side, perhaps on one of those over-stuffed, richly brocaded fauteuils on which many a member of her court, stiff with boredom and humble duty, must have prayed for those long evenings at Windsor or Buckingham Palace to come to an end. Let him share with Her Majesty this glimpse into the social life of her epoch. And let him remember, as he looks upon the scene, how long was the Queen's reign and how strange and startling must have seemed the traffics and discoveries which it encompassed.

Some of these, which then loomed large as life, have long since been forgotten; the Maynooth grant in 1845, for example, which gave financial aid to an Irish Catholic college and umbrage to many a choleric Protestant. Or the question of the Spanish marriages, that long-drawn-out and undignified imbroglio in which, for political reasons, England and France jockeyed for positions from which to influence the marriage of the Queen of Spain, a girl of sixteen. Other things, then of immense importance or concern, now evoke little more than the recollection of a name or a phrase – Disestablishment, the *Trent* affair, Home Rule, Majuba, Peace with Honour, *Goodbye, Dolly Gray*. Yet each at the time stood for something that aroused throughout the nation feelings of hope or dismay, of suspicion or relief, or created deep-seated crises of conscience. Perhaps a reminder of some of the more significant events that happened during the Queen's reign will help to put into perspective the ideas and occurrences discussed in later chapters.

Hindsight gives the historian a number of advantages, among them a sense of proportion. Political issues that once inflamed the conscience and rhetoric of opposing factions are cut down to size. To the early Victorians the parliamentary passions and conflicts of the period seemed like a struggle with destiny. Yet the truth is that politically speaking the first decade of the Victorian era was comparatively uneventful. In 1837, the year of the Queen's accession, there were demonstrations in Canada against United Kingdom rule, but these outbreaks were easily, if harshly, suppressed. In the following year there were the Chartist riots, when mobs up and down the country demanded – without success – electoral reforms.

In 1839 the Bedchamber Crisis gave the Queen's ministers an indication of that streak of obstinacy in her character which some of their successors were to find so trying. The Queen, still inexperienced in constitutional matters, forced the relationship between Crown and State into what might have been a dangerous impasse. In that year, Lord Melbourne, Prime Minister since the Queen's accession, resigned; the confidence of his supporters having wilted, or so he thought. His relationship with the Queen had become almost avuncular, her trust in him the trust almost of a devoted niece. The prospect of no longer having her 'good Melbourne' to help and advise her filled the Queen with horrid apprehensions. She burst into tears, then, with characteristic obedience to the promptings of duty, dried her eyes and sent for Sir Robert Peel, the leader of the Opposition. Sir Robert was stiff in his manners and opinions and was as unsympathetic to the young Queen as Melbourne had been congenial. He explained to the Queen that in order to give her unqualified support to the Government he intended to form, the principal ladies of the royal household, Whigs to a woman, should be invited to retire in favour of an entourage sympathetic to the Tories. The Queen flatly refused to yield up even a lady-in-waiting. Sir Robert likewise remained his adamantine self. An irresistible force had met an immovable object. For once this interesting problem in dynamics was to find a solution. Politely but firmly Sir Robert refused to form a government unless his stipulation was agreed to. The Queen appealed to Melbourne, who sounded members of his former cabinet. Lord Palmerston, the ex-Foreign Secretary and the rogue elephant of Victorian politics, would have no truck with the rights or wrongs of the case, but treated it simply as a matter of personal loyalty to the Queen and was supported in this view by other members. It was by their conduct as gentlemen, not as politicians, that posterity would judge their actions, and their plain duty was to stand by the Queen. Melbourne, as was his habit, bowed gracefully to the inevitable and agreed to carry on.

It sounds like a storm in a teacup. But the significance of the Bedchamber Crisis lies not so much in the issue at stake as in the evident signs it gave of the Queen's character and the lengths to which she was prepared to go in order to get her own way. It is safe to assume that this was not lost on aspiring politicians such as young Mr Disraeli, who had entered the House of Commons in the year of the Queen's accession, and Mr Gladstone who, although younger, had held office in Sir Robert Peel's first administration in 1835. Neither could have failed to appreciate that the sovereign whom they might yet be required to serve was a woman of exceptional determination and self-assurance. Time was to show them and the nation the advantages and drawbacks of these formidable qualities.

By far the most eventful happening of the early years of the Queen's reign was the repeal of the Corn Laws. During Lord Melbourne's administration there were some minor political crises, but no radical departures from the *status quo*. The defeat of the

The young Mr Disraeli; from a drawing by Daniel Maclise.

Whigs in 1841, two years after the Bedchamber Crisis, meant the replacement of the Queen's 'dearest kind Lord Melbourne' by the Tories, still led by Sir Robert Peel, then regarded by the Queen as 'a low hypocrite', but by the time he died, a trusted friend who 'could less be spared than any other human being'. Under Sir Robert, the fateful decision to repeal the Corn Laws was taken by Parliament in 1846. Briefly, the effect of their repeal was to transform British agriculture, for long a protected industry, into one dependent on the machinery of free trade. In the words of Disraeli's biographers, Moneypenny and Buckle: 'The repeal of the Corn Laws was the first decisive step in that policy of sacrificing the rural life of England to a one-sided and exaggerated industrial development which has done so much to change the English character and the English outlook.' It was, of course, a painful decision for the Tories to have to take, though perhaps not quite so ill-omened as it seemed to the apprehensive Moneypenny and the dubious Buckle. The Tories had always been the advocates of Free Trade, but were converted to the policy of protection by a fear of famine and the ruin of the agricultural system. Both inside and outside Parliament echoes of their change of heart were to reverberate loud and long down the perspective of the Queen's reign in arguments over the question of Free Trade versus Protection.

Equal in the passions it aroused and, in the long run, even greater in significance, was the question of electoral reform. No parliamentary measure of the Victorian era produced more vital effects than the Second Reform Bill of 1867. The first, passed just five years before the Queen's accession, had enfranchised most of the middle class. It had also infuriated many people at opposite ends of the social scale: at one end the parasitic élite and the well-to-do commercial community, who saw Reform as the thin end of a democratic wedge; at the other, the working man, whom the Bill left without a vote. The Second Reform Bill was to relieve his discontent. It gave the vote to most factory workers, thereby doubling the size of the electorate and once more whipping up the fears of the leisured and the merchant classes. A third bill, passed in 1885, completed their discomfort by extending the vote to those workers whom the two previous bills had excluded.

To electoral reform and repeal of the Corn Laws must be added a third factor of vital significance to the Victorian populace. This was the railway boom, which was gradually to sweep away the coaching system, perhaps the most efficient of its kind in Europe, and not only to transform the travelling habits of the entire population, but to leave its mark, as Michael Robbins says in *The Railway Age*, 'on the

The Queen's Coronation in Westminster Abbey on 28 June 1838 was an exhausting ordeal. The ceremony began soon after half-past eleven and did not end until nearly six o'clock in the evening. Despite this the Queen, in her own words, 'came home . . . really *not* feeling tired', and added, 'I shall ever remember this day as the *proudest* of my life!' This picture of the event was painted by John Martin.

A few months after her accession the Queen paid an official visit to Brighton, where she stayed at the Marine (now the Royal) Pavilion, her uncle George IV's oriental caprice. 'A strange, odd Chinese looking thing', was how she described it, from which she could 'only see a little morsel of the *sea*'; detail from a sketch by I. Caldwell.

physical landscape, on social organisation, on political groupings. . . .' When the Queen came to the throne the total length of railway track in England amounted to barely five hundred and forty miles, but already the great trunk lines that still form the backbone of the railway system were being established. Within ten years there were more than three thousand miles of track, and long before the end of the Queen's reign the system had spread its steel tentacles and cindery residue across the length and breadth of the land.

A factor of incalculable importance in establishing the strength of Britain's commercial position overseas was the dynamic effect of the railway boom on trade and industry and on the speed of communications. Early in the Queen's reign their speed had been given a boost by a new-fangled device, the electric telegraph. The first long-distance line in England, between London and Portsmouth, had been inaugurated in 1830 with an experimental transmission. An account of the affair in Bogue's *Anecdotes of the Electric Telegraph* reminds us that, in spite of life's increasing dependence on scientific aids, that incalculable gremlin, the human factor, can never be left entirely out of account. On the day of the experiment:

The signal was given at the Vauxhall terminus, and every eye was fixed upon the needle; but the signal was not answered; it was repeated, but with the same want of success; it was tried a third time: at last the needle began to move, and the letters they signalled were, 'Fast asleep by the fire', which indicated the condition of the clerk, whose drowsiness had, for a time, caused no little mortification to the experimenters.

The Tower Subway, now closed, runs for a quarter of a mile beneath the Thames between Tower Hill and Bermondsey. Built to reduce pedestrian traffic jams, its construction in the 'seventies was regarded as a miracle of engineering.

The Queen's first Privy Council, held at Kensington Palace on the morning of her accession, 20 June 1837. Although Sir David Wilkie's painting shows the Queen wearing a white dress, she was in fact in deep mourning.

FAR LEFT: Viscount Melbourne, who for the first four years of the Queen's reign combined the office of Prime Minister with the role of confidential friend and adviser.

LEFT: Sir Robert Peel, the Queen's second Prime Minister. Misled by his aloof manner, the Queen at first detested Peel, but later grew to like and admire him.

OPPOSITE: The House of Lords debating Home Rule for Ireland, 9 September 1893. By an overwhelming majority their lordships rejected the bill advocating the measure, and thereby bequeathed to England a legacy of hatred and frustration that was to poison Anglo–Irish relations for many years.

Viscount Palmerston, the high-handed and erratic *enfant terrible* of successive administrations, who became Prime Minister in 1855 at the age of seventy.

William Ewart Gladstone, pious, inflexible and oracular, four times Prime Minister, on the last occasion at the age of eighty-two.

Benjamin Disraeli, Earl of Beaconsfield, the wily, sarcastic and life-long opponent of Gladstone, became Prime Minister twice.

ABOVE: An extension of the franchise and reform of the Poor Law were among the aims of the Chartist movement, which at the beginning of the Queen's reign affrighted many who saw the movement as the thin end of a democratic wedge. In 1839, in 1842, and again in 1848, Chartist petitions were presented to Parliament, but with little effect. The illustrations show (LEFT TO RIGHT) 'T. Duncombe, Esq: presenting the Petition'; 'Procession attending the Great National Petition of 3,317,702 to the House of Commons'; and 'Members of the National Convention'.

LEFT: Behind the agitation for the repeal of the Corn Laws lay fears of famine and agricultural distress. The poor, dismayed at the rising price of bread, flocked in their thousands to sign Anti-Corn Law petitions.

Gladstone, the Grand Old Man of Victorian politics, found in forestry a congenial alternative to chopping down his opponents in the House of Commons.

Prince Albert at the age of twenty;
from a miniature by Sir William Ross.

The Prince Consort; engraved from a photograph, c.1860, by Oscar G. Reylander.

OPPOSITE: A popular exhibit at the Great Exhibition was this carved walnut chair inset with a porcelain plaque of the Prince, after a portrait, also by Sir William Ross, painted at the time of the Prince's marriage.

The first test of the telegraph as a vital channel of government communication came with the Crimean War, when messages that would previously have taken ten days to arrive from headquarters at Balaklava were received in London in twenty-four hours. In view of the attitude that the War Office adopted in its conduct of the campaign, the uses to which it put the telegraph hardly seem surprising. By the French it was used for technical instruction and urgent advice; by the British to enquire about the health of Captain Jarvis who, sad to say, had been bitten by a centipede, and for a discussion on whether beards were an advantage to deserters, of whom the numbers were infinitesimal.

In the whole of the Queen's reign there was no greater disaster than the Crimean War (except the Irish famine of 1844, in which nearly a million people died). The war began in September 1854 and dragged on to an inglorious peace eighteen months later. The British and French forces, fighting more than two thousand miles from home, were supported by contingents of the Turkish and Sardinian armies. Opposed to the Allies were incalculable masses of stubborn, well-equipped Russian soldiers, yet it was they who were eventually forced to give up the struggle. From the beginning to the end, it was for the British army the old story, the moral of which we seem as a nation to have some difficulty in learning – too little and too late. The callous ineptitude of the Government, led by Lord Aberdeen until the outcry from a shocked and anxious public forced him to quit, caused far greater casualties and suffering than were inflicted by the Russians. To this humiliation was added that of watching the triumphs of the French and the knowledge of our repeated failures to give them proper support. Yet the guts and heroism of the British Army at the Alma, at Inkerman, and before Sebastopol have never been surpassed. The trouble was the incompetence and snobbish folly of those at the War Office in giving preference to social status over worth and experience in the choice of commanders. The war was a savage rebuff to Victorian pride and self-confidence and the lessons of the campaign were dearly bought. Yet, sixty years later, as the Queen's nephew, Kaiser Wilhelm, was then to discover, they had largely been forgotten.

The causes of the Crimean War are obscured in a jumble of religious, economic and nationalist motives. The pot had long been on the boil, yet only three years before the war began, the Victorian vision of peace and prosperity had never seemed more substantial. 1851 was the year of the Great Exhibition, the precocious foster-child of a doting parent, Prince Albert. Under his approving gaze it was not only to attract the nations of the world to Hyde Park, it was

ABOVE: On 27 February 1854 the Scots Guards left London for the Balkans in anticipation of war in the Crimea, a declaration of which was to follow a month later.

LEFT: The Earl of Aberdeen, who, as Prime Minister, led Britain to humiliation and disaster in the Crimean War.

BELOW: The reading of orders in camp at Balaklava; from a photograph by Roger Fenton.

OPPOSITE: Florence Nightingale at Scutari in Turkey, where in the damp and filthy barrack hospital she battled against death, disease, and the obstructive tactics of the War Department. This detail is from a painting by Jerry Barrett.

THE
GREAT EXHIBITION QUADRILLE.

COMPOSED
BY
JULLIEN.

DUETTS. 4/
SEPTUOR. 4/
FULL ORCHESTRA 3/6
MILITARY BAND. 5/-
10/6

ENT. STA HALL

LONDON, PUBLISHED BY JULLIEN & Cº AT THE ROYAL MUSICAL CONSERVATORY 214, REGENT STREET & 45, KING STREET.

ABOVE: Sir Henry Cole, master-mind of the Great Exhibition, whose vision and capacity, backed by the Prince Consort's enthusiasm, brought a dream to life in the creation of the Crystal Palace.
OPPOSITE: Thousands used their talents, ingenuity, or wits to cash in on the success of the Great Exhibition, among them Jullien, 'the eminent musico'. The popularity of his *Exhibition Quadrille* may be judged by the variety of combinations for which it was scored. These included duet, septet, full orchestra, and military band.

to see them falling over themselves to fill the order-books of British tradesmen and industrialists. To the Queen it was a matter of life-long regret that the inestimable qualities that she saw in her Consort were never fully appreciated. 'It puzzled him, as it puzzled Queen Victoria, that anyone could be at once so good and so little liked.' Thus the painful truth is stated by Christopher Hobhouse in his *1851 and the Crystal Palace*. The formal and Teutonic manners of the Prince put him at a disadvantage with the jocular, insular British. He never managed to become, as the Queen had hoped he would, a popular figure. Indeed, so far as the public was concerned, nothing about him, except his death, caught their interest so much as the Great Exhibition with which he was so closely associated.

Although the Queen maintained that the inspiration was Albert's, and although he was one of the first to be consulted about the idea, the Exhibition was in fact the conception of Henry Cole, a civil servant, who had been much impressed by the Paris Exposition of 1840. Cole decided to try and mount an even more ambitious exhibition to promote British trade. He was a man with a passion for organisation and for getting things done, though whether so much would have been done so successfully without the firm support and hard work of the Prince Consort seems doubtful. Objections to the idea were many and various: the whole thing would be a waste of money; manufacturers would never give it their support; there was nowhere to hold it; not enough visitors would come. Implacably, courteously, the Prince, as President of a Royal Commission appointed to examine the scheme, torpedoed one objection after another. And once plans for the Exhibition had been approved, no obstacle was too formidable for his imagination to overcome, no detail too small for his attention. In the incredibly short space of two years, almost to the day, since he had first been consulted about it, the Exhibition opened its doors.

Its success exceeded even the hopeful vision of Albert himself. When it was over, contrary to the squawks that had been uttered by various birds of ill-omen, there was a surplus of more than £186,000. The Prince suggested, and the Commissioners of the Exhibition agreed, that the money should be spent on furthering opportunities for education. A site of seventy acres was bought – with help from the government – in South Kensington, and there in due course arose the complex of colleges and museums which have helped ever since to feed the imaginations and encourage the skills of students to whom the memory of Albert the Good is as dead as the dodo which gazes with vacuous eye from its case in the Natural History Museum, itself a by-product of the Great Exhibition.

MANCHESTER in 1851

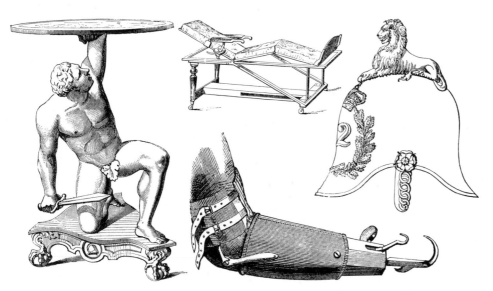

TOP: George Cruikshank's contrasting impressions of Manchester and London, from Henry Mayhew's *The World's Show, 1851*, highlights the vast provincial exodus caused by the magnetic attraction of the Great Exhibition.

LEFT: A few of the more bizarre objects pictured in the Exhibition catalogue: Fletcher's Gladiatorial Table, carved from solid Irish oak; Minter's Invalid Carriage, 'capable of adjustment . . . without the removal of the patient'; Landon & Moreland's improved Infantry Helmet in papier mâché; and Major Little's apparatus 'contrived to meet the loss of the right hand'.

OPPOSITE: The royal family at the opening of the Exhibition on 1 May 1851.

One of the smaller objects shown at the Great Exhibition, Messrs Roberts & Halls' Registered Toast Rack in silver plate. The ribs are emblematic of wheat-ears.

CENTRE LEFT: In the Baroque taste, 'a looking-glass and console table ornamented in gilt'; from a design by Charles M'Lean.

CENTRE RIGHT: The South Transept of the Crystal Palace, unfurnished. The architect, Joseph Paxton, drew on experience gained in planning the huge conservatories at Chatsworth, the Duke of Devonshire's estate in Derbyshire.

FAR RIGHT: The design of the Crystal Palace, combining efficiency with elegance, was the obvious model for the Exhibition of 1862, built in South Kensington where the Natural History and Geological Museums now stand. Although it was larger than the Great Exhibition and attracted more visitors, it was financially far less successful.

BELOW: The West Nave of the 1851 Exhibition, where United Kingdom manufactured goods were shown.

The death of the Prince Consort in 1861 was an abrupt turning point in the Queen's life and in her relationship with her people. The Queen was a woman of obstinate prejudice, with a built-in conviction of the divine right of queens. Yet as time went on she came to depend more and more on Albert's judgment and advice – perhaps not always consciously – and on his steadying and sagacious influence. Not till these comfortable props were knocked away in untimely fashion, launching her down a slipway of prolonged grief into the chilly waters of a self-imposed isolation, did she realise the extent to which she had come to rely on him in matters both great and small. The Prince's death left her stunned; and stunned she decided to remain. She withdrew from public life, partly perhaps to protect herself from the trials and vexations of affairs of state which she did not feel equal to coping with alone; partly through an illusion, not uncommon in public personages, that she was too often and too heavily put upon. Her seclusion, and with it an increasing unpopularity with the public, lasted for almost fifteen years, until under Disraeli's skilful stage-management she emerged from her long, neurotic hibernation. Many had tried and failed to purge the Queen's melancholy and tempt her back into public life. It is one of the ironies of history that it should have fallen to the unlikely lot of an elderly and sycophantic Jewish dandy to succeed.

But history abounds in ironies, as it also abounds in paradoxes. Some are cruel, some just, some merely comic. It is the paradox of Queen Victoria's place in history that as a reflection of the era to which she gave her name, her image is decidedly out of focus. It is beside the point, however tempting, to speculate on what sort of person she might have become if greatness had not thrust itself upon her at so early an age. There are some signs that under the influence of a consort less sedate, less earnest and more worldly than Albert, she might have developed into a different and in some ways more likeable woman. The pity is that she and Lord Melbourne were not more of an age. The period of his tutelage came too late for him to teach, or her to learn, much more than the ambiguous art of being a constitutional sovereign. By the time she came to the throne there was not much left of the zest of Melbourne's earlier years, and Peel's influence, when he became Prime Minister, was hardly calculated to add to the gaiety of nations; nor were his successors, Russell, Derby and Aberdeen, formed by nature to counteract the influence of Albert's solemnity on his young and dutiful wife. It is not surprising in the circumstances that Victoria, an unsophisticated, headstrong and impressionable girl, became in time solemn, introspective and distrustful of new ideas.

Mementoes of the royal marriage took
an infinite variety of forms.
ABOVE: Three views of a glazed saltware
mug symbolising the loyalty of the
agricultural community.
BELOW: A pair of miniature china busts.

ABOVE: A medallion designed to
commemorate the opening of the Great
Exhibition on 1 May 1851.
OPPOSITE: The Albert Memorial in
Kensington Gardens, designed by Sir
Gilbert Scott and erected in 1876 – a
reminder of zeal and virtue of the much
misunderstood.

In the sobriety of her behaviour, in her industrious habits, in her bourgeoise tastes, and in the fixity of many of her beliefs the Queen was certainly an epitome of her era. But in other and no less important respects, she was not. She gave little or no reflection of its surging enterprise, of its intellectual energy, or its scientific curiosity, and certainly none whatever of its facetious humour.

The period of the Queen's reign coincided with profound changes in national ideals, tastes, and habits. National self-satisfaction blossomed like a giant chrysanthemum, manured by the swift expansion and consolidation of the Empire and Disraeli's magical insolence in transmuting a Queen into an Empress, the final euphoric shot in the arm before the chastening episode of the Boer War. The justice of the motives for which the territories of Empire were acquired or the wisdom of the methods by which they were got hold of were not in dispute, for the Victorians were seldom troubled by doubts about the wisdom or justice of their proceedings. Casuistry is the opiate of conscience and though grammarians may seek to prove that 'empire' has no connection with 'empiricism', the Victorians knew better. The justification for the Empire was that it worked. Not only that; it worked, on the whole, a good deal better than other peoples' empires; the Belgians', for instance, or the Germans'. Disagreeable things have often been said, sometimes with truth, about the actions of the British in their Empire, but on balance the advantages they have brought to most of its former peoples probably outweigh the burdens they imposed upon them in the past.

The more pragmatic as well as the more sanctimonious of the Victorians would certainly have been pleased to think so, and it is easy to think of them as being both. Pragmatists and prigs abounded in Victorian life, as they did in Victorian literature. Mrs Proudie and Mr Pecksniff are more adhesive characters than some we might have preferred to meet, but once in the mind they stick there because they grow too big to be got out.

This mild form of gigantism was a disorder more common in Victorian times than it is in our own. By no stretch of reverence would it be possible nowadays to claim the existence of an élite so large and luminous as that which shed its lustre on Victorian society for over thirty years. Among its members were Acton, Matthew Arnold, Bagehot, Browning, Carlyle, Cobden, Darwin, Dickens, Disraeli, George Eliot, Faraday, Gladstone, Hardy, Huxley, Macaulay, Manning, Mill, Newman, Florence Nightingale, Ruskin, Scott, Tennyson, Thackeray and Trollope. This, though far from being an exhaustive list, may help to explain why the Victorian era is one of such persistent fascination.

OPPOSITE: Periodical works, such as *Heath's Picturesque Annual*, were popular reading throughout the Victorian era. Comprising poetic gems and snippets of history, topography, botany or other innocuous subjects, they made only slight demands on the understanding and were prettified with sentimental illustrations.

A drawing, probably of the Princess Royal, by Queen Victoria, etched by Prince Albert.

Affectious Offering.

Printed by Lefevre & Kohler, 52 Newman St

Flower after flower comes forth in Spring,   Till copse and field in richest bloom

OPPOSITE: The photograph album, in
plush or tooled leather, with a gilt
clasp to ensure the safety of its
treasured contents, was a fixture in
most parlours from the 'seventies
onwards. Here the likeness of a
Victorian *demoiselle* is framed with
eglantine and cineraria entwined,
which, in the language of flowers,
symbolises 'poetry, always delightful'.

The pantheon of Victorian letters
included many deities to whom we still
pay homage, among them (*left to right*)
Sir Walter Scott, George Eliot,
William Makepeace Thackeray, Alfred
Lord Tennyson, Matthew Arnold,
Thomas Carlyle, Robert Browning,
Anthony Trollope and Thomas Hardy.

For thirty years or more after the Queen's death little interest was shown in the Victorians. And even now, as Cyril Connolly has observed, 'no one can mention the Victorians without self-consciousness . . . they are still too near, and everyone is for or against them or determined to be bright and ironical'.

This tendency, fortunately for us, since in the long run history will show where prejudice has marred our judgment, seems at last to be declining. But in the 'twenties it was felt that the Victorians had had their day and inevitably a reaction had set in against many of the things they were thought to stand for – 'a self-satisfaction engendered by the great increase of wealth . . . conscious rectitude and deficient sense of humour; and an unquestioning acceptance of authority and orthodoxy'. Thus are they described in *The Oxford Companion to English Literature*. To this uncompromising catalogue may be added their particular type of sentimentality, which fostered and was fostered by such artificial sentiments as those of the syrup-dipped romances of Mrs Henry Wood and the pseudo-pathos of Little Nell. To Oscar Wilde is attributed the remark that it would be a hard-hearted man who could read of the death of Little Nell without laughing. To later cynics the pathos of the situation may seem to lie in Dickens's admission of his own grief at having to kill off Little Nell. Viewed from the 1920s, the pomposity, the complacence, and the sentimentality of the Victorians seemed not so much ingenuous as slightly absurd. Their art, their literature, except of course for that which was associated with the great names, their clothes, their furniture, in fact their tastes in general were regarded for a long while merely with amused tolerance.

Support for this attitude was given by Lytton Strachey's two famous studies, *Eminent Victorians* and *Queen Victoria*, the first published in 1918 and the second in 1921. Strachey's cynical and detached appraisal of the period was irresistible to the generation of the 'twenties, impatient of the stuffiness, the humbug, the bourgeois sense of values, and the jingoism it had come to associate with the Victorian era. As *The Times* remarked of Strachey, 'he contrived by means which must always delight but cannot always command respect to fix in the twentieth-century mind the conception of the typical Victorian as a verbose hypocrite'. We have had our own share of verbose hypocrites since then, but they have been no more typical of our times than Mr Stiggins or Mr Slope may be considered typical of theirs. The truth is that no such being as a typical Victorian ever existed. Could any two men have been less alike than, for example, Dickens and Ruskin? Or than Carlyle and Disraeli? Or two women than Florence Nightingale and the seductive Cora

Balmoral Castle, Aberdeenshire, the granite snuggery to which the Queen retired as often as the cares of state would allow.

Pearl? Yet each represented in his or her own way the quintessence of Victorian thought or conduct. If they had anything in common, it was not something that can be given a neat historical label; it was something much too amorphous, yet at the same time as incontrovertible as the supreme triumph of Victorian science, the discovery of the origin of species: all of them were members of the Middle Class.

Before the advent of the middle class:

The great world . . . was limited in its proportions, and composed of elements more refined, though far less various. It consisted mainly of the

ABOVE: John Brown, the insolent Scottish retainer to whom the Queen's strange subjection for over thirty years remains a mystery; from a bust by Sir Edgar Boehm.
RIGHT: From time to time the Queen took a short holiday abroad. Here, under a white parasol and the watchful eye of Brown, who acted as a rearguard, she ambles towards the Rochers du Basta at Biarritz.

great landed aristocracy. . . . Occasionally an eminent banker or merchant invested a large portion of his accumulations in land, and in the purchase of Parliamentary influence, and was in time admitted into the Sanctuary. But those vast and successful invasions of society by new classes which have since occurred, though impending, had not yet commenced.

So said Disraeli in *Endymion*.

The Middle Class was born by a process of parthenogenesis. It was the natural, the inevitable child of the Industrial Revolution, which brought into being a whole new species of society. It was a species not rooted in the land, from which the only two classes that existed previously had drawn their livelihoods: it was a species that was dependent for its existence on the hard logic of scientific progress and the dreary precepts of economic doctrine.

It is the essence of a revolution that it should be short and sharp. A revolution that is prolonged loses its impetus; it either collapses or becomes a civil war. The Industrial Revolution was not really a revolution at all, but a process of evolution that gained in power the longer it lasted. In a sense, it may be said to be still going on. The discovery and harnessing of atomic energy are as fundamental to the twentieth-century as those of the power of steam and electricity were to the nineteenth. But if it was not a revolution, its begetters still suffered from the occupational handicap from which most revolutionaries suffer: they could only guess at the ultimate effect of the changes they were trying to initiate. Scientifically, the Victorians of the 'sixties were in much the same state of mind as their descendants a hundred years later. As industry expanded and urban populations grew, steam and gas came to be accepted as part of the natural order of things. But it was as impossible for a mid-Victorian to visualise the changes electricity would eventually bring to the lives of ordinary citizens as it is for those living in the middle of the twentieth century to imagine the full effects of atomic power on a generation not far distant.

Whether the Victorians were really made happier by the changes that science brought into their lives, is difficult to say. It is less difficult to perceive that on the whole they were not made much wiser. War and want persisted, and so did harsh inequalities. To the great unwashed and under-educated working class few substantial changes were noticeable. The enormous gap between their own poverty and the opulence that existed at the other end of the economic scale cast too heavy a shadow over their lives for them to be able to view the effects of scientific developments with an objective eye. Those Victorians who did so sometimes viewed with apprehension the effects of mechanical progress on the lives of the working

OPPOSITE: The gibe attributed to Napoleon about a nation of shopkeepers seemed to the Victorians more of a compliment than a criticism. To get into Society was all very well; to get into Trade was, for the majority, even better.

population. Men like Peel, Cobden and Shaftesbury, though they were politicians, were actuated as much by conscience as by their political principles, for it is the distressing part of politics that one must sometimes choose between the two. For those who were not engaged in politics the problem was simpler: whether to plump for *laissez-faire*, or to concede the moral responsibility that attaches to wealth.

The Victorian middle class did not find it difficult to make up its mind. It was not deeply interested in moral responsibility. It went to church regularly, it prayed, it believed, no doubt quite sincerely, in alternative hereafters. But it did not believe in God exclusively; it also believed in Mammon, and it was the strength of this belief that gave such a powerful impetus to Victorian commerce. It was the age of a kind of optimism unknown in England before or since, an age of unquestioning belief in the idea that all progress was necessarily beneficial. In the common enthusiasm for this proposition it was easy to forget the sacrifices and inequalities, the dislocation of settled lives, and the unyielding demands on defenceless minorities which then, even more than now, were often the price of progress. Professor R. B. Mowat in *The Victorian Age* summarised the attitude of those to whom 'progress' seemed as inevitable a part of life as the natural functions:

It was their belief in progress which chiefly distinguished the Victorians from those of other ages. They did not hold (as many people of the eighteenth century believed of themselves) that they were at the apex of civilisation. . . . They were pleased with their achievements, their rich literature, their scientific discoveries and inventions, their missionary and philanthropic efforts; but they also thought that they could do better, and that subsequent generations would do better still. They took it for granted that there would be 'progress', not just in this or that direction, but generally throughout society. 'Progress' was not a conception of particular improvements, though these were worked for and welcomed, but of an ever further advance towards the divine perfection.

ABOVE: The Earl of Shaftesbury, whose life was spent in combating the abomination of child labour.
RIGHT: Worship of Mammon involved the sacrifice of small children in mines, potteries and factories, or as climbing boys apprenticed to chimney sweeps. Lucky the lad whose master provided more than a minimum of food and bedding.

This utopian faith was more or less universal, though it was naturally to the middle class that it made the strongest appeal, for it was from the middle class that the great Victorian entrepreneurs of industry and commerce came – Bessemer, the steel engineer, Brassey, the public works contractor, Cubitt, the builder, Hudson, the railway king. Such men undoubtedly brought enormous benefits to the public, yet in so doing they began the systematic ruin of the English countryside. Their grubby and gigantic footsteps were the price of progress.

It was a high but inevitable price, and as inevitable is an inclination to think of the Victorians as being concerned mainly with materialistic aims. It cannot be denied that there is some truth in this, yet at the same time the Victorian era was one of enormous intellectual activity. Moral and philosophical controversy flourished; in theory and in practice science made tremendous strides; it was a golden age in English literature, and if in painting and in music it was an age of baser metal, this was because we have never had it in us to excel in either sphere. The reputations of artists like Mulready and Burne-Jones, and of musicians like Balfe and Stanford have not worn well, but the reputations of men such as Darwin, John Stuart Mill and Ruskin have remained very much alive. The reason is partly one of education. The appetite for learning feeds on itself and as a result, interest in science, in economics and in philosophy is even greater now than it was then.

But religion, except in the Roman Catholic church, no longer exerts the powerful influence on our imaginations that it exerted then. It is difficult in the half-atheistic atmosphere of today to realise just how deep and widespread was the preoccupation with religion in those days, how intense the zeal, how sharp the schismatic bickering, and how boring the theological controversy must have been to a great many. Even so subtle and profound an advocate as Newman was not free from the temptation to waffle. As Sir Kenneth Clark remarks in the *Gothic Revival*, 'Too often the prophetic mantle muffles speech, and we search darkly for truth in a broth of words'.

It is the sad dilemma of the truly religious being that the more deeply he becomes concerned with the spiritual plight of man, the further he drifts from the object of his consideration. The monk in his cell, the brahmin in his temple, is about as far removed from the pressures and temptations of existence, and therefore to an understanding of the human problems to which they give rise, as it is possible to get in this fast-shrinking universe. The religious leaders of the Victorian age were far from monastic in their behaviour.

Victorian art appealed by and large to the emotions, not to the intellect. Every picture told a story, to be judged by its moral worth, and was praised or criticised for its surface effects. Landseer's *Stag at Bay* and Burne-Jones's *Mirror of Venus* typified mid-Victorian taste in painting, a taste for obvious sentiment and smooth execution, in short, a taste of honey.

ASSEMBLY ROOMS,

SALISBURY.

FOR TWO DAYS ONLY!

MONDAY and TUESDAY, MAY 19th and 20th,

Afternoons at 3. Evenings at 8 each day. *Carriages at 4.30 and 9.30.*

The Wonderful Talking Machine

EDISON'S LATEST

PHONOGRAPH,

Master of all Languages!
Servant of all Nations!
The Greatest Marvel of Science
and Practical Utility!

Mr. C. R. C. STEYTLER,

Of the Edison Phonograph Company, will exhibit and describe the

Greatest Wonder of the Age,

Edison's Latest Phonograph

OR TALKING MACHINE,

WITH NUMEROUS

REPRODUCTIONS OF VOICES AND MUSIC

Recorded in America and elsewhere.

☞ See Programme on Inside.

IMPORTANT NOTICE.

During the Entertainment, the entire audience will hear repeated by the Talking Machine,

Songs and Musical Selections originally Sung and Played before the Phonograph in the United States and various parts of Great Britain.

This statement may appear incredible to persons who have not had an opportunity of hearing the Machine It is nevertheless strictly correct. This Phonographic Entertainment is the most important and interesting exhibition ever offered to the British Public, and from all the varied points of view of practical utility, scientific triumph, inventive genius, amusement, instruction, wonder, and delight, is absolutely unique.

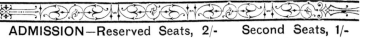

ADMISSION—Reserved Seats, 2/-   Second Seats, 1/-
Back Seats (a Limited Number), SIXPENCE.
Plan may be seen and Seats secured at Aylward & Spinney's Music Saloon, The Canal, Salisbury.

PAUL BROS., Printers. Southampton.]

LEFT: The ideal Victorian amusement was one with which a modicum of instruction was combined. This ideal was fulfilled by the phonograph, which first cackled into the ears of a wondering audience in 1876.

OPPOSITE: Ten years later, another scientific novelty had become all the rage: the stereoscope, a device for giving three-dimensional interest to the showing of camera portraits and holiday views.

OVERLEAF: Much of what was produced in the way of popular literature was cheap and nasty, in which it often reflected life. Twenty years before readers of the Gem Pocket Library were curdling their blood with stories such as *A Bitter Secret* and *Done to Death*, newspaper readers were still being treated to accounts of public executions, like that of Elias Lucas and Mary Reader, hanged at Cambridge on 13 April 1850 for murdering Lucas's wife.

HOGARTH HOUSE GEM POCKET LIBRARY

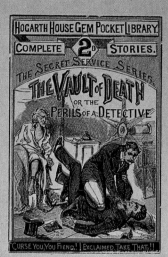

Each Book Contains 128 pp. of New and Original Text, Illustrated.
BOUND IN COLOURED WRAPPER

PRICE TWOPENCE EACH.

TO BE HAD OF ALL BOOKSELLERS EVERYWHERE.

LONDON: HOGARTH HOUSE, BOUVERIE ST.. FLEET ST.

THE DYING WORDS and CONFESSION OF

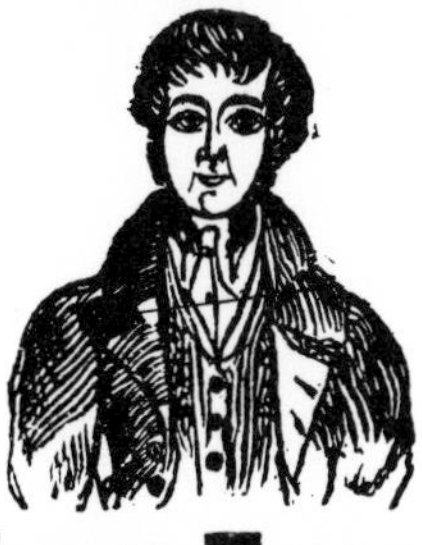

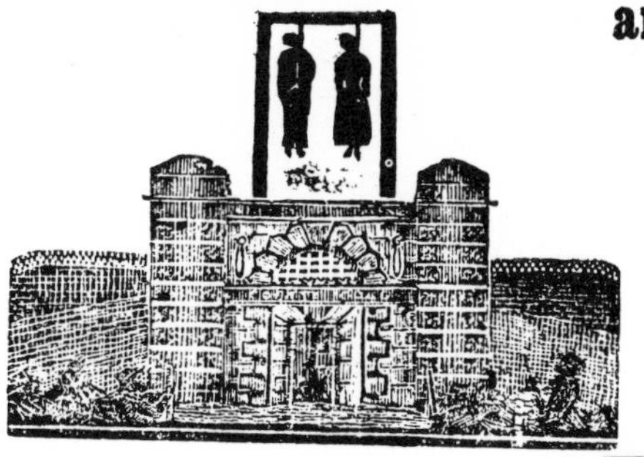

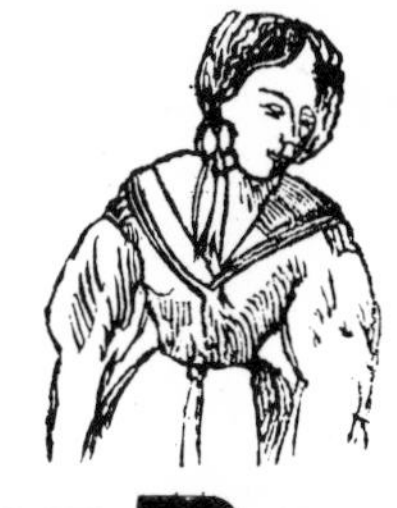

Elias Lucas AND Mary Reader,

Who were Executed this morning (April 13) in front of the County Goal at Cambridge, for the wilful MURDER of SUSAN LUCAS.

LIFE, CHARACTER, &c.

The unhappy beings who this day forfeited their lives to the offended laws of their country were brought up in industrious habits and humble circumstances at Castle Camps, about three miles from Haverhill. Lucas was an agricultural labourer, and lived with his wife at the above named village; his partner in crime was his wife's sister, and his victim the wife herself. Lucas was a strong muscular looking man, about 25 years of age, and up to the time of his committing this foul and unnatural crime, bore an excellent character, and was noted for his easy and cheerful disposition. The female was short and plump, and her features were even & good; the expression of her face bore the marks of innocence; her hands were remarkably white and small; and although stated in the calendar to be 20, she seemed not more than 16. Lucas and his wife had been married between 4 and 5 years, and appeared to have lived on excellent terms. The wife's sister lived as servant in Cambridge, to Mr. Miller, a carpenter, residing in Castle End, not far distant from the scene of her trial and melancholy exit; she continued in his service for a period of 15 months, and left on her own accord towards the end of last year, stating that her chest was bad; her master and mistress found no fault with her, and those who lived in the neighbourhood and had opportunities of judging her conduct and character, state that she appeared a well conducted modest girl, and conld hardly credit the fact that Ann Reeder, the quiet, good looking, and willing girl they knew so well, could have rushed into a crime so horrible in its nature, so frightful in its effects; She shortly afterwards became servant to Mr. Cross, a farmer in Camps, in whose employ was Lucas. Mr. Cross, it seems, entertained some suspicion there was something wrong between Lucas and his sister-in-law; but no suspicion was entertained by Luças's wife, for hearing that Mary Reader again complained of illness, Mrs. Lucas invited her sister to live with her, as by paying her attention she thought she could benefit her. Well was that kindness repaid! Well was the unsuspecting victim requited for her sisterly love! Lucas and Mary Reeder not many days after she became an inmate there, planned the poor creature's death. The former had had unfortunately and thoughtlessly by his employer, some poison entrusted to him destroy or make away with; instead of which he took it home, kept it several months, and at length tutored Mary Reeder to place a portion it in a mess of bread and water, which the unsuspecting wife ate for supper. For an account of the agony the poor creature suffered the reader is referred to the report of the trial which follows, and their blood will curdle with horror as they read from those who witnessed the poor wife's death, and the cold-blooded atrocity with which the crime was perpetrated. It will scarcely be believed that hardened man, as he saw his innocent and unsuspecting victim eating the deadly poison, and expressing a disgust at the taste, it being thoroughly seasoned with arsenic, brutally exclaimed to her complaint, "O dall it, mitress, I'll eat mine if it kills me." The brutal joke was understood by his companion in crime; and on his trial there surely never was greater levity displayed by the most hardened criminal than by this man. He frequently turned to laugh at his companions in court; and even when a tin box was brought into court, which held some part of his wife's stomach and intestines, he laughed right out. A few weeks before her death the prisoner's wife was confined; at the time he made an anxious enquiry whether the child was likely to live, and on the nurse remarking it was a fine healthy child, he seemed displeased, and muttered "he hoped it would die." On other occasions he was heard to express a hope that it might not live. That the child did die shortly after its birth is a matter of fact. Mrs. Lucas had 4 children, but only one survives. Lucas accompanied his wife when she went to be churched after her last confinement; on returning to their cottage he seemed absent in thought, at last he said, "wife I have had bad dreams of late; I have dreamed thrice I shall be either hanged or transported; she bade him banish such thoughts from his mind as only tending to make him miserable. It is but just to the memory of the poor woman to state, that she was a good and affectionate wife. The prisoner had never breathed one word against her, but acknowledged she had been a kind, good-hearted, aud unsuspecting woman; and he acknowledged more—he has admitted that an improper intimacy had existed between himself and Mary Reader, and which commenced last Christmas, and shortly after her leaving Cambridge and taking up her residence at Cambridge; and that being the case the cause of the murder soon suggests itself. Those who knew Lucas by reaiding in the same village, and looked upon him as a well-disposed light-hearted young man, can hardly believe him to be guilty of a crime so wicked and monstrous. He would sing and whistle about his employment, and was as blithe and gay as any of the village rustics with whom he companied. Vice, however, triumphed over the ill-fated young man and young woman.—They have this day met a disgraceful death, convicted of the most atrocious crime, by the hands of the common hangman.

TRIAL and CONVICTION.

Elias Lucas, and Mary Reader, were indicted for the wilful murder of Susan Lucas, by adminstering to her two drachms of arsenic.— Mr. Sanders stated that the prisoners were indicted for the murder of the wife of the male prisoner aud the sister of the female prisoner. Lucas had been married about four years to the sister of the other prisoner, who, having left her service at the house of Mr. Cross, near Castle Camps, where Lucas was also employed as an out-door servant, took up her residence at the house of Lucas about the end of January last. About that time it appeared that the deceased who had given birth to three or four children, had been confined, and had lost her child. In the course of a month, however, she had quite recovered, and was in excellent health on the 21st Feb. On the next day she died—Thomas Reader: I live under the same roof with the prisoners in a double tenement, am uncle to the deceased. I saw the deceased at four o'clock on the 21st. Maria Reeder came to my house next day, and asked me to fetch three penyworth of brandy, for her sister was sick. She gave me the money, and I took it to her. Before I had finished dinner, Maria Reeder called to my wife to come and see her sister, who had fallen out of bed. I went and found the deceased on the floor in the bed room. She was undressed. I helped to put her into bed..—The prisoner Lucas and the deceased seemed to live happily together.—Susan Potter: I was fetched by Thomas Reeder to go to deceased the day she died. She was in bed, and rose up and began to retch violently. She held up her hand, and said, "Elias, go for a doctor." I said so to. He said, "I do, don't I." He left the room immediately· he did not speak to his wife.—Cross examined: He did not stop a minute after she told him to fetch a doctor.—Frederick A. Cramer: I am assistant to Mr. Martin, the surgeon, of Haverhill. On the 22d Feb. Lucas came to me as his wife was dangerously ill.· I went, but before I got there was told she was dead. I went to the house, saw Maria Reader. Reeder said, "Sister had been poorly from disease of the chest, had been subject to it some years; they had given her castor oil morning before," She also said they had a mess of water and bread the evening before. Lucas came in and went out again; he said, "She has been very sick—she had complained very much of pain in her chest." I went up to see body; it was warm. I observed she had died in a state of collapse. The fingers were clenched as a bird's claw. Examined the body, found marks of recent confinement. It was supernaturally blue. The symptoms made me think the woman had died from cholera or poison: I suspected the latter. Something was said about a burial. I said I could not account for the death of deceased, and should not give a certificate to the registrar. Maria Reeder said, "To tell you the truth, she has been a deal worse since the water mess last night, and we all think there was something in it which caused her death. Sister complained that it tasted like lime, and offered me some in a spoon. I tasted it, but finding it like what sister described I spit it out. We gave some to the cat, who had also been ill." She also said that her sister 20 minutes after the mess, went to the front door, and, leaning against the sill, vomited into the garden, saying, "I am a dead woman." She never spoke after. She said she had crumbed the mess, and her sister had poured the water upon it. I asked both prisoners whether they had any poisonous substance in the house; both said, "Not they knew of." Went next day and opened the body. The chest was healthy, except some inflammation. I placed the stomach and part of the intestines in a bladder. Went the next day and completed the examination. Asked Lucas if he had ay arsenic in then house—he said he had told Tilbrook (the constable) he had it—it was on the shelf in the back place—that his mistress had given it him to destroy; he shewed it me, I produce it now as I found it. The parcel weighed 15 ounces. Reeder said arsenic could not have got into the basin by accident, for it was on the opposite end of the shelf." I said it was unfortunate for them that arsenic should have been found in the house. Reeder said, "I call God to witness I am innocent of poisoning my sister, though I am aware the world says to that effect.' Alfred Taylor: I fonnd in the stomach water, mucous fluid, and arsenic. There were two grains of metallic arsenic in the stomach, and from the result of my experiments I am prepared to say that death was produced by arsenic given to the deceased in large quantities. Professor Taylor proved that the substance produced in the parcel was arsenic. Mr. Cross proved at the last wheat sowing he gave Lucas nearly a pound of arsenic to destroy. Mr. Justice Wightman (to the witness); For the future I would advise you to take care how you deal with so dangerous an article as that before you. You should have seen it destroyed yourself, and I would caution you against the passession of so large a quantity. Mary Butterfield, was midwife when Sucan Lucas was confined. Lucas came in two hours after; he said he wished he was not married, and if he had known what he did then he would not have married her if her father had given her a 1000l." I told him not "to say anything then, as it was a difficult time" This was not in the room where is wife was. He afterwards went to her room and said the same to her, I believe. He then came came down and went out to work. I found his wife crying. On the Sunday after he asked me if the child was like to live or die. I said I thought it did not look like a dying child. I went away on Monday. The deceased had a good getting-up. Mary Butterfield: I am the daughter of the last witness. I went to replace my mother. I stayed till the Saturday. Lucas had eight pigs. I used to feed them. He came home one day in the week and," said He thought his pigs grew well, and he would keep the little cad-pig (the least of the lot) till he married again, and have a green leg of pork for his dinner. He said he should marry this Mary Reader, and went into the house. So did I. He told her he would keep this cad-pig till he married her sister. She said," That would never be, for they never would allow him to marry my sister." He said they can't help themselves, if in case I go a little way from home. Ann Ives heard Lucas say he "wished he could rid of his wife." He did not like a married life. Elizabeth Webb heard him say that his wife "was muddled away in a funny manner.—He said when his wife complained of the mess tasting so bad, he said, "mine is good enough" "D—n it I would eat it if it killed me." He gave the remainder of the mess to cat; she ate some and was sick and bad, but did not die." Mary Carlton went to see deceased on the 26th, and saw Maria Reeder in the garden. I was with her father. I aid to him, "Is this poor Susan's sister?" She said, "Yes." I hope you do not think me guilty of taking my poor sister's life?' I said, "I hope you are not—but God only knows, I do not; We then went in, and she said "Elias only came home at 10 o'clock last night, and said my case was worse than his, and I said "No; his was worse 'he got the aasenic.'" I said to her, "Why did you not get a doctor for your poor sister?" She said, "He was her husband though; I was her sister." I said to her afterwards in Susannah Reeder's house, "I heard the poor creature was worked upwards and downwards all night." Maria Reeder said." So she was; if you was to kill me I could not tell you how many times she got up in the night. Not that I know it by seeing her, for I slept at her back at her desire, and slept soundly, and so did Elias." F. Crick.—I went to Mr. Cross's for a sack chaff on the 27th of February. Lucas brought it to me. He said he was in great trouble about his wife. They said she was poisoned, and were agoing to hang him. I said "They cannot hang you if you did not do it," He said that when he wenn he went home he found three water messes, and on his saying he did not like it, his wife said she would put two spoons of sugar in it if he would eat it.." He said then he ate his, and when his wife had half eaten hers she said, "Dear me, Elias, my mess tastes very nasty," and with that "she fished and fished about, and and found a gob of arsenic in it." We were alone then. Next day I went to Haverhill with Mr. Cross and Lucas said, "D—n it, master, I'll stand a bottle of gin if I get off this job, to thiuk that I am a single man again; if the girl and I will keep our counsel they cannot hurt us."

Mr. Couch then addressed the jury on behalf of the prisoners; after which the Learned Judge in a clear and able manner summed up the evidence. The Jury after consulting a short period, returned a verdict—GUILTY against both the prisoners. Mr. Justice Wightman, after putting on the black cap, in a solemn and feeling address passed sentence of DEATH on the culprits, urging upon them the necessity of using the short period of time they had to exist in this world in penitence and prayer, and imploring mercy from that Being whose commandments they had broken, and who alone can pardon their transgression.

On hearing sentence pronounced, Lucas (who had conducted himself throughout the trial with the greatest levity) waived his hands, vociferating, "I am not guilty, good bye, ladies and genlemen, I am innocent."

CONFESSION.

However marked by levity and unconcern the conduct of Lucas during his trial, his deportment after his condemnation underweut a salutary change. Both of these young and unhappy people shortly after leaving the Court became fully sensible of the awful condition their crimes had placed them in, and appeared at once to make up their minds to meet the ignominious punishment that awaited them with penitence and contrition On finding their fate was inevitable, they both became attentive to their religious duties, and appeared frequently to engage earnestly in prayer—Lucas expressing his sanguine hope and confidence that the Almighty would forgive the crimes he had committed through earnest supplication and repentant prayer. Mary Raeder the night after her conviction fully confessed the part she took in the horrible transaction through which herself and her companion in guilt were now about to suffer. She stated, that persuaded by Lucas, she crummed the messes, and, unseen by her sister, conveyed nearly a table-spoon full of arsenic into the bason intended for Mrs. Lucas; but that she now bitterly lamented having been led to commit so great a crime. Lucas for some time persisted in his innocence, and declared that it was not his hand that placed the deadly poison in the basin; but when told of the female's confession—that she had done the act under his direction, he remained silent and appeared quite confounded. He has subsequently confessed to Mr. Orridge, as well those attending upon him in his cell, his participation in and guilty knowledge of the murder. He frequently expressed that he deserved to die, and the sooner the time arrived for his quitting this world the better—and that he felt great hope by praying to his Maker he should be forgiven.

The Condemned Sermon preached on Sunday by the Rev. Mr. Roberts, (in the absence of Mr. Ventris, unable to attend through indisposition) appeared to make a great impression upon both the unhappy culprits. They listened with deep and sorrowful attention to the Rev. gentleman's feeling and admonitory address, and seemed deeply affected throughout the whole of the service.

On Monday the female prisoner was again visited by her father, accompanied by her grandfather, who was much affected at parting. in bidding a last farewell to their wretched and unfortunate offspring. The final parting with her relatives was harrowing in the extreme.

Both the culprits previous to their death acknowledged the justice of their sentence; Lucas frequently repeating, "I deserve to be hanged," "I brought it on myself." Not alone did the wretched man confess the criminal intercourse which had existed between them, but within the last few days his companion in guilt made no scruple in acknowledging that it was that infamous passion which induced her to commit so foul a deed as the murder of an unsuspecting, affectionate, and kind-hearted sister.

The female prisoner a short time before her death (contrary to her former statements) persisted in declaring that Reeder was not aware of her intention to take the life of her sister, and that she alone was implicated in the horrid transaction. She further stated that she had something of importance to communicate which she hoped would not be made public until the moment of her death.

EXECUTION.

Shortly before 12 o'clock the culprits were removed from their cells, when the Executioner commenced the ceremony of pinioning their arms and preparing them for the awful trial they were about to undergo. The mournful cavalcade then slowly proceeded (the chapel bell tolling a solemn sound) towards the platform erected in front of the principal entrance to the goal, which, by the means of a ladder the culprits ascended, accompanied by the Rev. Mr. Roberts, Mr. Orridge governor of the goal, and Calcraft, the well known "finisher of the law." Shortly after the wretched beings were placed under the fatal beam, and after a few moments spent in prayer, the chaplain reading the usual portion of the burial service—the ropes being adjusted, on a signal given the fatal plank fell, and the wretched beings were launched into eternity, in sight of the countless muultitude of spectators, who filling the avenues and surrounding the Castle Hill, had assembled to witness the melancholy exit of two youthful criminals who had alike outraged the ties of nature, the laws of their country, and the sacred ordinances of God.

The bodies, after hanging the usual time, on being cut down will be buried within the precincts of the prison.

Seventeen years has elapsed since an execution took place in Cambridge. The last victim to public justice was John Stallon, the Shelford incendiary, who after his condemnation acknowledged being guilty of twelve fires out of thirteen which occurred in that village. Had the severity of the criminal code not been relaxed since that period, from the number of capital offences in the late calendar, we should in all probability have witnessed the melancholy spectacle of more than twenty human beings yielding their lives to the outraged laws of their country.

COPY OF VERSES
Written the night previous to Execution.

O God for mercy we do cry,
To-morrow we are doom'd to die,
Our sins we own are very great,
For which we meet a dreadful fate.

The crime of murder all allow
Is greater than any sin below,
And by the law it is decreed,
On the gallows we shall bleed.

A deadly poison we confess,
We put into our sister's mess,
Hoping when quiet in her grave
More guilty intercourse to have.

God's all-seeing eye doth watch
The actions of the guilty wretch
Wicked deeds he brings to light
Sure as day succeeds the night.

For murder now condem'd to die
And end our days with infamy,
A crime unequalled to be found,
If you search the world around.

A warning take now by our fate
And shun the evils that await
A guilty passion which did tend
To bring us to this fatal end

They preached, they sang, they wrote assiduously. They travelled far and wide, still preaching, still singing, still writing. Yet like the monk in his cell, it was with the delicate and transcendental problems of theology that they were mostly concerned, not with the coarse and pressing problems of Christianity. Man's inhumanity to man was discussed less widely and less vehemently than the nature of his duty to God. The worker priest, had he arisen in those days, would have had a rough deal, one feels, at the hands of Dean Farrar or Dr Spurgeon.

Yet in spite of a variety of Factory Acts, the exploitation of cheap labour and much unthinking cruelty in its employment went on for the greater part of the Victorian age. Practical interest in social problems was confined to a high-minded minority. Manifestations such as the Chartist movement, which reared its ugly head in 1838 and soon began to show its blackened teeth, may have dismayed these less complaisant few, but it can hardly have caused them much surprise. Queen Victoria had been on the throne for less than a year. It was a bad beginning to the history of labour relations during her reign.

But the lot of the working man was not really very interesting to anyone except himself. There were too many other things to think about. The large and growing middle class, enjoying a sense of security and a modest standard of genteel living, was hankering after an improvement in both. The upper class was preoccupied, not unnaturally, with trying to preserve the *status quo*. Neither had much time to spare for such distractions as the fine arts. The Grand Tour, which had often aroused in the previous generation, a latent interest in art and architecture, was no longer fashionable. Patronage of the sort that had flourished for the past two hundred years was declining, and opportunities for commissioning grand schemes of design or decoration were becoming fewer. No longer were the civilised canons of Georgian and Regency taste exerting their effect, and few manufacturers were enlightened enough to realise that good design has an influence on the mind as well as on the eye; an obtuseness reflected in the peculiar ugliness of many household objects made in the latter years of the Victorian era.

All art reflects the taste of its time. The taste of the early Victorians was for the romantic, for moral uplift, and for exaggerated delicacy of feeling. Dora Spenlow's winsome vapourings aroused no desire in Dickens' readers to thump her; her way of behaving was the correct conduct for a young lady of refined upbringing, and she is not the only one of her kind to be found in the novels or paintings of the period. It was the period of the Gothic Revival, that prolonged architectural experiment in which moral uplift and romantic appeal were combined. The Revival, which had begun towards the end of the eighteenth century, was still going strong nearly a hundred years later. Its influence was at first mainly on church architecture, but by degrees it extended with painful results to interior decoration and furniture. These side-effects did not appeal to everyone. Even Augustus Welby Pugin, high priest of the Revival, and, with Sir Charles Barry, designer of the most famous edifice built on Revivalist principles, the Houses of Parliament, was moved to criticise the work of some of his disciples. In his *The Principles of Christian Architecture* Pugin discussed the effects of the Revival on the domestic hearth: 'The fender is a sort of embattled parapet, with a lodge-gate at each end; at the end of the poker is a sharp-pointed finial, at the summit of the tongs is a saint'.

This is perhaps as near to a witticism as Pugin is likely to have got, though it was not said simply as a joke. The Gothic Revival had been inspired by a hazy belief that Gothic surroundings would help to induce a return to mediaeval forms of worship. But there was no such mystical hope to justify some of the strange, florid and derivative forms displayed in other types of mid-Victorian art and architecture. Railway stations were built to look like Gothic cathedrals, banks and offices like Florentine *palazzi*. The public's taste and its approval of the Pre-Raphaelites, after the storm of controversy aroused by their early works, encouraged artists to look backwards rather than forwards. William Morris, a true original, and founding father of the arts and crafts movement, although seduced by the prevailing fashion, swam almost alone against the tide in taking from mediaeval art and design that which was best and brightest instead of what was dull and clumsy. As a result, his fabrics and wallpapers look as fresh and pretty today as most others of that time look drab.

In the late years of the period there was a move towards a self-conscious Bohemianism. It was the period of W. S. Gilbert's 'greenery-yallery-Grosvenor-Gallery' clique, whose antics and artificiality gave the Victorian philistines a pretext for deriding the *avant garde* art of the period. Eventually, Whistler and *art nouveau* arrived to scandalise the pundits and bring a breath of cold clean air into the hothouse of academic art.

The decline of a tradition in art, like the death of an artist, is often followed by a slump in values. The decline of the Victorian tradition of academic realism, to which Whistler was among the first to give a pinprick, was a long process. It was not until more than a decade after his death in 1903 that the slump in Victorian art

The Gothic Revival, though chiefly concerned with architecture, had its effect inside as well as outside the home. Typical of domestic appliances in the Gothic taste was Doulton's water purifier, masquerading as a religious vessel.

touched rock-bottom. At the same time, interest in Victorian architecture, painting, furniture, the domestic arts and much of the period's literature was also extinguished. It appeared to most critics that this decline of interest in the Victorians had reached a point of no return. Even as late as the 1940s it seemed to so discerning an eye as that of Raymond Mortimer, glancing nostalgically at the Victorian era in his *Channel Packet*, that it was unlikely that Victorian art would ever become popular again. But there is no accounting for 'the wild vicissitudes of taste'. Late in the 1950s Victorian art, particularly of the anecdotal type, began to return to favour. But it takes more than the whims of a fashionable coterie or the inflationary tactics of a few dealers to bring about such a change in taste. No doubt it is partly due to the fact that the supply is still equal to the demand and that the works of Victorian artists are less expensive than those of even minor Old Masters. But there is also another factor. Some see in the revival of interest a reaction from the obscurity of much contemporary art, the idioms of which are becoming more and more difficult for most people to understand. It is not necessary, as most Victorians seemed to think, that every picture must tell a story, but painting, whatever else it may be, is primarily a means of communication, and if it is used by the artist merely for the purpose of talking to himself, the onlooker, however knowledgeable or sympathetic, is inclined to feel that he has been cheated.

In *The Shape of Content* the American artist, Ben Shahn speaks of the futility of placing too great a reliance on the subconscious and on the accidental element in art: 'The very act of making a painting is an intending one; thus to intend and at the same time relinquish intention is a hopeless contradiction'. In Victorian art there are no such contractions. There are characteristic faults and even absurdities, but there is always a sense of certainty. Perhaps this is the element that appeals most to present-day sentiment, for life in the twentieth century is menaced by uncertainties of a kind that not even that strange, sad Victorian, Thomas De Quincey could have dreamt of in his laudanum-soaked slumbers.

Before its decline in popularity, Victorian art had had a good run for its money, and that, taking into account the value of the Victorian pound, amounted to a tidy sum. A successful artist could afford to live in style and comfort. Millais at the height of his fame estimated his income at £40,000 a year. Rosa Bonheur, for one of her studies in turbulent horseflesh, could net a cool £4,000. Frith's painting, *The Railway Station*, was sold for £5,250, *The Monarch of the Glen* by Landseer for £7,245. Today, the sale-room value of paintings such

The architectural fashion of aping Continental styles led to the rebuilding in 1845 of Osborne House, the Queen's Isle of Wight retreat, in the manner of a Florentine *palazzo*.

It would have been more tactful, perhaps, to have chosen a design a little less like that of Osborne when Billingsgate fish market was rebuilt in 1854.

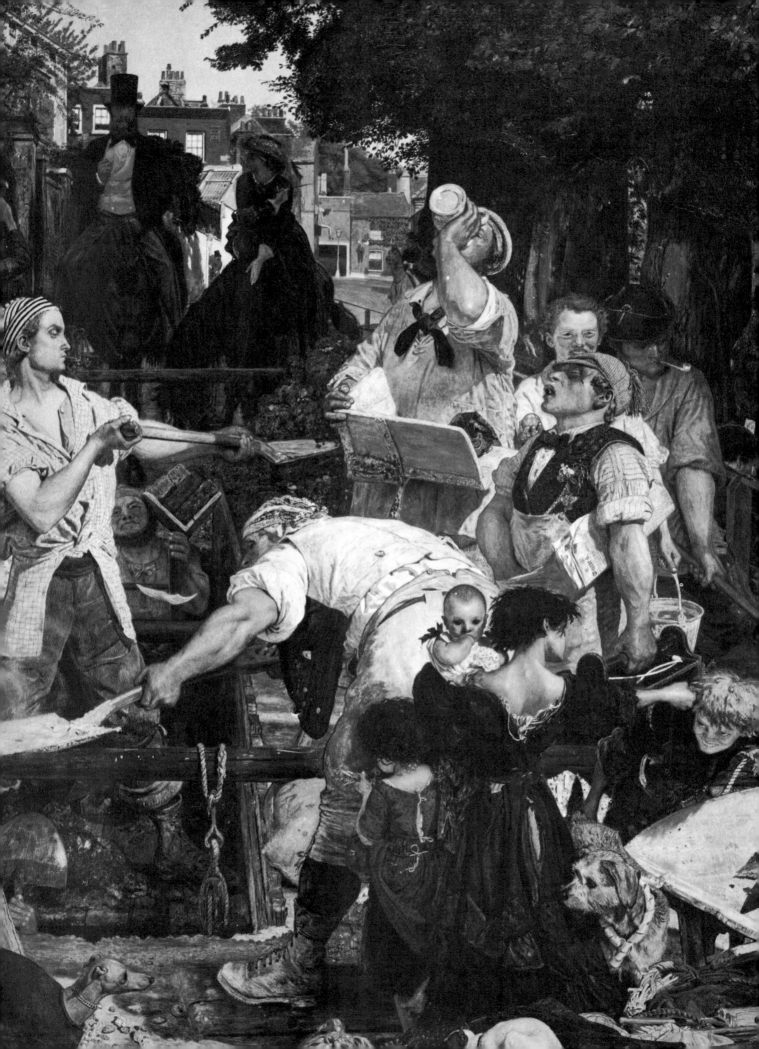

ABOVE: Though models from the antique were generally acceptable, Victorian artists on the whole resisted the influence of their foreign contemporaries, such as the Impressionists. An exception was the neglected N. F. Potter, painter of *The Music Lesson* (1887).

OPPOSITE: Social significance was the theme of much Victorian art. Ford Madox Brown's *Work*, from which this detail is taken, epitomised the central problem of Victorian society, the great divide between the leisured and the labouring classes.

as these, which not long ago could have been bought for a few hundred pounds, cannot be far short of the prices paid by their original owners.

It is not only in Victorian art that interest has revived. In varying degrees it has also revived in the architecture, the politics, the sociology, and the manners and morals of the period. This cannot always be due, as seems to some extent arguable in the case of painting, to an instinctive reaction against the obscurity of contemporary trends. It has followed naturally from the exploration of the Victorian era by latter-day historians and critics, to whom the perspective of time gives the advantage of an objective view that earlier authorities, writing from personal experience, could not have possessed. The judgments of men like Sir Edmund Gosse, E. F. Benson, Algernon Cecil or Lytton Strachey, however shrewd, could not fail to be coloured by their own recollections of the period.

In February 1948, there began a long series of broadcasts from London on the 'Ideas and Beliefs of the Victorians'. *The Times*, discussing this remarkable and ambitious project – there were eighty-three programmes in all, to which more than a hundred speakers contributed – described it as 'the climax of a reaction against the idea of Victorian England which prevailed amongst

55

educated Englishmen twenty years ago'; and in the opening talk Professor G. M. Trevelyan declared: 'The period of reaction against the nineteenth century is over; the era of dispassionate historical evaluation has begun'. Since then, the rich Pre-Raphaelite panorama of the Victorian age, its foreground crowded with diverse and fascinating figures and its middle distance crammed with inexhaustible detail, has been examined from innumerable angles and under innumerable types of lens. Its architecture and its churches have been discussed with evangelical fervour by John Betjeman, its clothes and habits by James Laver, its transport by Michael Robbins; A.J.P. Taylor has dissected its politics, Roger Fulford its princes; its leading lights have been acutely observed by Raymond Mortimer, its taste analysed by John Gloag, its art by William Gaunt; the discerning eye and sensitive intelligence of Dame Edith Sitwell has been brought to bear on its poetry; Mrs Cecil Woodham-Smith has resurrected the grim realities of its war and pestilence; examination of its society has been made by Peter Quennell, Hector Bolitho, Professor Asa Briggs, and many others; and biographies of its sovereign have been innumerable. Through the eyes of this host of explorers and interpreters we have begun to view the Victorian era with greater detachment than before and, helped by their guidance, to reassess the values which the Victorians placed on their own achievements.

This is not the place to discuss those achievements in detail. That must be left to the historian, and this is not a work of history, as has already been made clear. Its purpose is to present, chiefly to the eye, an impression of the vitality and variety of the Victorians' day-to-day existence. Much has been left out that a more ambitious study would have included. The aim has been to concentrate on a number of essentials. Apart from shelter, food and clothing, and politics aside, the Victorians were mainly preoccupied, as we are – except in one significant respect, religion – by two considerations: employment and the means of spending their leisure. Less vital to them than to us, though still of urgent importance, were the problems of education and the means of getting about. The influence of these various preoccupations on the conduct and habits of the Victorians was profound and inescapable. Let us look at some of their effects.

The old Queen; from a drawing by Phil May.

THE ENGLISHMAN'S HOME

Chapter 2: The Englishman's Home ¶ Home, Sweet Home ¶ Slums Old and New ¶ Stately Mansions ¶ On the Parish ¶ Royal Residences ¶ Ventilation and Sanitation ¶ Model Dwellings ¶ Making Room for Railways ¶ Parlour Furniture ¶ Staying in Hotels ¶ A Taste for Bric-à-brac

We tend to think of the Victorian home in the same way as we tend to think of the Victorians themselves – as essentially middle-class and more often than not placed in the middle of the Victorian era. So wide a prospect cannot be taken in at a single glance and the middle of the era is a convenient observation post. From it we can look back to the beginning of the period, when urban development was in its infancy and Regency influences in the home still much in evidence, and forward to the 'eighties and 'nineties when developments in science and in art had transformed much of the architectural landscape and the domestic scene. It is from this vantage point, too, that we tend to regard Victorian painting, which instinctively calls to mind not the names of Turner or Samuel Palmer, still less those of Whistler or Sickert, but of painters like Frith and Augustus Egg, whose work typifies the taste of the mid-Victorian middle class. Pictures such as theirs are an affirmation of the values of a bourgeois society. The moral tone of the period is implicit in almost all their works. The rewards of virtue and the penalties of vice are depicted in painstaking detail; the compositions are often ingenious and well-ordered, the colours clean and bright, the execution smooth. The seamier side of life is swept under the good hard-wearing Axminster carpet, or if partially exposed, is shown for some didactic purpose.

In the early years of the era taste was less genteel, in the later years signs of the ostentatious and inelegant styles of the Edwardian era are already to be seen. How wide was the gap between the two

OPPOSITE: The Victorian doll's house reflected in miniature Samuel Smiles' dictum, A Place for Everything, and Everything in its Place. The generations segregated, a room for this, a room for that (though nothing so unmentionable as a lavatory), and nothing where it shouldn't be. What the doll's house never reflected was the type of dwelling (RIGHT) in which many thousands had to live – and die, sometimes no doubt being glad to do so.

may be observed by comparing the early with the late Victorian drawing room. Almost their only point of similarity is shown in a fondness for clutter. The influence of the Gothic Revival, not always for the best, which was strong on the domestic scene at first, had disappeared by the end of the era. So had those reminders of the Regency taste which supplied a refinement usually lacking in a Gothic teapot or a Gothic sideboard. In their place we see effects borrowed from the Orient, or oozing from those recesses of the imagination from which *art nouveau* originated.

Furniture in the earlier period was on the whole more comfortable and less grandiose and interior decoration simpler. In the later period the domestic *mise-en-scène* seemed to reflect the growing complexity of life.

The drawing-room, in humbler households the equivalent of the parlour, was essentially, if not in origin, a middle-class apartment, a kind of halfway house between a sitting room and a *salon*. Few except the richest of the middle class aspired to a *salon*, but a library, formerly the prerogative of a gentleman, as distinct from someone engaged in trade, became essential for the master of many a middle class household, whether he was intellectually inclined or not. The possession of a library was regarded, as is the possession of a swimming pool in certain circles today, as a status symbol.

The nice distinction of a breakfast-room, a morning-room, a smoking-room or, after the 'sixties when billiards became popular, a billiard-room, depended on the size of the house and of the family. The habit of indiscriminate proliferation, which so often blighted the lives of the working classes, assumed the look of a pious duty when it occurred among the middle class. A family of eight or ten children, or perhaps even more, was by no means a phenomenon; indeed was a matter for paternal pride until the late 'seventies, when the euphoric vision that had persisted for so long, of unending prosperity and overseas expansion, began suddenly to fade.

In these post-Freudian days the idea that children should be seen and not heard seems fraught with dangers of maladjustment. To a Victorian mother, not too well-off and with ten or more children to look after, the eldest perhaps only thirteen or fourteen, it must often have seemed a consummation devoutly to be wished. The upper, and to a lesser extent the middle classes, were seldom so inconvenienced. The problems of parenthood were solved by the simple expedient of segregating the children from the grown-ups, to whom they were allowed access only at stated periods of the day. Washed and starched and on their best behaviour, they were allowed down from the nursery or the schoolroom at specified hours to be shown off

OPPOSITE: Family feeling and the home beautiful. It must have been a loving and forgiving nature that found room for this mass reminder of relatives, a typical feature of the décor of the 'nineties with its chinoiserie, pampas grass and *lunaria biennis*.

Cleanliness is next to Godliness, and Saturday night was the time to impress upon infant minds the sin of atheism.

OPPOSITE: Irony, the favourite weapon of Sir W.S. Gilbert for debunking pretentiousness, strikes home at Grims Dyke, his house at Bushey in Hertfordshire. Designed by Norman Shaw, it was a monument to Victorian pretence and opulence.

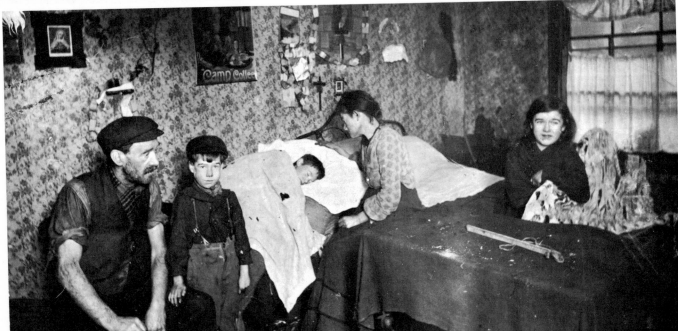

to visitors or converse with their parents, or on Sunday to walk with them to church. The poorer classes had to put up with the perpetual inconvenience of having their families about them at all times. There is not much privacy in a slum or in a labourer's cottage, and most of the working population lived in one or the other.

Professor G. M. Trevelyan, discussing the early nineteenth-century origins of the slums that are still with us, speaks of

... the rampant individualism, inspired by no idea beyond quick money returns, that was the generating force in creating huge areas of jerry-built back-to-back dwellings on the outskirts of many an industrial centre. ... Town-planning, sanitation and amenity were things undreamt of by the vulgarian makers of the new world, while the aristocratic ruling class enjoyed its own pleasant life apart, and thought that town building, sanitation and factory conditions were no concern of the government!

Throughout Victoria's reign rampant individualism and the profit motive remained the governing factors in the housing situation. We still see their results in the oppressive contiguity, the meagre amenities, the appalling visual monotony of street after street in many an industrial town. Yet to those who knew the look and smell of Victorian slums, such streets, when they were newly-built, must have seemed infinitely preferable to the warrens and rookeries, the foul courts and fouler tenements, the broken garrets and streaming cellars in which tens of thousands of the very poor were herded with as little consideration for human needs as if they had been rats living in a rubbish heap.

Between 1841 and 1844 Charles Knight, the publisher, a typically indefatigable Victorian, produced the six volumes of his *London*, a fascinating compendium of lore and learning. In it is included a description of the district known as St Giles's, lying between Soho, Bloomsbury and Holborn, as it was in the early 1840s:

Cellars serving whole families for 'kitchen and parlour and bedroom and all' are to be found in other streets of London, but not so numerous and near to each other. Here they cluster like cells in a convent ... it is curious and interesting to watch the habits of these human moles when they emerge, or half emerge, from their cavities. ... Their infants seem exempt from the dangers which haunt those of other people: at an age when most babies are not trusted alone on a level floor, these urchins stand secure on the upmost round of a trap-ladder, studying the different conformations of the shoes of the passers-by. The mode of ingress of the adults is curious: they turn their backs to the entry, and, inserting first one foot and then another, disappear by degrees. The process is not unlike (were such a thing conceivable) a sword sheathing itself. They appear a

Market Court, Kensington (TOP), was typical of innumerable courts in mid-Victorian cities, all equally gloomy, squalid and insanitary. It was demolished soon after this photograph was taken in the late 'sixties. But the attitude of mind that bred and tolerated such slums was not to be demolished. The lower photograph, taken some thirty years after Market Court had disappeared, shows the mean and filthy conditions in which many thousands still lived.

63

Sufferers from Lambeth floods was the title of this photograph, taken in the 'seventies. Almost every year, to the accompaniment of illness and often severe loss, families living near the Thames at Lambeth were temporarily flooded out of their homes.

'Nowhere to go.'

short-winded generation, often coming, like the otter, to the surface to breathe. In the twilight which reigns at the bottom of their dens you can sometimes discern the male busily cobbling shoes on one side of the entrance, and the female repairing all sorts of rent garments on the other. They seem to be free feeders: at certain periods of the day tea-cups and saucers may be seen arranged on their boards; at others, plates and pewter pots. They have the appearance of being on the whole a contented race. . . .

There follows a description of the region of St Giles's known as 'the Rookery':

It is one great maze of narrow crooked paths crossing and intersecting in labyrinthine convolutions, as if the houses had been originally one great block of stone eaten by slugs into innumerable small chambers and connecting passages. There is no privacy here for any of the over-crowded population; every apartment in the place is accessible from every other by a dozen different approaches. Only at night, when they are asleep – and not always at night – can their redundant numbers find room; for so long as they are lively enough to turn and be aware that anything presses them, there is squeezing and jostling, and grumbling and cursing. Hence whoever ventures here finds the streets (by courtesy so called) thronged with loiterers . . . the stagnant gutters in the middle of the lanes . . . piles of garbage . . . pools accumulated in the hollows of the disjointed pavement . . . filth choking up the dark passages which open like rat-holes upon the highway. . . . It is a land of utter idleness.

In Birmingham, Manchester, Glasgow and a dozen other cities there were districts no better than St Giles's, and although some of the worst areas were swept away in course of time, even while they still existed people of wealth and position continued to devote enormous sums of money and unlimited building resources to re-housing themselves in luxury and splendour. In the late 1840s the Earl of Ellesmere, a cultivated and intelligent man and distinguished public servant, delighted to watch the progress being made in the building of Bridgewater House, his new town residence, which today stands beside Green Park, a monument to the strange indifference of most of his kind to the circumstances of the poor. The south front of the building, we are told in Walford's *Old and New London*, is 140 feet long,

. . . the west 120 feet; and there are two small courts within the mass to aid in lighting the various apartments. The ground-plan itself comprises a perfect residence – drawing-rooms, dining-rooms, ladies-rooms, chamber, dressing-rooms, etc. The first floor is, with a small exception, appropriated to state-rooms, dining-room, drawing-room, the splendid picture-gallery, etc.

64

Bluegate Fields, Shadwell, in the East End of London, c. 1860. Gustave Doré's impression shows the apathy and squalor in which its inhabitants lived, but conveys nothing of the stench, the lack of sanitation, and the danger of epidemic diseases.

RIGHT: The sham period residence appealed to many Victorians, who dwelt with satisfaction in mock-baronial, mock-Tudor or mock-Renaissance houses. In Sir Frank Dicksee's painting, *The Housebuilders*, Sir W. E. Welby-Gregory and his wife contemplate the plans for Denton Hall in Lincolnshire, erected in the late 'seventies on the site of an earlier house demolished to make room for a dwelling in the Elizabethan taste. Some architects included extravagant whims to gratify the taste or vanity of the owner. In 1867 Edward Welby Pugin, son of Augustus, the high priest of Victorian Gothic, designed for Mr Thomas Kennedy, of Leeds, The Towers (ABOVE). Distinctive features of this bizarre habitat included an Italian marble staircase and chimneys hollowed from stone blocks, also from Italy.

OPPOSITE: Bad news in the breakfast room. W.P. Frith's sad picture, shows this forgotten sanctum with all its details lovingly observed. The ladies, all too soon perhaps, may have to exchange its comforts for a different type of feeding place, such as that (OPPOSITE BELOW) of St Pancras Workhouse (1901).

In Frith's respectable milieu Notice to Quit was as rare as it was scandalous. In circles less comfortably established it was not uncommon, nor as a rule was there much to be removed.

Within the next three or four years a number of such palatial houses arose in London. The handsome squares and stuccoed streets in parts of Knightsbridge and Pimlico, then a rather more fashionable neighbourhood than it is now, arose to accommodate the large families to which the rich no less than the poor seemed prone. Street after street of new houses sprang up. Londonderry House, in Park Lane, now no more, but then 'one of the most spacious and splendid in London', was built by the third Marquess of Londonderry in 1850; Dorchester House, also in Park Lane, a year or two later by Mr R. S. Holford. The Knightsbridge mansion which is now the French Embassy and whose first occupant was George Hudson, the railway magnate, dates also from this time. These and others, all of considerable size, were designed and built with little regard for expense. Such housing projects must have seemed, for all their grandeur, in questionable taste to those who had bothered to enquire into housing conditions in St Giles's or the slums of the East End.

At the opposite end of the scale from the mansions of the rich was the dreaded workhouse. It was the economical policy of the Poor Law Commissioners to make workhouse conditions so detestable and their administration so brutal that those who found themselves without means of support might be tempted to commit suicide rather than 'go on the parish'. It amounted to the same thing in the end. If starvation, cruelty and vermin failed to achieve the Commissioners' purpose, loneliness, ignominy and lack of hope could generally be counted on to have the desired effect. Yet some among the destitute still preferred the casual ward of the workhouse to the prospect of a night under the open sky, especially in winter. But it was forbidden to use the same ward too often and anyone detected doing so could be 'punished' by the workhouse master; the punishment at one London workhouse being a three-day stint at picking oakum, a task that soon split your nails and made your fingers raw. Many of the old or infirm had no alternative but to 'go on the parish'. Walford records that in 1858 no less than 117,000 people in England and Wales were suffering the rigours of parochial hospitality. Throughout most of the Victorian era workhouse administration remained a scandal and poverty a stigma on the poor rather than on those sections of society that accepted its worst manifestations with such placid indifference.

The Queen's situation was, of course, rather different from that of the nobility so elegantly housed in St James's and Belgravia. A certain degree of sumptuousness was considered indispensable to the authority and dignity of her position. But between her lavish scale of living, which was often eagerly adopted by those who could aspire to copy it, and the conditions in which masses of her loyal subjects were condemned to live, there existed a discrepancy that was, to say the least of it, decidedly injudicious. Yet the Queen appeared unaware of this. For once the common sense that often characterised her actions seemed to desert her. It is understandable that she should have longed for a place that she could call her own, where she could escape from the cares of state and the formality of life at Buckingham Palace, but her extravagant means of gratifying this desire were questionable. In 1845 she bought Osborne House in the Isle of Wight for what was then the very considerable sum of twenty-six thousand pounds. Soon afterwards, at further cost, the house was knocked down and rebuilt in the form of a massive Italian *palazzo*. A year later twenty thousand pounds was voted by Parliament for altering and refurbishing Buckingham Palace. For four years, from 1850 to 1854, the Queen rented Balmoral House in Aberdeenshire. She then decided to buy it and, as in the case of Osborne House, promptly pulled it down, this time in order to erect a sham castle. There is much that is difficult to understand in the Queen's character, but nothing so perplexing as her inconsistency, as for instance in her genuine dislike of subterfuge and her love of flattery, in the deference she expected from her ministers and the familiarity with which she allowed John Brown to treat her, or in the reversal of her attitude towards Sir Robert Peel. Equally difficult to reconcile are her genuine concern for the conditions of the poor and the wilful extravagance of her own housing arrangements. It is not surprising that from time to time public criticisms were made of the amount it cost the nation to maintain the royal family in accordance with the Queen's notions of what was right and proper.

Until the latter part of the century the houses of both rich and poor were badly drained and often very imperfectly ventilated. Not until 1851 was the window tax repealed. This ingenious means of raising money dated from the seventeenth century when a tax was levied on all houses, except those subject to Poor or Church rates, according to the number of windows in the house. Consequently, those who could not afford to pay the tax had to forfeit light and air by blocking up their windows. The tax also encouraged the building of houses in which privies, passages and semi-basement rooms had no windows at all.

That there was any connection between health and ventilation was not a matter likely to trouble the conscience of a speculative Victorian builder. Nor were government or local authorities unduly concerned about the effects of sanitation on public health. For the greater part of the Queen's reign water supplies were inadequate

Osborne House in the Isle of Wight, bought by Queen Victoria in 1845, as it appeared after its reconstruction.

and often liable to contamination, and arrangements for cleaning the streets were of the most primitive kind. It is not surprising that illnesses and epidemics were frequent. In 1848 cholera appeared in London for the second time since the turn of the century. Yet the government was reluctant, and remained so until 1855, to enforce comprehensive measures for the improvement of city sanitation. This was a cause, like the abolition of child labour, for which the Earl of Shaftesbury struggled almost alone and for so long, that had for years a lone champion, Edwin Chadwick. It is no exaggeration to say that the safety and efficiency of London's water supply and drainage system are very largely due to the solitary efforts of Chadwick, who by his example inspired other cities to improve and modernise their own systems. Chadwick began life as a barrister and, after acting as secretary of a royal commission on the Poor Laws, became a member of the Board of Health, set up in 1848 for improving water supplies and drainage and keeping towns clean. He had none of Shaftesbury's influential connections, nor at the start much political support. Still less had he Shaftesbury's sense of discretion or of when his ultimate aims might best be served by compromise. He said exactly what he thought about men and institutions without any regard for personal feelings, corporate dignity, or cherished traditions. Worse still, he insisted on finding out or confirming everything for himself, and thereafter rode roughshod over every obstruction, whether caused by indifference, carelessness or the preservation of vested interests. The measure of his unpopularity in official circles may be gauged from the fact that in spite of the immense improvements in sanitation brought about in London as a direct result of his efforts, he was nearly ninety before his services were recognised by the award of a knighthood.

More than Chadwick's single-mindedness and determination would have been needed to avert the creation of what were to become the twentieth century's slums. As the impetus of the industrial revolution got under way, more and more people were attracted into the mining and manufacturing districts in the Midlands and the North. By the beginning of the Victorian era overcrowding was already a serious problem, but serious only to those who had to endure the dangers and inconveniences that it caused. It was easy money for the unscrupulous landlord and the jerry-builder. Families were packed several at a time into old and decrepit houses. Acres of land were covered with cramped dwellings built back-to-back without proper foundations, ventilation or drainage. Sometimes twenty or more houses would be grouped round a court-yard, each house being jammed with as many families as it would

ABOVE: Sir Edwin Chadwick, a pioneer in matters of public health, to whose vision and implacable attitude to opposition, from whatever quarter it came, London and other great cities owe the purity of their water supplies and the efficiency of their drainage. The danger of epidemics, though to some extent reduced by gradual improvements in sanitation, remained for long a serious possibility. Public disinfectors (BELOW) with portable ovens helped to lessen outbreaks by fumigating on the spot belongings of persons who had died from infectious diseases, or were suffering from them.

hold, with only one pump and one privy to serve the needs of all the inhabitants.

Efforts to improve this state of affairs were sporadic and usually due not to the initiative of local authorities, but to the imagination of individuals. Prince Albert, adopting a characteristically practical approach, initiated the planning and building of some model houses for labourers as an external feature of the Great Exhibition in Hyde Park, where some 350,000 people went to inspect them. But the Prince was not the first person to interest himself in improving the housing conditions of the poor. In 1842 a society had been formed which was called, with typical Victorian verbosity, the Metropolitan

ABOVE: The luxury of a porcelain finish was rare for baths in the 'sixties; utilitarian zinc was the rule.

ENAMELLING WITH
Aspinall's
Is "Pastime Passing Excellent"—*Shakespeare.*

She: "I intend but only to surprise him". Timon of Athens. V.2.
He: "Wert thou thus surprised sweet girl?" Titus Andron. IV.1

OPPOSITE: For those who could afford it (they were in the minority) a bath was a regular ritual, sometimes observed in a Thermal Bath Cabinet (TOP LEFT), sometimes, though rather less comfortably, in a Sitz Bath (CENTRE), and in infancy (BOTTOM) in a Patent Hammock Bath. The washing-machine (TOP RIGHT) and mangle (CENTRE AND BOTTOM), if more laborious, were as essential to the housewife as the twin-tub and spin-dryer are today.

LEFT: The Victorian bourgeoise was invariably a house-proud spouse, a martyr to convention, diligent in her efforts to keep up with the Jones's, and ever ready to surprise her lord and master with some colourful touch to brighten up the home.

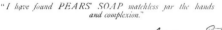

"I have found PEARS' SOAP matchless for the hands and complexion."

ABOVE: The matchless voice of Adelina Patti, of whom we are here afforded an intimate glimpse, can only have been due to nature. Not so, it seems, her matchless complexion.

BELOW: How much more sociable Doulton's Improved Three-Person Tip-up Lavatory in solid mahogany than the solitary pedestal basin of the modern bathroom.

ABOVE: The Victorians' reverence for cleanliness is reflected in the ecclesiastical appearance, often typical of such establishments, of Cookridge Street Public Baths in Leeds (1882).

SPECIALLY DESIGNED THREE PERSON LAVATORY.

Association for Improving the Dwellings of the Industrial Poor (shades of the United Metropolitan Hot Muffin and Crumpet Baking and Punctual Delivery Company). Through the efforts of this society blocks of tenement flats began to appear. Although there may have been much about them that could be criticised, they were a vast improvement on the mean, mass-produced dwellings which in many areas were stretching out in dingy rows to form new industrial suburbs. But the rent for a model flat was usually in the neighbourhood of 4s a week, and this was a good deal higher than most working men could afford, unless they were in regular employment and earning good wages. In 1850 the average weekly wage of a fully-employed man was only about seventeen shillings. By 1880 it had risen by six shillings, but there were still many wage-earners who were condemned to occupy houses that were either shabby and broken-down, if old, or shoddy and ill-planned if new.

A scheme on somewhat similar lines resulted twenty years later from the generosity of George Peabody, an American business man who had established a business in London in 1837. Over a period of four years Peabody gave what was then the enormous sum of £350,000 'to ameliorate the condition of the poor . . . and to promote their comfort and happiness' by the erection of model tenements. In London a number of these tenements, known as Peabody Buildings, still serve their original purpose of housing working-class families.

The housing problems of the London poor were often complicated by the operations of railway companies. Families in their hundreds were displaced to make room for cuttings, viaducts and stations, a process that went on intermittently throughout the whole of the Victorian era. The building of Euston station between the years 1835 and 1839 is said to have displaced twenty thousand people and in 1898 as many as 1,750 families were estimated to have lost their homes as a result of the building of Marylebone station. Arrangements for rehousing those who had been dispossessed were supposed to be made by the railway companies, but their primary interest was in getting stations built and tracks laid and consequently the welfare of those who had been made homeless took second place. Sometimes there were long delays in getting new houses built and often when they became available the rents were so high that those for whom they were intended could not afford to occupy them. Instead, they crammed themselves into already overcrowded districts or moved *en masse* into cheaper and inferior accommodation, thus creating new slums.

A symbolic tribute to George Peabody, the American businessman and philanthropist who spent a fortune in improving the housing conditions of London's poor.

What a House Should Be.

VERSUS

DEATH IN THE HOUSE.

A COMPANION BOOK TO

"*HEALTHY HOMES,*

AND

HOW TO MAKE THEM."

Illustrated with Sanitary Dwellings and Sanitary Appliances.

By WILLIAM BARDWELL,

ARCHITECT, AND SANITARY ENGINEER.

AUTHOR OF

"*Ancient and Modern Temples,*" "*Ancient and Modern Westminster,*" "*Villas and Labourer's Cottages,*" "*Essays on Sewage,*" &c.

SALUS POPULI SUPREMA EST LEX.

LONDON: PUBLISHED FOR THE AUTHOR, BY DEAN & SON.

A growing concern for the welfare of the poor was reflected in innumerable publications, such as those of the architect and sanitary engineer, William Bardwell.

Peabody Square (1871), Blackfriar's
Road, a demi-paradise to slum-dwellers
re-housed in its trim, if somewhat
penitentiary, buildings.

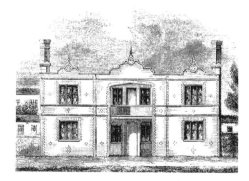

Prince Albert, a practical zealot in
matters of reform, inspired the design
and erection of this four-family living
unit built in Hyde Park as an adjunct
to the Great Exhibition.

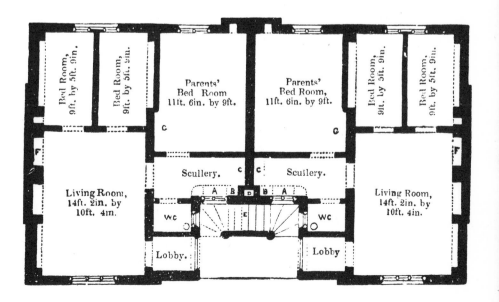

73

The coming of the railways affected the middle classes in precisely the opposite way. Instead of concentrating them in populous districts, it dispersed them on the outskirts of the towns and in the rural areas that surrounded them. They became, in fact, the first commuters. Their dispersal resulted in architects and builders producing a rash of country and suburban houses, most of them of a fairly modest order, designed to appeal to a variety of tastes, ranging from the Gothic to the Swiss, from the Italianate to the Baronial, and from the Rustic to the neo-Regency. Only the rich landowner or the plutocratic businessman could afford the huge ornamental mansions that went up between the 'forties and the 'sixties, erected on foundations deep-laid in hopes for their perpetual grandeur, but which in so many cases have suffered sad changes, often ending up as regional headquarters of government departments or as training colleges, remand homes, or asylums.

It was an expensive business to keep such residences in good repair. This was one anxiety the poor were spared. Their houses showed little change from one generation to the next. They always looked shabby and were always inadequately furnished, usually with bits and pieces either inherited or bought secondhand. Good taste was still a luxury and its indulgence still synonymous with wealth. Those who could afford that indulgence kept the pendulum of fashion swinging. In 1837 the neo-classical influence of late Georgian taste was still apparent to some extent in architecture, decoration and design. By 1851, the curlicues and rotundities of a bastard rococo style were grafting themselves onto every sort of manufactured object, from bird-cages to bath-chairs, from hat-stands to harmoniums. No doubt there is a psycho-aesthetic explanation for this divergence from an earlier standard of elegance, but whatever it may be, its effects were clumsy by comparison with those produced by Sheraton, Hester Bateman, the silversmith, or architects and designers such as the Adam Brothers, Soane, and Nash. Overemphasis replaced restraint. It became the fashion for the middle class parlour to be crammed with bric-à-brac and furniture to be decked with flounces and antimacassars. No mantelpiece was complete without its valence, ruched and fringed with bobbles, no shelf without its china ornaments or family photographs in plush frames.

Towards the end of the century an oriental influence began to creep in. The influence of Japan was noticeable in such things as screens, fans, vases and the venerable aspidistra; that of India in Benares brass, hard teak furniture, and Agra rugs and carpets. In the homes of the intelligentsia, a class without distinction from the

Throughout most of the Victorian era the universal means of illumination, apart from candles, was the oil lamp, on the efficiency and design of which much ingenuity was lavished.

The ornate and hideous solidity of this
late-Victorian bedroom (ABOVE)
compares sadly with the elegance in
design of the 'forties and early 'fifties:
bedsteads in papier mâché (LEFT) and
cast iron (RIGHT), shown at the Great
Exhibition in 1851.

75

ordinary well-educated until the coining of that convenient nuance, life was starker and simpler. Morris wallpapers, Voisey furniture, de Morgan tiles, Whistler etchings, and willow-pattern china made a chill though not unhealthy contrast with the exuberance and eccentricity which hitherto had debased much Victorian design.

Folie de grandeur was an occupational disease of Victorian architects. No doubt in some it was congenital. In others it was contracted through their attempts to translate into brick and stone the grandiose ideas of the ignorant *nouveau riche*. The symptoms of the disease were not confined, however, to stately homes or town mansions; public buildings, railway stations and hotels often became grotesque parodies of Rhineland castles, Flemish guildhalls or Angevin châteaux. For that matter, hotels themselves were something of a novelty until towards the end of the century. The sightseers who came to London in their thousands for the Great Exhibition were mostly accommodated in inns or lodging houses, or slept in the open air. The reputation for discomfort and indifferent food that many British hoteliers and landladies still strive so hard to justify was established quite early on. Macaulay, writing from a Brighton hotel in 1843, complained that the coffee room was 'ingeniously designed on the principle of an oven, the windows not made to open; a dinner on yesterday's pease soup, and the day before yesterday's cutlets, and no ice'. Dickens, in his description of a Ramsgate lodging house a few years earlier, was equally dissatisfied:

... a dusty house, with a bay window, from which you could obtain a beautiful glimpse of the sea – if you thrust half your body out of it, at the imminent peril of falling into the area ... terms ... five guineas a week ... *with* attendance.... (Attendance means the privilege of ringing the bell as often as you like, for your own amusement.)

In 1889 the Savoy Hotel was opened in London. It was one of the first to compare with the type of luxurious establishments to be found on the Continent and had, according to the *Illustrated London News*, 'many features quite novel to London'. These included 'smoke-rooms and other conveniences which are the outgrowth of modern civilisation', an artesian well more than 420 feet deep, and a Turkish bath. In the bedrooms were 'pile carpets, brass "twin" bedsteads, inlaid cabinets, and suites of mahogany, walnut, or enamelled ash, carved dados and mantelpieces, wall hangings of Japanese papers, or of tapestry designs, friezes of gold, and pottery of the choicest description'. Nothing was 'wanting to please the educated eye or gratify the taste, as well to ensure comfort'. But the Savoy was an exception to the rule that continental standards of comfort and convenience are an unnecessary luxury in Britain.

William Morris, founding father of the arts and craft movement, as seen from the rear by his friend, Sir Edwin Burne-Jones.
OPPOSITE: The ideas and influence of Morris, a man of immense energy and diverse talents, had a profound effect on interior decoration. His wallpapers especially, such as this 'Pimpernel' design (1876), changed the look of many a fashionable home.

OVERLEAF LEFT: Following the success of Morris, whose wallpapers, fabrics and furniture appealed strongly to the educated classes, Doulton's, famous as makers of bathroom and lavatory equipment, took a lead in improving industrial design. By commissioning tiles from artists such as Walter Crane, whose direct linear style was well suited to their manufacturing process, Doulton's gave ceramics a new look.
OVERLEAF RIGHT: The hideous necessity of the water-closet (its representation was confined, of course, to builders' catalogues) could in some measure be mitigated by the beauty of its design. Seldom can *art nouveau* have been put to better use than in the decoration of this tasteful pan, equipped for 'simple seat-action ... or by a pull handle as shown'.

Nº 38ᴬ.

Nº 100.

Nº 227.

Nº 184.

Nº 69ᴬ.

Nº 325.

Nº 64.

Nº 179.

Nº 169.

Nº 178.

Nº 166.

Nº 77.

THE LAMBETH
PATENT PEDESTAL
"COMBINATION" CLOSET

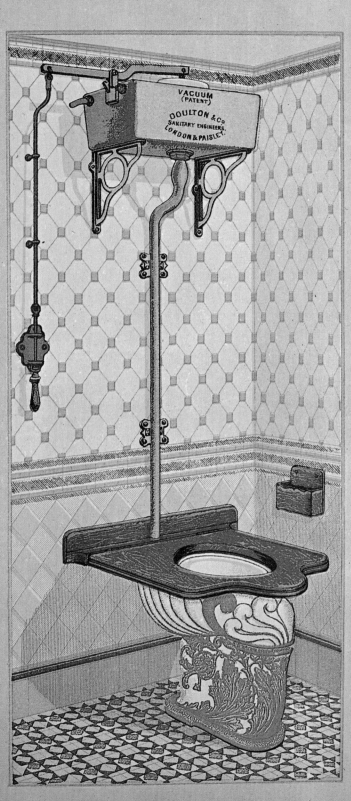

ADVANTAGES.

Front of Basin Lipped to form Urinal and Slop Sink when the seat is raised.

A water area equal to size of hole in seat, reducing the possibility of soiling basin.

Can be readily fixed, either square or across the corner of a room.

Self-contained, and all parts open to inspection.

Depth of water retained in basin, 1½ ins.

It may be flushed by simple seat-action arrangement, or by a pull handle as shewn.

THE LAMBETH PATENT PEDESTAL "COMBINATION" CLOSETS are made both in STONEWARE, WHITE QUEENSWARE, and STRONG GLAZED WARE, The former being especially adapted for places where they are liable to rough usage, as, by reason of their great strength, they are not likely to be damaged.

THE WHITE QUEENSWARE, are specially well finished and suitable for higher-class work.

These Closets are strongly recommended for HOSPITALS, ASYLUMS, PUBLIC INSTITUTIONS, FACTORIES, TENEMENTS, MODEL DWELLINGS. Also MANSIONS and PRIVATE HOUSES, they are made both PLAIN & ORNAMENTAL, and can be supplied either with Turned-down (**S**) or Shoot-out (**P**) Traps.

THE WATER CLOSET—SLOP SINK—AND URINAL COMBINED.
This Closet has been designed by DOULTON & CO., and was awarded
THE GOLD MEDAL at the HEALTH EXHIBITION.

For Prices and Full Particulars, see Pages 4, 5, 6, 7.

RIGHT: A preoccupation with the antique led to extensive borrowings from Greece, Rome and the Renaissance for the design of household objects and garden ornaments. Asia, too, was raided for inspiration. The transfer jug (BELOW) made in about 1840, bears the influences of both China and Japan.

RIGHT: By 1900 Japan and Whistler had between them created a distinctive vogue in interior decoration. It was not one, however, that always allied itself comfortably with the trappings of home-life in Putney or Norwood.

RIGHT: Externally, the Gothic influence for long remained predominant. The Grove at Harborne in Worcestershire (1877) typified the taste for living in surroundings with an ecclesiastical flavour.

OPPOSITE: A touch of old Damascus in Holland Park Road. The Arab Hall of Leighton House was designed by George Aitchison and built in 1865 for Frederick Leighton, afterwards President of the Royal Academy, a peer of the realm, and a pillar of Victorian society.

The complaints of Macaulay and Dickens give some idea of the inconveniences of travel in the early and middle years of the era. Few and far between were the lodgings or hotels in which anything approaching the comforts of home could be found. And to the Victorians, with their passionate fondness for possessions, home comforts meant a lot. Today, ornaments and bric-à-brac of the kind the late Victorians collected, of stone, ormolu and bronze, of sandlewood and teak, lacquer and papier mâché, the painted vases and transparent pictures, the silver-mounted ostrich eggs, the elephants' feet, the stuffed birds under glass domes – today such paraphernalia, where it survives, is thought hardly worth the trouble of dusting. Gone, too, are the texts and samplers, the silhouettes and steel engravings, gone is the oleograph of Riviere's *Sympathy* and Landseer's *Monarch of the Glen*. In their place we have the oxydised features of Tretchikoff's Chinese shop assistant or a skein of ducks by

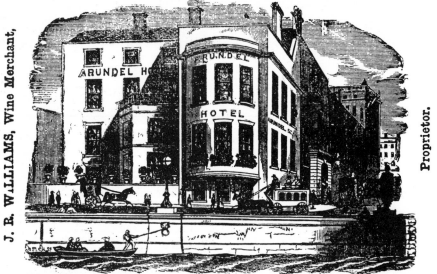

ARUNDEL HOTEL

ARUNDEL STREET, STRAND, W.C.

OVERLOOKING THE THAMES EMBANKMENT.

Passengers travelling from any part of the NORTH, SOUTH, or WEST of ENGLAND, can arrive at the TEMPLE STATION (NEXT DOOR TO THE HOTEL).

J. B. WILLIAMS, Wine Merchant,

Proprietor.

This HOTEL, now the largest Private Hotel in London, is **situate on the NEW VICTORIA EMBANKMENT.** The charge, including Breakfast, Luncheon, Dinner (5 courses), and Tea, a good Bed Room, and use of well-appointed Sitting Rooms, is **SIX SHILLINGS AND SIXPENCE PER DAY.** It is largely patronised by Professional Men, Officers of both Services, also Americans and their Families, for whom is especially provided a free "**WATER COOLER.**" The sleeping Rooms are large and scrupulously clean. Private Sitting Rooms, from **3s. per day.** Service, 1s. No other extras. Wines of the finest quality, including "Roederer," "Perrier Jouet," "Möet," &c., &c., charged at **8s. per bottle,** and all others at a like moderate rate. **An elegant appointed Suite of Rooms appropriated for Wedding Breakfasts, &c.** Hot and Cold Baths. A Night Porter. Ici on parle Francais. Mein spricht Deutsch. [Lo.-339

LEFT: The private hotel in its heyday was not, as are so many of them nowadays, a permanent resort of the elderly and genteel, living uncomfortably on small incomes. It was more often a thriving establishment with a rapidly changing clientele, patronised by foreigners as well as middle-class English families.

OPPOSITE: The Russell Hotel in Bloomsbury, designed by C. Fitzroy Doll and built in 1898, was a different class of establishment, which set out to impress guests by its phoney Renaissance grandeur rather than to reassure them with an atmosphere suggestive of a home from home.

Peter Scott. Is it any wonder if the temptation is less strong than it used to be to enquire with Emily Brontë,

> *. . . what on earth is half so dear —*
> *So longed for — as the hearth of home?*

Few people nowadays would regret the ostrich eggs or the elephants' feet, the one a useless eccentricity, the other ugly and cumbersome, and not many would deplore the eclipse of Briton Riviere, whose sentimental animal paintings are of a kind no longer appreciated. But now that we are getting far enough away from the Victorian era to see and judge it in perspective, we are coming to realise not how different, as we once thought, but how alike our tastes are in a good many respects. In architecture, painting, furniture, textiles, china and other spheres of design the Victorians, for much of their era, produced works that still have an appeal, not merely because of what is vaguely known as period charm, but because they satisfy modern standards of taste, comfort and convenience.

Cowslip now, and willow herb
Crushed 'neath sett and granite curb;
Fast in the speculator's hand
England's green and pleasant land.

APPETITES AND VICTUALS

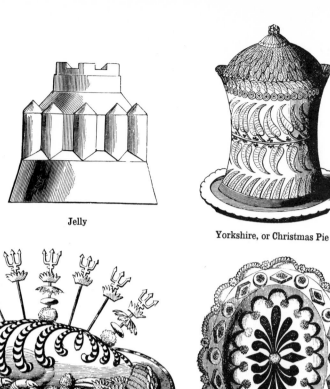

Jelly

Yorkshire, or Christmas Pie

Jelly

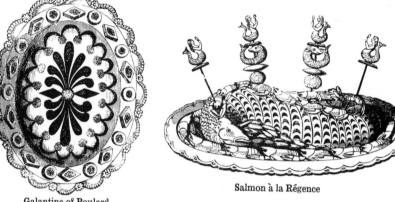

Capon à la Godard

Galantine of Poulard,
with aspic jelly

Salmon à la Régence

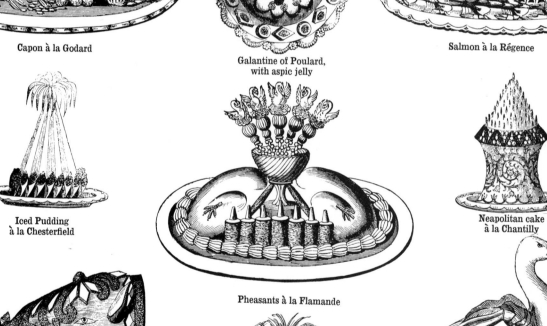

Iced Pudding
à la Chesterfield

Pheasants à la Flamande

Neapolitan cake
à la Chantilly

Boar's Head with aspic jelly

Galantine de Dinde à la Volière

Salade de Grouse à la Soyer

STUDY OF THE STOMACH IS THE STUDY OF MORALITY.

THE FESTIVE SEASON.

How to enjoy good food, which otherwise disorders the digestive organs, causing Bilious Headaches and Impure Blood, use

ENO'S FRUIT SALT.

Also as a refreshing, Cooling, and Invigorating Beverage, use **ENO'S FRUIT SALT.** It is the best preventive and cure for Biliousness, Sick Headache, Skin Eruptions, Impure Blood, Pimples on the Face, Giddiness, Feverishness, Mental Depression, Want of Appetite, Sourness of the Stomach, Constipation, Vomiting, Thirst, &c., and to remove the effects of errors of eating and drinking.

Experience shows that porter, mild ales, port wine, sweet champagne, dark sherries, liqueurs, and brandies are all very apt to disagree; while te wines, and gin or whiskey largely diluted with soda-water, will be e least objectionable. **ENO'S FRUIT SALT** is particularly adapted for titutional weakness of the liver; it possesses the power of reparation estion has been disturbed or lost, and places the invalid on the right health. A world of woe is avoided by those who keep and use **ENO'S** SALT, therefore no family should ever be without it.

NG AN OVERDRAFT ON THE BANK OF LIFE.—Late hours, fagged atural excitement, breathing impure air, too rich food, alcoholic drink, eumatic, and other blood poisons, feverish colds, biliousness, sick headache, tions, want of appetite, sourness of stomach, &c.—Use **ENO'S FRUIT** t is pleasant, cooling, health giving, refreshing, and invigorating. You erstate its great value in keeping the blood pure and free from disease.

THING BUT THE PLAINEST FOOD DISAGREES WITH ME.— slow Gardens, London, S.W., September 10, 1882.—Sir,—Allow me to o you my gratitude for the wonderful preventive of Sick Headache which given to the world in your **FRUIT SALT.** For two years and a half I much from sick headache, and seldom passed a week without one or more Five months ago I commenced taking your **FRUIT SALT** daily, and have one headache during that time; whereas formerly everything but the food disagreed with me. I am now almost indifferent as to diet. One our medicine has above others of its kind is that to it the patient does not slave, and I am now finding myself able gradually to discontinue its use. thank you sufficiently for conferring on me such a benefit; and if this a be used in any way, I shall be really glad, merely begging that the ly of my name may be published.—I am, Sir, yours gratefully, TRUTH.

ON.—*Examine each Bottle, and see that the CAPSULE is marked "ENO'S* SALT." *Without it you have been imposed upon by worthless imitations.* ll Chemists. Directions in Sixteen Languages How to Prevent Disease.

pared only at **ENO'S FRUIT SALT WORKS, HATCHAM, LONDON, S.E.,** by **J. C. ENO'S PATENT.**

ABOVE: Among the Victorians, morality and indigestion were both excessive. Relief of the stomach no doubt alleviated also that sense of guilt that comes from greed.

OPPOSITE: The Victorians' taste for elaborate ornament, characteristic of much of their architecture, their household goods, their appearances, and their rhetoric, extended even to their cooking. Two favourite 'culinary manuals' were *The Gastronomic Regenerator* and *The Modern Cook*, from which has been compiled this selection of favourite specialités.

The dinner table was crowded. . . . In the centre stood a magnificent, finely-spun, barley-sugar windmill, two feet and a half high, with a spacious sugar foundation. . . .

The whole dinner, first, second, third, fourth course – everything, in fact, except dessert – was on the table. . . . Before both Mr and Mrs Jorrocks were two great tureens of mock turtle soup, each capable of holding a gallon, and both full up to the brim. Then there were two sorts of fish: turbot and lobster sauce, and a great salmon. A round of boiled beef, and an immense piece of roast occupied the rear of these, ready to march on the disappearance of the fish and soup – and behind the walls, formed by the beef of old England, came two dishes of grouse, each dish holding three brace. The side-dishes consisted of a calf's head hashed, a leg of mutton, chickens, ducks, and mountains of vegetables; and round the windmill were plum puddings, tarts, jellies, pies, and puffs. . . .

Jorrocks' Jaunts and Jollities – R. S. Surtees

How did they do it? How did the Victorians manage to get through such gargantuan meals and still survive? We, who live lives far more abstemious, who balance our diets with care, and watch our figures, absorb far more remedies for dyspepsia than the Victorians ever dreamt of. Whether statistics would have proved that they suffered from indigestion to the same extent as we do seems doubtful. If they did, one would have expected to find some hint of their sufferings in the writings and advertisements of the period. A greater delicacy in Thackeray than in Dickens or Surtees might have prevented his referring openly to flatulence, but there is never a mention even of heartburn let alone apoplexy through over-eating; and except for an occasional testimony to patent lozenges, or gripe water or milk of magnesia, the dyspeptic seems to have been left to writhe in peace.

We like to think that our more moderate appetites reflect a more rational approach to the subject of nutrition. But the truth is that it is not only our respect for the findings of science that limits our intake of calories, proteins and other substances of which the Victorians were ignorant; it is also that for many of us the pace and pressure of existence prevents us from enjoying our food in the way the Victorians enjoyed theirs. We have neither the time nor the

ABOVE: The high priestess of Victorian domestic economy, Isabella Mary Beeton (1836–65), whose *Household Management*, published in 1859, was of incalculable influence on the eating habits of middle-class England.
BELOW: 'A *coup-d'oeil* of the matchless culinary arrangements of the Reform Club.' Alexis Soyer, the celebrated chef, supervised the construction of the kitchens, which, under his direction, gave the Club a gastronomic reputation that was second to none.

inclination for large and leisurely meals. Yet curiously enough there is a greater interest now in food than there has ever been. There are cookery books of all kinds and from all countries. Those that were published in the Victorian era dealt mainly with traditional English cooking. Mrs Beeton's was of course the most famous and most successful; within a decade of its publication two million copies had been sold, even though a good many of the recipes must have been beyond the abilities of anyone but a skilful cook. To this assumption of culinary expertise Mrs Beeton now and then added a flattering belief in the omniscient understanding of Victorian housewives. 'All fish,' she declares in *Every-day Cookery*, 'in consequence of its highly nitrogenous character, requires the abundant use of starchy foods in combination with it.' Then comes a table showing the relative proportions of water, nitrogenous matters, fat and mineral matters in salmon and sole – which leaves us with a rather different picture of the Victorian cook than that of a plump, simple-minded kitchen autocrat. To follow Mrs Beeton faithfully, it seems that she must also have been a scientific dietician and statistically inclined.

A close rival to Mrs Beeton was Alexis Soyer, the famous chef of the Reform Club, who published three cookery books. First was *The Gastronomic Regenerator*, which he described as being 'adapted for the highest class of epicures'; then 'for the easy middle class', came *The Modern Housewife*, of which some thirty thousand copies were sold. And in 1854 *A Shilling Cookery for the People*. This followed a visit to the Crimea, which Soyer made on his own initiative in order to see

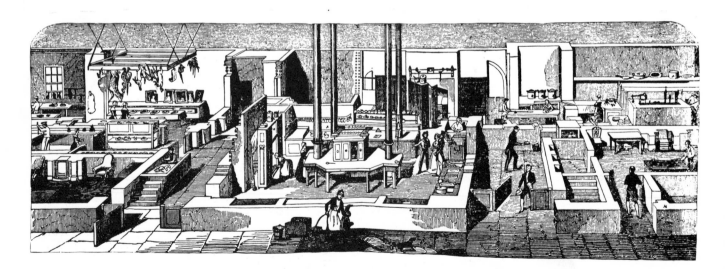

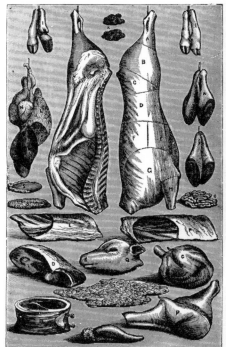

*, Hind Knuckle; *B*, Fillet; *c*, Loin, Chump end; *D*, Do., best end; *E*, Breast; *F*, Neck; *G*, Shoulder; *H*, Fore Knuckle; *I*, Feet; *K*, Kidneys; *L*, Lights; *M*, Liver; *N*, Heart; *O*, Brains; *P*, Leg; *Q*, Head; *R*, Tongue; *S*, Sweetbread; *T*, Caul.

Following Soyer, Mrs Beeton also produced a *Shilling Cookery Book*, which was for long a best seller. Its information included instructions in the anatomy of beef, mutton, veal, etc. But working-class wives still learnt mostly by experience, with monotonous and often uneconomic results. In 1873, Mr Catlin, an East End missionary, concerned for the body as well as the soul, organised cooking lessons (BELOW) in his mission hall, which were sometimes attended by as many as two hundred ladies.

what advice he could offer on catering for the army. It was typical of the attitude of those in charge that his suggestions for the more nutritious and economical use of food in the British camp were received with very little enthusiasm; and but for the support of Florence Nightingale, of whom the generals seemed more scared than of the Russians, Soyer's proposals would almost certainly have been ignored. After making a tour of investigation, he reorganised the catering and messing arrangements, replaced amateur messmen with trained cooks, did away with the automatic practice of boiling everything, improved the baking system, and devised new ways of using army rations.

In the gloomy history of the Crimean campaign few episodes occurred to raise the spirits of the British soldier, but Soyer's visit to the front, the results of which were to affect a permanent improvement in catering and cooking throughout the army, was something for which every man in the ranks had reason to be grateful.

In his preface to *A Shilling Cookery for the People*, Soyer explained what had prompted him to write it:

My readers will easily perceive that, whilst semi-buried in my fashionable culinary sanctorum at the Reform Club, surrounded by the *élite* of society, who daily honoured me with their visits. . . . I could not gain, through the stone walls of that massive edifice, the slightest knowledge of Cottage life. . . . I found that the only course I had to pursue was to visit personally the abodes, and learn the manners of those to whom I was about to address myself.

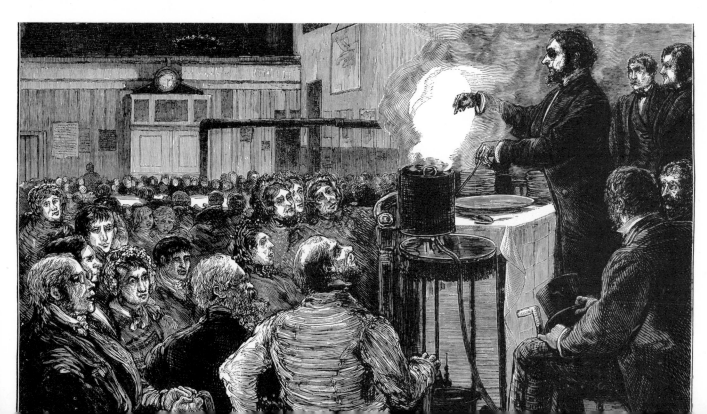

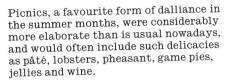

OPPOSITE: The food preserving industry was already flourishing in the 'fifties, unhampered by hygienic restrictions such as would have prevented food from being left on the floor.

Picnics, a favourite form of dalliance in the summer months, were considerably more elaborate than is usual nowadays, and would often include such delicacies as pâté, lobsters, pheasant, game pies, jellies and wine.

Alfresco meals of a more formal but more economic kind were a popular form of plebeian jollity. Parties provided their own food and drink, but had to rely on obliging cottagers to lend tables and chairs.

A *Shilling Cookery* was, in other words, the result of a long tour of investigation into the gastronomic habits of the poor throughout the British Isles. Soyer's approach was severely and typically practical, but at the same time he appealed for a more imaginative attitude towards cooking. He wrote with considerable sympathy on the general ignorance of the poor in cooking; he instructed them in marketing, in the economy of roasting by gas, and on the selection and cooking of vegetables. He also gave instructions for preparing French *pot-au-feu*, *Hints on the Pig*, *Observations on Bottled Preserves*, and hundreds of other cheap, simple and ingenious recipes. Soyer's intention was admirable and the book had a huge sale, but its effect on the eating habits of the 'people' was disappointing. They remained on the whole as lethargic and unenterprising as ever.

It was not the basic material but more often the will that was lacking. Food was cheap and abundant and with a little ingenuity simple fare could be made delicious. In our present day enthusiasm for foreign cookery, which, better late than never; has overcome our ancient gastronomic prejudices, we have forgotten about some excellent and inexpensive dishes that the Victorians enjoyed. Perhaps

BELOW: Pepin's cast-iron 'Digester', forerunner of the pressure-cooker. According to its inventor, it was guaranteed, for those who enjoyed such exotic *bonnes bouches*, to reduce a felt hat to a jelly in four hours.

there are too few larks, and no doubt too many upholders of the rights of small birds, for us to be able to enjoy roast larks and bacon with a clear conscience; but what of Young Rook Pudding (no farmer would object to fewer rooks), Eel Pudding (made with beer or wine), Devilled Bones, or Herrings in Whiskey, all of which Soyer recommends? What of Hot Codlins, or Lampreys? What of Ramekins, Aunt Nelly's Pudding and Victoria Buns?

Too often we are inclined to accept as typically Victorian the idea of a table loaded with succulent food, the Rhenish and the claret flowing, and steaming punch to follow. With such an agreeable picture in one's mind it is easy to forget that at the same time there were many thousands, particularly in the industrial towns, where there were fewer extras in the way of food than in the country, who hardly knew what it was like not to feel hungry. Even in the country, the farm labourer's mid-day meal, the principal one of the day, must have been, according to present theories of nutrition, shockingly inadequate, lacking as it did the proper amount of vitamins and protein. In *Lark Rise*, which describes life in a farming community during the 'seventies, Flora Thompson describes the sort of meal her father and brothers ate:

At twelve by the sun . . . the teams would knock off for the dinner hour. Horses were unyoked. . . . and given their nosebags and men and boys threw themselves down on sacks spread out beside them and tin bottles of cold tea were uncorked and red handkerchiefs of food unwrapped. The lucky ones had bread and cold bacon, perhaps the top or the bottom of a cottage loaf, on which the small cube of bacon was placed. . . . The less fortunate ones munched their bread and lard or morsel of cheese; and the boys with their ends of cold pudding were jokingly bidden not to get 'that 'ere treacle' in their ears.

Breakfast too would probably consist of bread and home-made lard flavoured with rosemary – butter was too expensive – and tea without milk, for only the farmer kept a cow. How different from the breakfast which Squire Headlong provided for his guests. Although *Headlong Hall* was written some thirty years earlier, breakfast in the house of the gentry still meant a good solid meal and a variety of dishes to choose from. At Headlong Hall it began at eight, for those who liked to get up early, and went on till two, so that less energetic guests might not be made to feel that there was any need to hurry. The side-table, from which the meal was served by a butler, was 'copiously furnished with all the apparatus of tea, coffee, chocolate, milk, cream, eggs, rolls, toast, muffins, bread, butter, potted beef, cold fowl and partridge, ham, tongue and anchovy'.

The habit of toasting is now mercifully confined to formal or official functions. George Cruikshank's Mr Lambkin, a typical ass-about-town of the 1840s and never at a loss for words, was always in demand for toasts at the innumerable parties where he spent so much of his time.

And now let Mr. Lambkin speak for himself.

"Ladies and Gentlemen, unaccustomed as I am... (Bravo)...return...
(Bravo) on the part of Miss... (oh! oh! ha! ha!), I beg pardon, I mean Mrs
Lambkin (Bravo) and myself for the great...hum... ha...hum.... and
kindness, (Bravo) In return hum...ha...pleasure to drink all your healths
(Bravo),—Wishing you all the happiness this world can afford (Bravo)
I shall conclude in the words of our immortal bard—"may the single
be married and the (hear! Hear! hear! Bravo) married happy."
Bravo! Bravo!! Bravo!!!

1. *Open Jelly with whipped cream.*　　　2. *Yorkshire Pie and Aspic Jelly.*
3. *Trifle, Ices and Jellies around.*
4. *Christmas Pudding.*　　　5. *Jelly of two colours.*

DINNER TABLE—OLD-FASHIONED STYLE.

In the laying of the table, whether for luncheon, tea, or dinner, precision was the watchword of the butler, who supervised operations, and was likewise the bane of the parlour maid, who deployed the paraphernalia of the pantry, the china cupboard, and the silver closet.

OPPOSITE: Victorian *haute cuisine* required almost as much time and trouble to be spent on perfecting the appearance of food as on the succulence of the elaborate dishes without which no fashionable dinner party was complete.

TEA TABLE.

For the sake of efficient husbandry it was as well perhaps that the labourers of *Lark Rise* were spared the temptations of *Headlong Hall*. But a breakfast of only bread and lard does not seem much for a growing boy or a man working in the fields for perhaps nine or ten hours a day, six days a week. Yet most farm labourers managed not only to survive but to keep strong and healthy, though against this fact it must be remembered that the death-rate, particularly among children, was enormously high: in the early 'sixties forty-two years was the average expectation of life.

There was little variation in the working man's diet, either in town or country, except that in winter there were fewer vegetables. The main sources of food were bread and potatoes. It was estimated in an official report of 1863 that at that period the amount of bread eaten by farm labourers averaged $12\frac{1}{4}$ lbs a week. In the part of North Oxfordshire where Flora Thompson's family lived there were more pigs and sheep than there were cows and consequently milk was a luxury. But eggs and fruit were easier to come by and so were more often eaten in the country than in town. On their way to school the children

... would creep through the bars of the padlocked field gates for turnips to pare with the teeth and munch, or for handfuls of green pea shucks, or ears of wheat, to rub out the sweet, milky grain between the hands and devour. In spring they ate the young green from the hawthorn hedges, which they called 'bread and cheese', and sorrel leaves from the wayside, which they called 'sour grass', and in autumn there was an abundance of haws and blackberries and sloes and crab-apples for them to feast upon. There was always something to eat, and they ate, not so much because they were hungry as from habit and relish of the wild food.

If they were less hungry than urban children, this was often because the country housewife had learnt a bit about the arts of cookery and economy, which the middle-class townswoman had very little chance to learn. It was the aim of every village mother to get her daughter into service. In a good place a girl not only got her keep, which meant there was one less mouth to be fed at home, but would usually learn plain cooking and sewing. If she were sensible and industrious she might also learn something about the management of a household, so that if she returned to the village, as girls often did, to marry a childhood sweetheart and settle down, she would have some practical experience of how to run a house and feed a family.

Although the prices of food were low a poor family could usually afford meat – pork and veal were favoured more than beef or mutton, which were too dear – only two or at most three times a week.

For two hundred years Covent Garden had been (as it still is) the centre of London's wholesale fruit and vegetable trade, a landmark in our culinary history.

Today the supermarket provides all that we want – except the personal touch and the delivery service that once made shopping for groceries a pleasure instead of a boring routine. With eggs at a penny each, margarine at fourpence a pound, and butter, cheese and bacon equally inexpensive, the pleasure must have been considerably enhanced.

PHYSIOLOGY OF TARTS, PIES AND PIE CRU

PORTRAIT OF AN APPLE PIE AS IT OUGHT TO BE
TAKEN FROM STILL LIFE

T. TURNER LITHO.

STRIKING LIKENESS OF AN APPLE TART IN A FIT AS THEY
OFTEN ARE (TAKEN FROM REAL LIFE)

ABOVE LEFT AND RIGHT: The Sunday
joint, with its Yorkshire pud, and the
apple tart which usually followed, were
often too big for the modest domestic
oven and would be taken round to the
local baker's where they could be
cooked for a penny each. But, as Soyer
showed in his *Modern Housewife*, this
was not always a success.

In slums throughout the country a
number of charitable institutions ran
soup kitchens, without which some of
the very poor would often have been
without sustenance.

A soup house was sometimes a last resort of the down-and-out before turning to the workhouse. Here a bowl of hot soup with potatoes and a slice of bread cost twopence, and trade was brisk all the year round.

Columbia Market in Bethnal Green was built in 1866 by the philanthropic Baroness Burdett-Coutts. Its ecclesiastical frontage reflected her pious hope that trading in such surroundings would be less fraudulent than elsewhere in the East End, where many butchers, grocers, dairymen and other shopkeepers were notoriously dishonest.

Even so, more meat was eaten in the towns than in the country because the bulk of it was sent away to market. In London it went to Smithfield or Islington, where cattle were slaughtered in conditions both brutal and insanitary. More humane and more precautionary methods would have seemed desirable not only for their own sake. In 1842 it was said that 'the deterioration of the meat from this brutality has been calculated at no less a sum than £100,000 per annum'. The scene at Smithfield in the early morning was

... one of terrible confusion.... The lowing of the oxen, the tremulous cries of the sheep, the barking of dogs, the rattling of sticks on the heads and bodies of the animals, the shouts of the drovers, and the flashing about of torches, present altogether a wild and terrific combination; and few, either of those who reside in the metropolis, or who visit it, have the resolution to witness the strange scene.

In poor districts a considerable amount of cooked food, and also a variety of drinks, was sold by street traders. A list drawn up by Henry Mayhew, that patient and observant chronicler of Victorian low life, writing of things as they were in the late 'fifties, shows what an astonishing array of food and drink was to be had from the trays and barrows of itinerant salesmen:

The solids consist of hot-eels, pickled whelks, oysters, sheeps'-trotters, pea-soup, fried fish, ham-sandwiches, hot green peas, kidney puddings, boiled meat puddings, beef, mutton, kidney, and eel pies, and baked potatoes. In each of these provisions the street-poor find a mid-day or

Hokey-pokey, now known as ice-cream, was one of many varieties of foodstuff sold in the streets of working-class districts.

ABOVE: Oranges, roast chestnuts and ginger-beer were among the cheaper and more popular forms of fare.
RIGHT: Oysters, at a penny each, though still something of a luxury, were eaten far more freely than they are today.

midnight meal. . . . The pastry and confectionery which tempt the street eaters are tarts of rhubarb, currant, gooseberry, apple, damson, cranberry and (so called) mince pies; plum dough and plum cake; lard, currant, almond and many other varieties of cakes, as well as of tarts; gingerbread-nuts and heart-cakes; Chelsea buns; muffins and crumpets; 'sweet stuff' includes the several kinds of rocks, sticks, lozenges, candies and hard-bakes; the medicinal confectionery of cough-drops and horehound; and, lastly, the more novel and aristocratic luxury of street-ices. . . . The drinkables are tea, coffee and cocoa; ginger beer, lemonade, Persian sherbet, and some highly-coloured beverages which have no specific name, but are introduced to the public as 'cooling' drinks; hot elder cordial or wine; peppermint water; curds and whey; water; rice milk; and milk in the parks.

Bread was the staple of the working-class diet, but some could only afford stale bread, which was sold in the streets for as little as a penny or sometimes even a halfpenny for a four-pound loaf. If there were a few pennies to spare they might be spent at a soup-house where for twopence or threepence you could buy 'a basin of prime soup, potatoes, and a slice of bread'. Charles Knight, in describing this, adds that 'the quantity sold every day at these houses is extremely large'. In the windows 'a goodly array of blue and white basins is displayed . . . from which emanate abundant clouds of odour-giving steam. Around the windows, too, a crowd of hungry mortals assemble on a cold day, and partake (in imagination) of the enticing things within'.

Coffee-stalls did a brisk trade all day in food as well as drinks. Few stalls are now left and most of those that survive are open only at night. In 1842 there were some three hundred in London selling, besides coffee, tea and cocoa at a penny a mug (as against sixpence now charged for a smaller cup), ham sandwiches, watercress, boiled eggs, baked potatoes, and slices of cake or bread and butter. Nothing cost more than twopence and a filling if not particularly nourishing meal could be got for sixpence. The proprietor of a favourite stall in Oxford Street estimated that he could 'take a full thirty shillings of a morning, in halfpence'.

For those who were somewhat better off than the patrons of the coffee stall or the street market there were innumerable chop houses, such as are often mentioned by Dickens, where for about one shilling and sixpence the City clerk could get an ample lunch. A plate of liver and bacon would cost tenpence, twopence would go on bread and potatoes, fourpence on cheese and celery, and about the same on a pint of stout. Or if by some improbable stroke of luck he were feeling flush, he might, like Mr Guppy in *Bleak House*, spring an

Suspicion of foreign food and cooking was widespread, except among a sophisticated minority. Even *groseilles au vin blanc* were sufficient to dismay the English housewife, as shown by John Leech in his painting of a Parisian *table d'hôte*.

French as it is spoken. Scene Paris, a Table d'hôte.
(Old Lady at Breakfast "The Garçon has been ordered to bring some Tea to the old Lady)

ABOVE: For most of the Victorian era many Londoners living near the Thames drew their drinking water from the river, into which hundreds of sewers poured their filth and riverside dwellers emptied their garbage.

ABOVE RIGHT: The coffee room at St John's Gate Tavern, Clerkenwell, 1860, formerly a haunt of Johnson, Garrick and Goldsmith. At such retreats, in contrast to the noise and bustle of a tavern bar, customers could drink and smoke at their ease.

OPPOSITE: On 9 November 1837 the Lord Mayor of London was the host at a banquet for the young Queen in the Guildhall. It was one of the most magnificent of her reign – and no doubt one of the most expensive: 570 guests were entertained by the Corporation at a cost of more than £8,000.

RIGHT: Regal hospitality required lavish arrangements below as well as above stairs. The kitchens at Windsor Castle, fifty feet in height, included every sort of up-to-date culinary device and under the watchful eyes of a *chef de cuisine* and two yeomen of the kitchen, a staff of twenty-four was employed.

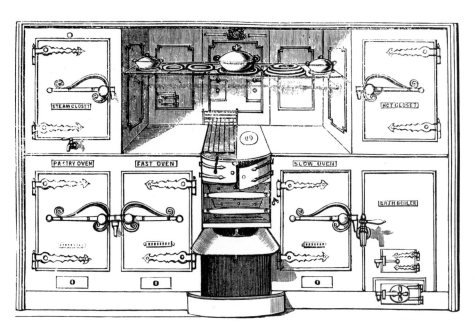

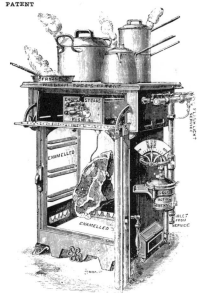

The housewife's dream in 1851 was Goddard's combined oven (LEFT), steam-closet and bath boiler, first shown at the Great Exhibition. Forty years later Sugg's Gas Kitchener (RIGHT), a less elaborate and more sophisticated apparatus, had superseded the heavier equipment of earlier days.

extra twopence; in which case the reckoning, for himself and friends, two in number, would be, as one of them declared:

Four veals and hams is three, and four potatoes is three-and-four, and one summer cabbage is three-and-six, and three marrows is four-and-six, and six breads is five, and three Cheshires is five-and-three, and four pints of half-and-half is six-and-three, and four small rums is eight-and-three.

which with threepence for the waitress comes to two and tenpence a head.

Mr Guppy's employer, Mr Kenge, was a prosperous and self-important solicitor, typical of the *haute bourgeoisie* of the 'fifties. The keeping of a good table would have been for Mr Kenge not so much a matter of gastronomic pride or pleasure as a means of ensuring that his friends and his clients were aware of his position in society. The period was one in which for persons like Mr Kenge the giving of formal dinner parties was deemed as necessary a tribute to Mammon as family prayers were to God. But whereas tribute was paid to God, if only nominally, in a submissive spirit, the feelings evoked by Mammon were rather different.

'Dinners,' says Thackeray in his *Sketches and Travels in London,*

. . . are given mostly in the middle classes by way of revenge; and Mr and Mrs Thompson ask Mr and Mrs Johnson, because the latter have asked

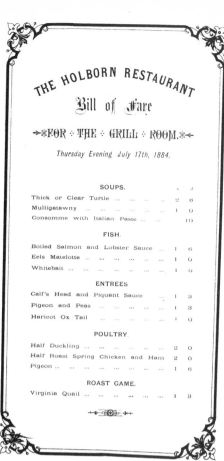

The Holborn Restaurant, now no more, was of a type popular with business men, combining ostentation with economy. The evening *table d'hôte* offered a choice of six main dishes, including salmon and quail, with musical accompaniment, all for three shillings and sixpence.

BELOW: The ritual of afternoon tea at its most formal was perfected in the 'seventies, when this drawing by Du Maurier appeared in *Punch*.

them. A man at this rate who gives four dinners of twenty persons in the course of the season, each dinner costing him something very near upon thirty pounds, receives in return, we will say, forty dinners from the friends whom he has himself invited. That is, Mr and Mrs Johnson pay a hundred and twenty pounds, as do all their friends, for forty-four dinners of which they partake. So that they may calculate that every time they dine with their respective friends, they pay about twenty-eight shillings per *tête*.

It seems a high price to pay for the tedium that such dinners must have involved, not to mention the monotony of the fare. 'Everybody,' says Thackeray, 'has the same dinner in London, and the same soup, saddle of mutton, boiled fowls and tongue, *entrées*, champagne, and so forth'.

Relatively, of course, it was not expensive at twenty-eight shillings per *tête*, and on the whole food remained remarkably cheap for a very long time.

Some twenty-five years after the publication of *Bleak House*, which made its appearance in 1852, the current edition of Mrs Beeton's *Everyday Cookery* showed that food prices had increased very

SOYER'S SAUCE.
Sold only in the above bottles, holding half-a-pint.
PRICE 2s. 6d.

BELOW: An annual ritual was the Christmas dinner, of which the climax was, as it still is, plum pudding blazing with brandy.

OPPOSITE: Several varieties of sauce were concocted by Alexis Soyer. The most popular, known simply as Soyer's Sauce, was a godsend to the bored or unimaginative cook.

Stanhope Forbes's painting, *The Health of the Bride*, shows in characteristic and touching detail that solemn Victorian feast, the working-class wedding breakfast.

little. Her book, of course, was intended for a public that was socially a cut above Mr Guppy's circle. Even so, the prices of meat, poultry and fish must seem astonishing to the housewife of today. Rump steak could be bought for tenpence a pound, so could saddle of mutton; chickens were two to three shillings each, grouse and partridges not more than five shillings a brace; salmon varied from between tenpence and three shillings a pound, and lobsters between sixpence and four shillings each; Whitstable natives were from one to three shillings a dozen. Fruit, vegetables and groceries were all correspondingly cheap and it was quite possible, as Mrs Beeton showed, to give a dinner party for ten people at a cost of about five shillings a head. This did not include wine, but with the best sherry at only sixty shillings a dozen and red and white wine equally inexpensive (an excellent Chablis could be bought for thirty-six shillings a dozen and a Chateau Lafitte for eighty shillings) and vintage port at forty-two shillings, the wine would have cost about the same as the food, the outlay for the whole dinner being something in the neighbourhood of four pounds.

The menu given by Mrs Beeton in her book is of interest not only for its breakdown of the cost, but also for the choice which it shows it was customary to provide:

MENU	Quantity	Average cost	
		s	d
Game Soup	3 pints	4	0
Turbot	1 fish	7	0
Lobster Sauce	1 tur.	2	6
Vol-au-vent of Oysters	1	6	0
Salmi of Black Game	1 dish	5	0
Saddle of Mutton	1 joint	9	6
Potatoes Sprouts	3 lbs each	0	9
Compote of Apples	1 dish	2	0
Banana Fritters	1 dish	1	6
Cheese Straws	1 dish	0	9
		£1 19	0

By the late 'eighties the production and distribution of food had become major industries, as distinct from being organised merely to supply local needs. Less was sold in the streets than in Mayhew's time and far more in the shops. Improved methods of canning and preservation, though still primative by modern standards, had added enormously to the variety of food that could be bought, and by 1891 more than half a million people were employed in manufacturing and distributing food.

By the middle of the 'eighties, the Victorian cornucopia had begun to run dry. The great tide of prosperity on which the country had been propelled for so long was receding. Forty years earlier the repeal of the Corn Laws had stimulated fears about the future of the country's agricultural situation, but these fears had been shown to be exaggerated. There had not been, as many farmers expected, an immediate increase in the amount of grain imported from abroad. This was largely because British farming methods were ahead of those on the Continent and so it was still cheaper to buy farm produce at home than from foreign countries. But a depression was beginning which before long was to hit both agriculture and industry. Economy became the watchword. But to the middle and upper classes it was a word that had an obnoxiously plebeian ring about it. Like democracy or atheism or syphilis, it was something one did not talk about. The long, formal and elaborate dinner parties which twenty years earlier had bored the Podsnaps' and the

The repeal of the Corn Laws in 1846, whereby restrictive tariffs were removed from British agriculture and the price of bread reduced, was the result of a long and widespread agitation fostered by Anti-Corn Law leagues (FAR RIGHT) in all parts of the country. The repeal was marked by the sale of innumerable emblems, among them crude statuettes of the Prime Minister, Sir Robert Peel (ABOVE) as well as commemorative china inscribed with words of thanksgiving (RIGHT).

GIVE US THIS DAY OUR DAILY BREAD

NATIONAL ANTI-CORN LAW LEAGUE,

is a *Registered Member*

Joseph Hickin *Secretary*

1609. Registered by

Veneerings' sycophantic guests now, as Du Maurier shows us, bored the guests of Sir Gorgius Midas and Mrs Ponsonby de Tomkyns, whose dinners were as tedious as a City banquet.

All banquets, of course, are tedious. No one except a toastmaster goes to a banquet for any other reason than that his sense of duty urges him to attend. Victorian banquets were of inordinate length and splendour and their effects on the digestion must often have been distressing. Probably the most magnificent banquet of her reign was that which the Mayor and Corporation of the City of London gave to the Queen in the year of her accession. It lasted from half-past five, when the 570 guests took their places in the Guildhall, until eight o'clock in the evening. The bill of fare for the company, not including those at the Queen's table, provided among its thirty-nine dishes, 220 tureens of Turtle, 45 dishes of Shell-fish, 2 Barons of Beef, 10 Sirloins, Rumps and Ribs of Beef, 50 Boiled Turkeys and Oysters, 80 Pheasants, 60 Pigeon Pies, 45 Hams, ornamented, 140 Jellies, 200 Ice Creams, 40 Dishes of Tarts, creamed, 100 Pine Apples, and a variety of other dishes.

The Victorian diner is more often pictured as greedy than as fastidious, but the menu at the Queen's table was calculated to activate the salivary glands of the gourmet as well as the gourmand. A choice of sixty-five dishes included such exotic items as Sultanne de filets de Sole à la Hollandaise garnis aux Excrevisses, Pierre grillé aux Vin de Champagne, Dindon rôti aux Truffes à l'Espagnole, Fontaine Royale garnie de Patisserie à la Genevoise, and Fanchonettes d'Orange garnies aux Pistache. With this enticing spread went champagne, hock, claret, burgundy, madeira, port and sherry.

The bill came to £1,971.17.6. But further charges for lighting and illuminations, gilding, upholstery, printing, music and incidental expenses (bellringers, £8.8.0, waiters' collars, £14.0.0, buttons, £24.4.5, perfumery, £12.1.3) made the occasion one of the most expensive banquets per head that the Corporation of London can ever have given. The final total came to £8,172.4.11.

For any guest who may have felt towards the end that he still had room for another mouthful, there might have been food for thought in the observation of Samuel Smiles, most typical of Victorians: *We each day dig our graves with our teeth.*

Chapter 4: Old Clothes and New ❡ Fashionable Intelligence ❡ The Well-Dressed Man ❡ The Etiquette of Dress ❡ Petticoat Lane ❡ Keeping up Appearances ❡ Silks and Satins ❡ Under-clothes ❡ The Queen and the Empress Eugénie ❡ The Aesthetic Movement ❡ The Shape of Things Departed

Plus ça change . . . that fashion is based entirely on whim and seldom has any connection with need, convenience or hygiene, was never better shown than by the bustle of the late 'eighties, perhaps the most incongruous period of Victorian fashion.

What is fashion? Hazlitt defined it as 'gentility running away from vulgarity and afraid of being overtaken'. The Victorians were nothing if not genteel, for although in their day the word had not acquired the undertones of affectation that it has since taken on, gentility, or an aspiration towards it, is one of the forms of self-consciousness that distinguish the middle from both the upper and the lower classes. The Victorians were intensely interested in clothes, and fashion was for many of them a permanent preoccupation, whether they could afford to indulge it or not. Even those who lived in the country and had few occasions for dressing in their best, except on Sunday, were never tired of hearing or reading about the latest fashions. This they did in fashion magazines, which were, comparatively speaking, no less popular then than they are now. In England the tendency at first was for such magazines to copy designs and information from Parisian journals rather than to display original fashions. But from the 'fifties onwards magazines began to appear which catered for the interests of a middle-class readership instead of for the exclusive tastes of ladies in high society, who preferred, as they still do, to be dressed by their own favourite *couturiers*.

In our own time well-designed clothes produced for the mass market have enormously improved the standard of appearances among both men and women. The latest styles are in the shops almost as soon as they have appeared at the spring or autumn collections. But although a new neckline or the raising or dropping of a hem may make headlines, fashions do not really change as much as designers and fashion editors like us to think. Fashion, in the sense of clothing that is merely up to date but not so very different from what was in vogue a few years earlier, depends largely on the fancy or prejudice of those designers who happen to be popular at the time. But fundamental changes in dress, as, for instance, the wearing of wigs by men during the seventeenth and eighteenth centuries, or the universal adoption of trousers by women in the twentieth, occur very seldom. As often as not, changes in dress have less to do with personal taste than with social conditions. The late Victorians, for example, were considerably more mobile than their parents; consequently they needed clothes that were suitable for faster and easier methods of travel than those of the 'forties and 'fifties.

The Victorian child had much to put up with besides Victorian parents. *Fashionable Wear for the Juvenile Nobility*, a plate from the early 'forties, shows that fun and games were not restricted merely by parental sanctions.

Fashions are not the sole creation of the designer. An influence more significant, if less direct, is sometimes exerted by the industrial scientists or the mechanical engineer. Technical developments in industries allied to the clothing trade may have effects of enormous importance. In Victorian days the discovery of new materials and improvements in manufacturing methods, though far fewer than in our own time, were still an influential factor.

Periods of national upheaval, such as war or revolution, may also have profound effects on clothing habits. But at home the Victorian era was a period of comparative tranquillity, and no abrupt or sensational changes in fashion occurred. The crinoline, which reached its most extravagant dimensions in the 'sixties, though incongruous and unwieldy, was only an enlargement *ad absurdum* of the type of dress that preceded it. This had a bell-shaped skirt supported with pads and petticoats, sometimes to the number of six or seven. In turn, the crinoline itself presently gave way to the bustle, which was at first a moderate variation on the same theme. It was not until the 'eighties that it began to take on the appearance of a physical deformity, suggesting that the wearer's behind was grossly enlarged, sometimes by as much as fifteen inches or more.

If there were no basic changes in the styles of dress, there was one change which left an influence that is only now showing signs of slackening. From the mid-forties the colours of men's clothing began to be more sombre. The bright and varied hues of the preceding years gradually gave way to the darker colours that were thereafter worn most of the time until the end of the century. A lighter waist-coat might be permissible on informal occasions and something less subfusc could be worn in the country, with a soft hat or a cap.

OPPOSITE: Ladies' headgear in the 'seventies was designed to decorate the head, not to cover it, and for this purpose was perched high on the coiffure. Parisian confections of straw or velvet were decked with ribbons, lace, passementerie, artificial flowers and feathers, with an effect that was singular rather than discriminate.
OVERLEAF: In gents' wear a sober look, in contrast with the elegance of Regency days, was already in vogue in the 'fifties and was to become more pronounced as time went on. Parisian influences lingered among the fast set, but subdued formality was observed by respectable persons.

LA MODE ILLUSTRÉE

Bureaux du Journal 56 rue Jacob Paris

Chapeaux de M.ᵐᵉ AUBERT. 34. r. de la Victoire.

December

Journa

THE CUTTERS'

of London

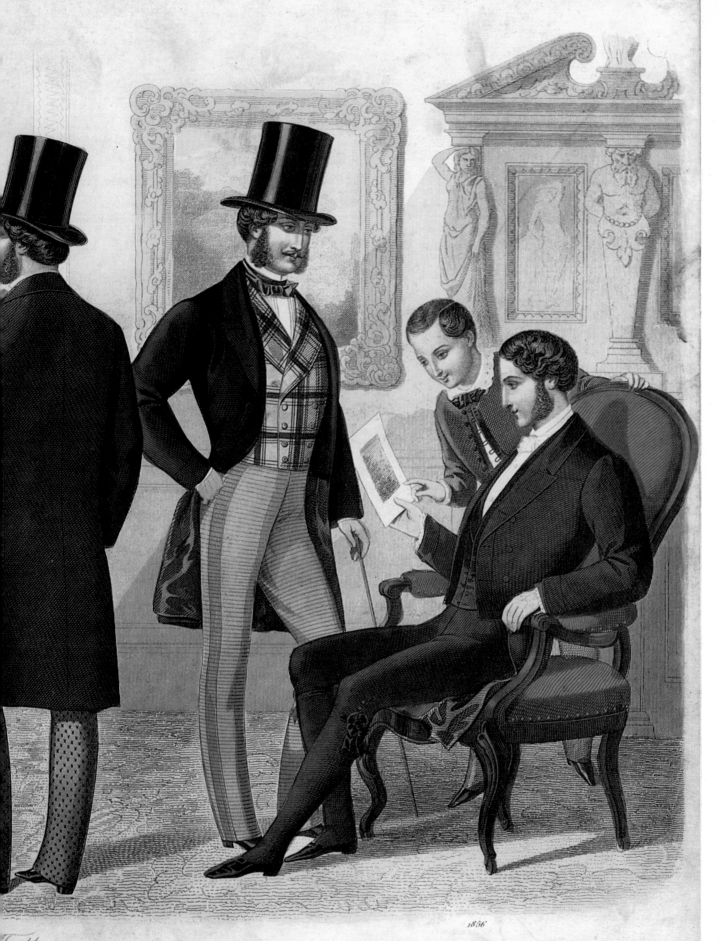

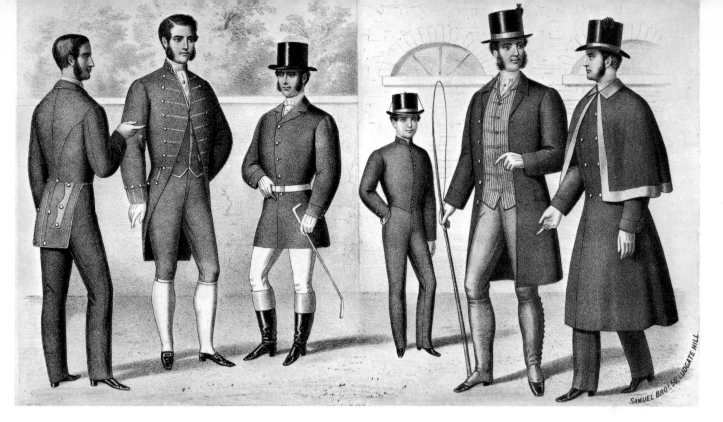

Beau Brummell made the cravat the keystone of a gentleman's toilette. The Victorian dandy, in his choice of neckwear as much as in the tying of a bow or a four-in-hand, was no less scrupulous than Brummell.

But in town a suit of dark clothes remained for long the only thing to wear, and with it, inescapably, a top-hat. The bowler, known when it first appeared round about the 'sixties as a billycock, was for fifty years or more a decidedly plebeian article.

Although in most essentials male dress remained the same throughout the Victorian era, in cut and colour there were considerable changes. In 1837

The coat – well padded when nature had been in any way unkind – fitted tight to the figure; the collar was prodigiously large and heavy, and exquisites would sometimes carry a small roll of lead sewed inside each pocket, so as to keep the garment well down and free from creases. Trousers were worn tight, while waistcoats were of satin, silk, velvet or other rich material, sprigged, shot or gaudily patterned in endless variety. The neck was swathed in a huge stock, cravat or neck-cloth. The hair, worn longer than at present [i.e. 1887], was often curled, and nearly always liberally supplied with scented oil or pomatum thoroughly well rubbed in. Whiskers were of the order known as 'mutton chop', and a civilian bold enough to wear a moustache would have been debarred from respectable society as a hopeless reprobate.

In the days when Queen Victoria's uncle was Prince Regent, his friend George Brummell had set Englishmen a standard of sartorial perfection that gave them the reputation of being the best dressed men in the world – a reputation that was to last for more than a century before influences from abroad began to diminish its lustre. Brummell's most notable successor in early Victorian days, Count d'Orsay, was, ironically, an Englishman only by adoption. This in itself was no doubt enough to prejudice him in the eyes of the middle classes, without his being well dressed into the bargain. This must

have seemed like adding insult to injury, for the Victorian middle class, like the middle class of today, was essentially conservative in matters of dress.

This attitude affected not merely style; there was a strict etiquette about dressing well, and its observance or neglect was a pointer to one's position in society. Considerably more time was spent than most people could nowadays afford, or would consider necessary, in making up one's mind what to wear or in changing clothes in order to be sure of being correctly dressed. The moments for wearing or discarding gloves and bonnets, the colours and materials appropriate to various uses and occasions, the precise degrees of distinction between formal and informal dress, what to do with coats and hats, parasols and canes, were matters of grave preoccupation to those who were intent on rising in society.

Since Neanderthal woman, furs have been fashionable wear for ladies. Their range in Victorian days included such forgotten items as dolmans, pelisses, paletots and muffs.

SHOW E
ROOME

Were Cowper's lines perhaps in Richard
Doyle's mind when drawing this
fashionable milliner's in 1849?

To those who had no hope of doing so, however, such things did
not seem important. The poor had to make do with whatever they
could get hold of, which as often as not meant second-hand clothing,
in which there was consequently an enormous trade. In London, the
region around Whitechapel's Petticoat Lane was where most second-
hand clothing was sold. Here, besides the stalls and shops of individual dealers, there were two large wholesale houses, the Old
Clothes Exchange and Simmons and Levy's, where many second-
hand dealers bought old clothes for the purpose of re-selling them.
A good deal of what was sold in these establishments was not bought
to be worn, but for making good or repairing other clothes. Mayhew
describes some of the ways in which 'left-off garments' were put to
other uses, according to the materials they were made of and their
condition.

The practised eye of the old clothes man at once embraces every capability of the apparel, and the amount which these capabilities will realise; whether they be woollen, linen, cotton, leathern, or silken goods; or whether they be articles which cannot be classed under any of those designations, such as macintoshes and furs.

A *surtout* coat is the most serviceable of any secondhand clothing, originally good. It can be re-cuffed, re-collared, or the skirts re-lined with new or old silk. . . . It can be 'restored' if the seams be white and the general appearance what is best understood by the expressive word 'seedy'. . . . If the under sleeve be worn, as it often is by those whose avocations are sedentary, it is renewed, and frequently with a second-hand piece of cloth 'to match', so that there is no perceptible difference between the renewal and the other parts. Many an honest artisan in this way becomes possessed of his Sunday frock-coat, as does many a smarter clerk or shopman, impressed with a regard to his personal appearance.

Trousers, waistcoats and cloaks were all in demand, not so much for their own sake as for the use that could be made of their material. From a worn-out suit of clothes enough good material might be found to make a boy's jacket and trousers, or from a discarded skirt a girl's dress. Dress or tailcoats, being worn by few members of the poorer classes, except waiters, were often cut up to make caps, for to go bareheaded, even in the summer, was virtually unheard of.

Of the rags worn by the many vagrant children who roamed about the poorer districts, children such as those whom Fagin gathered round him, Mayhew remarks: 'These rags are worn by the children as long as they will hold, or can be tied or pinned together, and when they drop off from continued wear, from dirt, and from the ravages of vermin, the child sets his wits to work to procure more'.

In working-class districts there was a perpetual movement in the supply of second-hand clothes and those who wore them, however shabby, were always likely to look a little more in the mode than the poor who lived in the country. Until fairly late in the century, agricultural workers tended to wear much the same sort of clothing as their grandfathers had worn: leather breeches and gaiters, stout hobnailed boots, and often the long smock made of coarse linen and sometimes elaborately tucked, with a brightly coloured kerchief

The moral climate of the mid-Victorian middle class permitted no 'sweet disorder in the dress' to 'kindle a gentle wantoness'. Middle-class fashions reflected the stiffness and formality of the middle-class mind.

125

round the neck and a round black felt hat. By the 'eighties the trend towards a sombre conformity in men's clothing had begun to affect even the farm worker's traditional get-up. Instead, most of them now wore suits of stiff brown corduroy, or trousers of the same sort and a 'sloppy', a loose jacket made of unbleached drill. It was a less picturesque but probably more serviceable outfit and was still quite often to be seen up to the First World War.

The British passion for respectability, or as it has come to mean, conformity, on the gratification of which so much time, money and emotion is still spent, was even stronger in the Victorian era than it is today. It was not confined to that virtuous, amorphous mass, the middle class. The working classes were for the most part as keen to put up a front of respectability as the traders and shopkeepers, who considered themselves a cut above the labouring man. In many families the perpetual struggle to look respectable involved hard-worked housewives in the careful renovation or altering of clothes already well worn. The few who were skilled and patient enough might sometimes make their own clothes, but this usually took time, and like most other commodities, there was seldom much to spare in a working-class household. Boots and shoes, particularly in large families, were an expensive item of the working-class budget and many a father did running repairs for his whole family.

For the women, silks and satins were of course out of the question, but it was still possible when the occasion demanded, as on Sundays, to look neat and clean in materials less showy. When in the 'forties Friedrich Engels first visited Manchester, ostensibly on business for his father, his egalitarian eye noticed, no doubt with approval, that most of the mill hands were dressed in cotton or fustian. Wool and linen were too expensive.

The importation of cheap mass-produced clothing, mostly from Germany, which began in the 'seventies, made in course of time a substantial improvement in the dress and appearance of the working classes. A few years later, after many false starts, the sewing machine, a miracle of American labour-saving ingenuity, gave a considerable boost to home dress-making, but the cost of machine and materials made this an occupation too expensive for the working-class housewife.

By contrast with the simple and monotonous clothing of the poor, the clothing of the upper classes showed perpetual variations in style and was often extremely expensive. Some of the materials that were then in use are now unknown, no doubt because they would be too expensive to make, but their effect upon the Victorian scene must have been rich and beautiful. There was, for example, Ottoman

The appearance of master and man were more clearly differentiated in the country than in town. Each had his own characteristic form of dress, in the master's case the tweed suit and gaiters, in the man's, the long linen smock frock and bandana choker.

By the 'eighties, the traditional country dress was being replaced by a suit of stout corderoy, but still retained the look of earlier days.

ABOVE: The crinoline reached its most extravagant dimensions in the early 'sixties. Its inconvenience barred its adoption by the working class, hence its absence from the huge displays of second-clothing in Petticoat Lane (BELOW), where many of the London poor bought their clothes. Others went to districts such as Seven Dials (OPPOSITE) or Hackney, where there were numerous old clothes shops.

satin, a rich shaded satin embroidered with flowers, which is included in a list drawn up by that encyclopaedist of fashion, the late Dr Willett Cunnington. Others that he mentions are Levantine *folicé*, a soft, rich silk with arabesque patterns; Algerine, a twilled shot-silk of green and red or blue and gold; Sultane, a mixture of silk and mohair, like fine alpaca, with alternate satin or *chiné* stripes; satin velouté, which is described as being 'as rich as velvet and as supple as muslin'; and Pekin point, a rich white silk painted with bouquets of flowers or foliage and with 'a light mixture of gold in the pattern'.

A fashionable material towards the end of the era was known as Victoria silk. This had the distinctive quality of producing that sound so alluring to Victorian ears and imaginations, 'the frou-frou of dainty underskirts'.

Colours were as exotic in their names as materials. Those in vogue, for example, during 1855 included Siberia, Raisin d'Espagne, Lucine, Garnet, Marron Claire, Fumée de Londres and Tan d'Or.

The often elaborate and expensive *toilettes* of the well-dressed woman in early Victorian society concealed underclothes that were by contrast surprisingly simple, consisting of a linen shift, a pair of linen pantaloons, reaching to just below the knee, where to begin with they were fastened like breeches, and several petticoats. A little lace trimming was permissable, but only a very little; it was not until the 'eighties that a profusion of frills and furbelows became the thing. Somewhat surprisingly, the immodesty of the *cancan*, in which drawers and all were shown, seems to have increased rather than diminished the popularity of elaborately trimmed underclothes. By that time, when early Victorian pantaloons had given place to short knickers, trimming had come to include threaded ribbons, as well as frills and lace, and silk and chiffon were beginning to replace linen.

The vogue for tricycling, which ladies took to in the early 'nineties, and for bicycling a decade later, involved some modifications of fashion. Clothes became simpler and slightly less restrictive. Ada Ballin, in *The Science of Dress*, warned ladies that 'tight lacing must be banished from the mind and body of the woman who would ride the steel horse'.

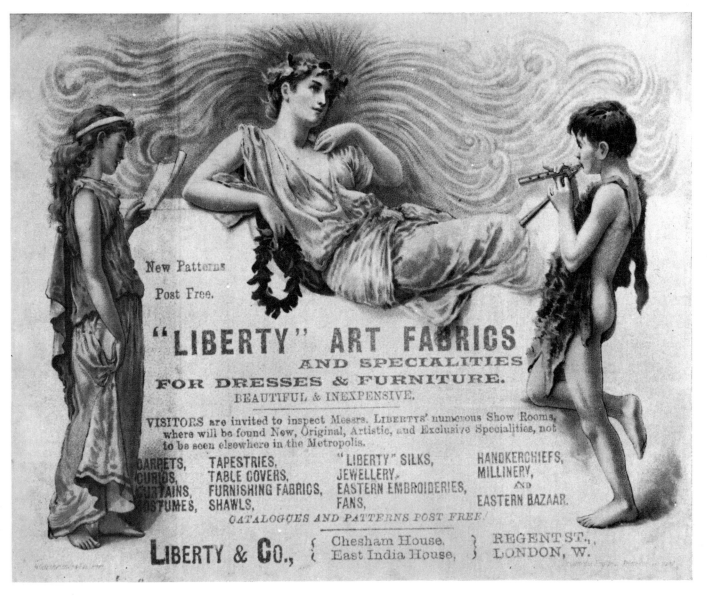

New Patterns
Post Free.

"LIBERTY" ART FABRICS
AND SPECIALITIES
FOR DRESSES & FURNITURE.
BEAUTIFUL & INEXPENSIVE.

VISITORS are invited to inspect Messrs. LIBERTYS' numerous Show Rooms,
where will be found New, Original, Artistic, and Exclusive Specialities, not
to be seen elsewhere in the Metropolis.

CARPETS,	TAPESTRIES,	"LIBERTY" SILKS,	HANDKERCHIEFS,
CURIOS,	TABLE COVERS,	JEWELLERY,	MILLINERY,
CURTAINS,	FURNISHING FABRICS,	EASTERN EMBROIDERIES,	AND
COSTUMES,	SHAWLS,	FANS,	EASTERN BAZAAR.

CATALOGUES AND PATTERNS POST FREE.

LIBERTY & Co., { Chesham House, } REGENT ST.,
{ East India House, } LONDON, W.

In the late 'sixties a boost was given to home dressmaking by the appearance at long last of efficient sewing machines. Since 1841 various models had been invented, but none had been successful. Then with the importation of American machines, which were comparatively cheap and easy to handle, dressmaking became a popular middle-class pursuit. Liberty art fabrics (ABOVE) were for many years favoured by ladies of the intelligentsia over materials of more conventional pattern.

Fashions in hairdressing (and in bonnets to fit the fanciful styles of the period) varied throughout the era, from the ringlets such as Elizabeth Barrett Browning wore in the 'forties to the elaborate styles of the 'seventies and 'eighties, involving the use of pads, coils, switches and, for evening wear, flowers.

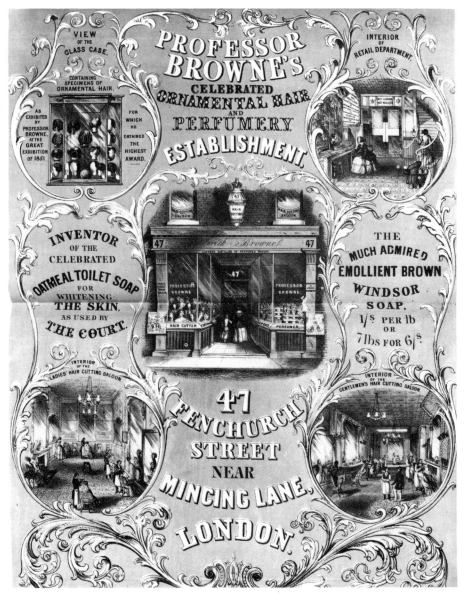

Already at the beginning of the era the Bond Street neighbourhood was the hub of the world of fashion, where the dressmakers, milliners, and hairdressers of the *haute monde* were to be found. Lesser salons, such as Professor Browne's in the City, drew their clienteles from a different but more numerous class.

Such depravity as this the well-undressed woman seemed to find no difficulty in accepting, but on one point she remained adamant: white was still the only permissible colour for underwear, except for ladies of the demi-monde, and so it remained till well towards the end of the era.

Men's underclothing showed very little change throughout the period and was comparatively simple. An uncomfortable Teutonic fad, the substitution of wool in place of linen, was the only significant alteration that occurred. Wool in Victorian days was a harsh and hairy substance and pants and vests, long in leg and sleeve, and later all-enveloping combinations, must have made the wearing of such clothes a ticklish and uncomfortable business.

In the matter of underclothes, the poor of both sexes, as usual, had often to do without, and it was not until mass manufacturing methods began to reduce the cost of clothing generally that the poorer classes were able to afford the luxury of wearing underclothes.

In spite of the amount of time, money and consideration that the feminine élite of Victorian society spent on their clothes, and on expensive accessories, they seldom succeeded in looking as elegant or as distinguished as fashionable Parisiennes, first among whom was the Empress Eugénie. In spite of origins less august than those of some of the English aristocracy, the Empress somehow made most of its ladies look decidedly dowdy. Ironically, the success of her *toilettes* was due largely to an Englishman, Frederick Worth, a Lincolnshire lad, who in the 'sixties made good, rather surprisingly, as a Parisian dressmaker.

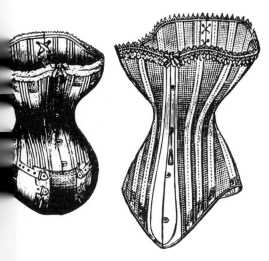

ABOVE: The wasp waist remained fashionable for more than thirty years, although the corsets that were worn to produce this effect were both uncomfortable and incongruous.
OPPOSITE: The growing popularity of women's sports did not do away all at once with the restrictive practise of tight-lacing. A waist of 22 inches, or even smaller, emphasised by the breadth of a leg-of-mutton sleeve, was the ideal of elegance in the 'nineties. The Rational Dress Society, formed in the 'eighties, aimed in its *Gazette* to publicise among other things the harmful effects of tight-lacing (RIGHT).

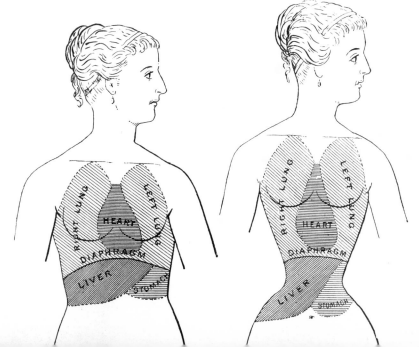

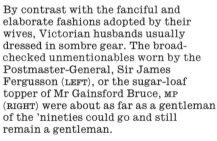

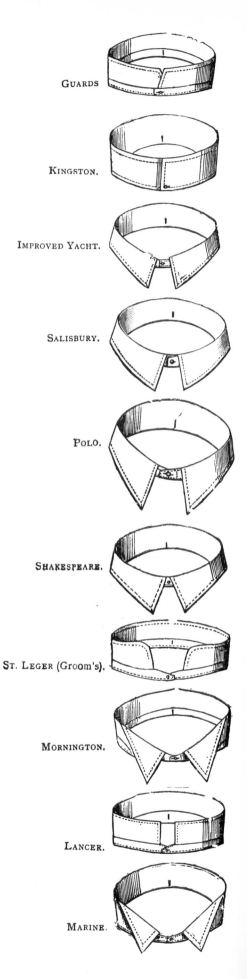

By contrast with the fanciful and elaborate fashions adopted by their wives, Victorian husbands usually dressed in sombre gear. The broad-checked unmentionables worn by the Postmaster-General, Sir James Fergusson (LEFT), or the sugar-loaf topper of Mr Gainsford Bruce, MP (RIGHT) were about as far as a gentleman of the 'nineties could go and still remain a gentleman.

Gents' accessories, especially in the way of collars, were as numerous as they are today and equally indicative of status. For a member of White's or Brooks' to have been seen in a St Leger, a style of neckware reserved for grooms, would have been unthinkable.

GUARDS

KINGSTON.

IMPROVED YACHT.

SALISBURY.

POLO.

SHAKESPEARE.

ST. LEGER (Groom's).

MORNINGTON.

LANCER.

MARINE.

SHOOTING CAPE.

With Straps.

Gentlemen's Golfing Capes.

ABOVE: The masher of the 'sixties, personified in the music halls by Arthur Lloyd, the Beau of Bond Street, was the sartorial ideal of every young man who wanted to be thought a dandy.

LEFT: In sports clothes a certain amount of licence was permissible. This did not go so far as to allow them to be comfortable, but did permit some informality.

LEFT: Sportswear, that unpleasing brain-child of some addled ad-man, was a term unknown to the Victorians. Most sports, especially those few permitted to ladies, could be enjoyed in clothes not very different from those worn every day; although in the 'sixties the crinoline added a minor hazard to rock-climbing.
OPPOSITE: Centre court aspirant, 1880.

LEFT: Boating party in the 1890s.
OPPOSITE: Bathing belles, 1900.

It is difficult to imagine that any woman, however eager to reach the forefront of fashion, would submit nowadays to the languid insolence with which Worth treated his customers. Hippolyte Taine, writing in *La Vie Parisienne* (then a comparatively respectable journal), gives a picture of Worth's method and manner:

Women will stoop to any baseness to be dressed by him. This little dry, black, nervous creature receives them in a velvet coat, carelessly stretched out on a divan, a cigar between his lips. He says to them, 'Walk! Turn! Good! Come back in a week, and I will compose you a *toilette* which will suit you'. It is not they who choose it; it is he. They are only too happy to let him do it, and even for that it needs an introduction. Mme B., a personage of the real *monde* and elegant to boot – went to him last month to order a dress. 'Madame,' he said, 'by whom are you presented?'

'I don't understand.'

'I am afraid you must be presented in order to be dressed by me.'

She went away, suffocated with rage. But others stayed, saying, 'I don't care how rude he is, so long as he dresses me'.

What would have been the effect on Queen Victoria's clothes if she had chosen Worth as her dressmaker, as did the Empress, it is hard to guess. For one thing, her person was less promising than Eugenie's. For another, she was averse by instinct to spending much time and thought on dress. She disliked fittings, which she found tedious, and was bored by consultations about clothes. Also, her preference was for effects of grandeur rather than elegance, and she had, too, an unfortunate penchant for the Royal Stuart tartan, a pattern rather too emphatic to suit her figure. Furthermore, her natural sympathies were never as warm towards the French as towards the Germans, in whose stolid and innate provincialism she seemed to sense an affinity closer to her own temperament than was that of the more volatile and sophisticated French. But by the time Worth had become the rage of Parisian feminine society, the Queen was already mantled in those garments of woe to which, in her tenacious and unsparing grief for the Prince Consort, she stuck for the rest of her life.

Until the Empress Eugénie's marriage to Napoleon III in 1853, the Queen had been the arbiter of English fashion. Thereafter her influence began to wane, not altogether surprisingly, for she had neither Eugénie's grace nor sense of style, as the French were quick to spot when the Queen and Prince Albert paid an official visit to the Emperor and Empress in 1855, following a visit by them to England earlier in the year. In the Queen's journal, in which she recorded detailed impressions of both visits, there are no less than fourteen references to Eugénie's *toilettes* and ten to her own.

The March of Fashion, 1840, 1847, 1863,
1872 ,1880, 1895.

The Queen was also quick to notice the splendid liveries of her hosts' servants, as well as the military uniforms of the French, which she recorded as being 'infinitely better made and cut than those of ours, which provokes me much'.

Her own appearance was observed with a discriminating eye by General Canrobert, who, until a short while before, had been in command of the French forces then fighting in the Crimea. Sitting beside her at dinner he noticed that:

She had plump hands with rings on every finger, and even on her thumbs; one of these contained a ruby of prodigious size and of a superb blood-red. She found it difficult to use her knife and fork with her hands thus laden like reliquaries, and even more difficult to take off and put on her gloves. On her head was a diamond aigrette, pushed well back; and she wore her hair in long loops which fell over her ears.

The Queen recorded in her journal that on this occasion her own dress was of green silk trimmed with lace and that there were roses and violets in her hair. The Empress was dressed in white organdie 'embroidered with blue and straw', and her jewellery was of diamonds and turquoises.

In spite of the sobriety of the Queen's disposition and her acute sense of decorum, she was by no means averse to a revealing *décolletage* – permissible of course only in evening dress – perhaps because it suited her better than other fashions which were less flattering to her dumpy figure.

It is a curious point about Victorian morality that a strict regard for propriety should have gone hand in hand with the seductive fashion of showing as much of the bust as could be revealed without actually displaying the naked breast. And this, oddly enough, at a time when ankle-length drawers were considered indispensible beneath the concealment of a crinoline. It is such strange ambiguities that make the psychology of dress so fascinating a branch of scientific study.

Not the least of its mysteries is the popularity of a garment at once so outlandish and so inconvenient as the crinoline itself; another, that the bustle of the early 'eighties, with its outline so reminiscent of the emu – not one of the most graceful or attractive of birds – should ever have been widely adopted.

By contrast with the changes that occurred in the feminine silhouette, that of the Victorian male remained more or less static from the beginning to the end. The frock-coat and top-hat of the leisured class and the bourgeoisie, and the short jacket and tweed cap, or later the billycock hat, of the working man, were as invariable

FAR LEFT: The Empress Eugénie in 1855; from a painting by F.X.Winterhalter. LEFT: The simplicity of early Victorian fashions suited the Queen, as may be seen in this picture by W.Corden drawn in the year of her accession. In the more elaborate fashions of twenty years later, however, she seldom achieved the elegance of the Empress Eugénie.

The Queen and the Prince Consort's state visit to the Paris Opera, 21 August 1855, accompanied by their hosts, the Emperor and Empress.

What the well-dressed undergraduate
and friend wore in 1898.

as the Prince Consort's virtuous demeanour. The only significant
departure from this staid tradition was made by the droopy fashions
adopted by the aesthetes of the 'seventies. This attempt to modify
the conformity of men's clothing – which, heaven knows, was never
in such need of a little gaiety as at that time – by introducing a touch
of the Renaissance, might have met with more encouragement if it
had not been coupled with absurdities of conduct such as Gilbert
parodied in *Patience*. It is a pity the aesthetes did not achieve their
aim. Their failure put back by almost a hundred years the first real
breakaway from the tradition of men's fashions that established itself
when the last vestiges of Regency elegance disappeared under the
stately folds of Prince Albert's frock-coat.

It is in the nature of things that women's clothes change more
often than men's. We do not know how many ways of wearing a
fig-leaf were tried by Eve before she found one that satisfied her, but
women are never satisfied with a fashion for long and in no com-
parable period of time have there been more changes in style than
in the Victorian era. From the bell-shaped skirt and neat bonnet of
the early 'thirties, fashion ranged through the various extravagances
of the crinoline, the swathed skirt and rustling train of the late
'seventies, and the bustle of the 'eighties, to the high-necked, wasp-
waisted and leg-of-mutton sleeves that were in fashion when the
era came to an end. The fluctuations of fashion are unpredictable,
but to the social historian invaluable. Within each of these categories
wide variations of style occurred, marking successive phases of public
taste as clearly as the history of the Victorian era is marked by its
political events.

A Little Learning

Chapter 5: A Little Learning ¶ The Dangers of Education ¶ Lancaster and Bell ¶ Extending State Aid ¶ Public Schools and Private Academies ¶ Mr Squeers and Co. ¶ Tuition at Home ¶ Ragged Schools ¶ Learning for Young Ladies ¶ Elementary Education ¶ The Universities

The educational system, such as it was, at the beginning of Queen Victoria's reign, was elementary, inefficient and bedevilled by factional disputes between those who wanted the system to be based on religious principles and those who believed that education was the right of every child, whatever its religion. To see this situation in its proper perspective one must look back to the early years of the century. It was by no means taken for granted then that education was in itself a desirable thing. Was it not men of education, men like Rousseau and Mirabeau, who had helped to instigate the French Revolution? Worse than that, some of its actual leaders had been highly educated men. To allow education to spread indiscriminately among all classes would seem to be asking for trouble.

Speaking in the House of Commons in 1807, Davies Giddy, who later became President of the Royal Society, expressed what quite a number of educated people felt about education:

> However specious in theory the project might be, of giving education to the labouring classes of the poor, it would in effect be found to be prejudicial to their morals and happiness; it would teach them to despise culture, and other laborious employments to which their rank in society had destined them; instead of teaching them subordination, it would render them fractious and refractory, as was evident in the manufacturing counties; it would enable them to read seditious pamphlets, vicious books, and publications against Christianity.

Not everyone agreed with sentiments of this kind. One who did not was Joseph Lancaster, a Quaker, living in London. Another was Andrew Bell, a Church of England clergyman, who had been the head of an orphan asylum in India. Quite by chance, and independently of each other, both had become impressed with the need for some form of national education, and both had independently hit on more or less the same idea. The plans they conceived were for a voluntary system of education organised on national lines. When Bell returned to England from India in 1797 he published a pamphlet called *An Experiment in Education*, in which he described his experiences while teaching in India. His work there had been hampered by a lack of trained staff and he had therefore adopted the system of enlisting what we would now call pupil-teachers. Much the same proposal was also put forward by Joseph Lancaster. Where they

The Lower School at Eton, cheerless, comfortless and inconvenient, was the nursery from which emerged some of the most gifted and most influential figures of the Victorian era.

failed to agree, as so many sensible and worthy Victorians often failed to agree, was on the question of religion. As a member of the Society of Friends, Lancaster took as his maxim that friendliest of exhortations, 'Suffer little children to come unto me'. All would be welcome, he said, whatever their creed. Not so Dr Bell. The mantle of the Church of England, though a capacious garment, was also a respectable one: it could hardly be expected to cover the naked indecency of Nonconformists. Such as they must get their education where they could.

The split between Bell and Lancaster was not merely over dogma: it was even wider over the fundamental question of who should order and direct religious teaching in schools. Was such teaching to be the prerogative of the Church of England, or should it be strictly undenominational? It was not an issue that allowed room for the exercise of that overworked faculty, the British genius for compromise.

One of Lancaster's supporters was Samuel Whitbread, an enlightened Whig politician, who tried and failed to get a bill through Parliament which was based, broadly speaking, on the theory advocated by Lancaster. The bill was thrown out by the House of Lords on the ground that any national system of education must be based on religious principles, and Whitbread's proposals failed to grant oracular powers to parochial clergy, by whom school teaching must be directed and controlled. Better ignorance and illiteracy than the dangers of Dissent.

It was clear that the only hope of extending opportunities for education lay in the voluntary principle. In 1808, a body called the Royal Lancastrian Society was formed to promote schools run on the lines advocated by Lancaster. If Dr Bell had needed a spur, this was it. Within a year the National Society had been formed for educating the poor in the principles of the Established Church, and Dr Bell was its director.

For many years religious differences continued to hamstring all efforts to get a proper system of education started. Only by slow degrees was money allotted by Parliament to promote the building of schools, and grants were conditional on their being run on Church of England lines. In 1837 the amount voted by Parliament was less than forty thousand pounds for the whole of England and Wales, but with the Victorians' passion for self-improvement and the growing demands of industry and business for trained and intelligent men, things gradually began to improve. In 1847 a considerable advance was made when state aid was extended to Roman Catholic and Wesleyan schools; four years later it was extended to Jews.

Apart from state-aided schools, there were others of various kinds

TOP: Joseph Lancaster (1778–1838), a Quaker who was a pioneer in the movement to establish a national system of education. Despite his own beliefs, he favoured the establishment of an undenominational scheme. BELOW: Dr Andrew Bell (1753–1832), advocate of a modified system applicable only to children of the Church of England. Ignorance and illiteracy seemed to many devout members of the Church lesser dangers than dissent.

Rugby School, 1841, where Dr Arnold, the foremost figure in Victorian education, sought to give proof to the startling theory that character is more important than brains.

to which a boy might be sent, according to the income or social status of his parents. (The idea of educating girls, except in deportment and the domestic arts, was still thought of as a suspicious eccentricity.) First, of course, there were the public schools. These were more or less the preserve of the sons of gentry, and there was a choice of nine: Eton, Harrow, Winchester, Charterhouse, Shrewsbury, Rugby, Westminster, St Paul's and Merchant Taylors'. All of them (except Charterhouse, 1611) had been established in the sixteenth century or earlier and their curriculums were still much the same as when the schools were founded. A grounding was given in the classics, but in little else. As temples of learning they were as bankrupt of ideas as they were of discipline and morals, on which

ABOVE: The dormitory of Christ's
Hospital, the Blue Coat school, founded
in 1552. Its austerity was in marked
contrast with the well-appointed
kitchens of Charterhouse (LEFT),
founded in 1611, which resembled
those of a luxurious restaurant.

ABOVE: Battle School in Sussex, built in 1847. This tasteful exercise in Victorian Gothic was no doubt as satisfactory to its sponsors as it was inconvenient to its pupils and staff.

RIGHT: The mortarboard and stiff collar of the public schoolboy or the academy pupil were calculated, like the appearance of the master, to impress by their dignity rather than to afford comfort.

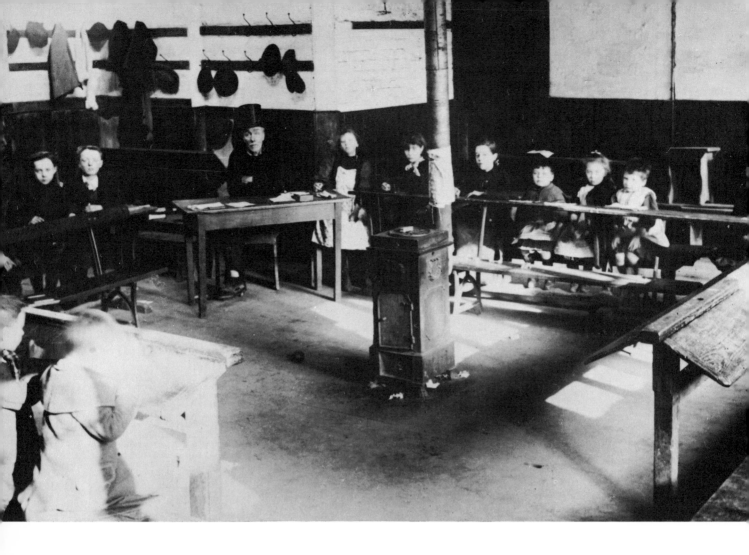

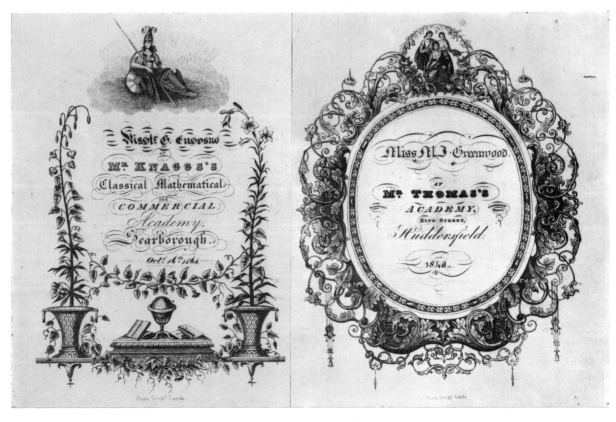

THE AMERICAN RACE.   17

hair, and dingy yellow or olive complexions. They are remarkable for considerable imitative powers, and are susceptible of a high degree of cultivation.

American.

The AMER′ICAN RACE, or *aborig′inal** inhabitants of the *North and South Amer′ican continents*, seem to be an admixture of the *Cauca′sian* and *Mon-*

ABOVE: The curriculum in most schools, except those for infants, was for a long time based on the Classics. A grounding in more practical, as well as more abstruse subjects – Ethnology among them – was occasionally added.

OPPOSITE TOP: The Education Act of 1870 put paid to the few private academies that still existed. In the London borough of Lewisham only one, Mr Williams's, was left.
OPPOSITE BELOW AND RIGHT: The better class of private academy provided its pupils with decorative exercise books designed to encourage elegant penmanship.

score it was the opinion of the Rev. Dr Bowdler, the man who knew better than Shakespeare, that the public schools were 'the very seats and nurseries of vice'.

For the sons of the up-and-coming middle class there were innumerable private academies. Like Dr Blimber's academy in *Dombey and Son*, most of them were still stuck in the classical rut:

Dr Blimber's establishment was a great hot-house in which there was a forcing apparatus incessantly at work. . . . Mental green peas were produced at Christmas and intellectual asparagus all the year round. Mental gooseberries – very sour ones too – were common at untimely seasons and from mere sprouts of bushes under Dr Blimber's cultivation. Every description of Greek and Latin vegetable was got off the driest twigs by boys under the frostiest circumstances.

Some headmasters, with an eye to the future and a glance not altogether disinterested, had added arithmetic and geography to Greek and Latin, but the public schools stuck to their old and increasingly useless syllabuses. Many a middle-class snob who wanted his son to become a gentleman, yet also to become as astute in business as himself, was torn between the idea of sending him to

Eton or Harrow and the advantages of his receiving a more practical education elsewhere. For such distracted parents one answer was to send their sons to one of the newer establishments with a wider educational perspective, such as Cheltenham, Marlborough, Radley, or Wellington, which in spite of their recent origins (the first was founded in 1841, the last in 1853) still qualified as public schools.

For the sons of less well-to-do parents there were the various grammar schools, which usually provided much the same sort of education as the public schools. Most grammar schools were ancient establishments and a good many had fallen on hard times, their original endowments, sometimes dating from the Middle Ages, having dwindled almost to nothing. This left the headmaster to make do as best he could – usually by charging as much as he dared for as little board and education as he could get away with.

Anyone who felt disposed to set up a school could do so, whether from an altruistic belief in the value of education or simply in order to make money. No qualifications were needed and methods and standards of teaching were for the schoolmaster to devise. Assistant masters were often sad and seedy individuals who were appointed not because of their learning, but because their services were cheap; and as there was no proper system of inspection or examination, it was every master for himself, and every pupil too. Men as illiterate as they were unscrupulous were to be found acting as headmasters in schools as little deserving of the name as pig-sties. Dickens, in his preface to the 1858 edition of *Nicholas Nickleby*, speaks of schoolmasters of the early Victorian period as 'blockheads and imposters'. Yorkshire, in which the earlier part of the novel is set, was notorious for schools kept by ignorant thugs who specialised in the reception of unwanted or illegitimate boys for inclusive fees that were sometimes as little as twenty guineas a year. Such men were, as Dickens described them, 'Traders in the avarice, indifference, or imbecility of parents, and the helplessness of children; ignorant, sordid, brutal men, to whom few considerate persons would have intrusted the board and lodging of a horse or a dog'. One such creature, who kept a school at Bowes, near Barnard Castle, was William Shaw, to whom Dickens gave egregious immortality in the character of Mr Squeers. In the churchyard at Bowes there are the graves of twenty-five of Shaw's pupils who died at the school between 1810 and 1834. Conditions such as those under which this blackguard carried on his nefarious trade lasted a good many years even after the publication of *Nicholas Nickleby* in 1838, but by arousing public indignation at the state of affairs in Yorkshire, Dickens gave the cause of educational reform a substantial boost.

'The internal economy of Dotheboys Hall', the school where Nicholas Nickleby became a master, and which was typical of a good many such establishments, was regulated by periodic 'physicking' with brimstone and treacle. Where the profit motive was all that mattered, economy rather than efficiency was the watchword and a healthy ignoramus was preferable to a delicate pupil of genius.

EDUCATION,
BY MR. SHAW, & ABLE ASSISTANTS,
At Bowes Academy.
NEAR GRETA BRIDGE, YORKSHIRE.

YOUTH are carefully instructed in the English, Latin, and Greek Languages; Writing, Common and Decimal Arithmetic; Book-keeping, Mensuration, Surveying, Geometry, Geography, and Navigation, with the most useful Branches of the Mathematics; and are provided with Board, Clothes, and every necessary, at TWENTY GUINEAS per Annum each. No extra charges whatever, Doctor's bills excepted. No vacations, except by the Parents' desire.

N.B. The French Language Two Guineas per Annum extra.

Further Particulars may be known on application to Mr. W. LANKSHEAR, Surgeon, Tottenham Court, New Road; Mrs. YOUNG, Plough Yard, Crown Street, Soho; Mr. WALKER, 37, Drury Lane; Mr. TOWNLEY, Chief Office of Excise, Broad Street; Mr. HAMPSON, 52, Long Lane, Smithfield; Mr. GARDINER, 80, Tottenham Court Road; Mr. PITT, 22, Crown Court, Soho; and Mr. WIGGINTON, 42, Museum Street, Bloomsbury.

MR. SEATON, AGENT, 10, FREDERICK PLACE,
Goswell Street Road,

Will give the most respectable References to the Parents of others at the above Seminary, as well as to those who have completed their Education with Mr. SHAW.

ALL LETTERS MUST BE POST PAID.

It is sad to think that Mr Squeers, the egregious brute who ran Dotheboys Hall, had his counterpart in real life. At Bowes Academy in Yorkshire, run by a Mr Shaw, no fewer than twenty-five pupils died during a period of twenty-four years from starvation, disease or neglect.
RIGHT: Mrs Hartley's School, though it was a considerably later foundation than Miss Pinkerton's academy, where Becky Sharp got what little learning she had, seems to have provided much the same curriculum.

HOPEWELL HOUSE, NORTH ROAD,
HORSFORTH, NEAR LEEDS.

Mrs. HARTLEY'S SCHOOL
FOR YOUNG LADIES.

Terms per Quarter.

FOR TUITION IN ALL THE BRANCHES OF AN ENGLISH EDUCATION:

	£	s	d
For Boarders above 12 Years of Age	£6	0	0
Ditto under 12 ditto	5	0	0
Weekly Boarders	4	0	0
For Day Pupils above 12 years of Age	1	1	0
Ditto under 12 ditto	0	15	0
Music	1	1	0
French	1	1	0
Drawing	0	10	6
Laundress	0	10	0
Single Dinners	0	0	6

Masters for French & Drilling.
Each Young Lady to be supplied with Slippers, Sheets, Pillow Cases, Towels, Toilet Soap, Fork and Spoon.
It is requested that each Day Pupil be provided with Slippers.

A Quarter's Notice required previous to the removal of a Pupil or a Quarter's payment.

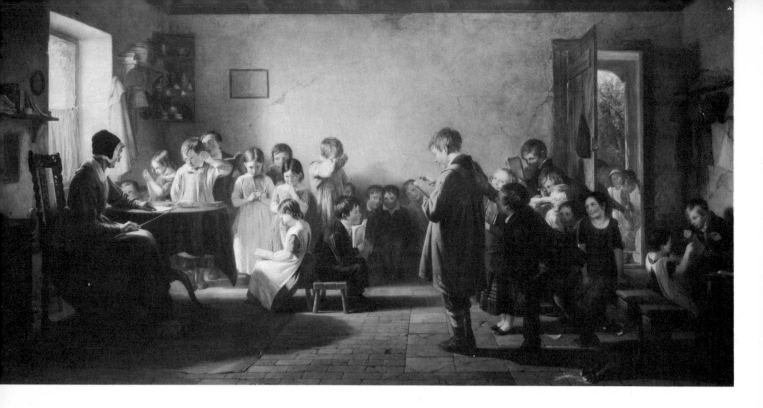

ABOVE: *A Dame School*, by Thomas Webster. The education of rural infants was for many years left to well-meaning but usually ignorant women, able to impart the elements of reading and scripture, but no more.
OPPOSITE: Irony, the schoolmaster's handiest weapon, shames the late-comer in *The Last In* (detail) by William Mulready.
BELOW: By 1900 standards of teaching and discipline had much improved. If the tots at Marhamchurch village school in Cornwall seemed less obstreperous than the pupils of an earlier generation, no doubt they knew quite as much, if not more.

W Water - lilies, whereon Fairies
delight,
To dance in the Summer, when shines
the moon bright.

X for Exotics, which Grandmamma
sends,
That Fanny may garnish the room
for her friends.

Y Yellow-lily, which John, with a
crook,
Is trying to reach from the bank of
the brook.

Z is for Zinnia, which has carried
away
The prize at the Grand Show of
Flowers to-day.

ABOVE AND OPPOSITE: An extract from
The Alphabet of Flowers, a teaching aid
of the 1850s. The use of such words as
'whereon', 'exotics' and 'garnish' may
seem sophisticated for a child not yet
in command of its ABC, but infant
prattle was still uninfluenced by such
educational aids as the comic strip and
the TV commercial.

It needed it. In spite of a change in the tone of public schools, inspired by the pious example of Dr Arnold at Rugby, there were still some lamentable defects in the system, which in some ways was no better than it had been at the beginning of the century. It was then, according to Lytton Strachey, 'a system of despotism tempered by anarchy'. Writing of his experiences at Harrow in 1848, Augustus Hare, whose reminiscences gave a lively and often touching picture of a juvenile's existence, recalled

... how terrible the bullying was in our time ... how little boys were constantly sent in the evening ... to bring back porter under their great-coats, certain to be flogged by the head-master if they were caught, and to be 'warped' by the sixth form boys if they did not go ... how, if they did not 'keep up' at football, they were made to cut large thorn sticks out of the hedges, and flogged with them till the blood poured down outside their jerseys. . . . I may truly say [Hare concludes] that I never learnt anything useful at Harrow, and had little chance of learning anything. Hours and hours were wasted daily on useless Latin verses with sickening monotony. A boy's school education at this time, except in the highest forms, was hopelessly inane.

Parents who preferred that their sons should be educated by private tutors rather than be exposed to the nameless horrors with which Dr Bowdler charged the public schools, sometimes prepared the way themselves for the higher education which it was hoped their darlings would receive at the hands of some studious, half-starved curate looking for a means of increasing his insignificant stipend. Again, in *The Story of My Life* Augustus Hare recalls how in the year 1839 he began the long and painful process of his education:

After breakfast I began my lessons, which, I now think to have been rather advanced for a child of five years old, as besides English reading, writing and spelling, history, arithmetic and geography, I had to do German reading and *writing*, and a little Latin. . . . Through plans, maps, and raised models, I was made perfectly familiar with the topography of Jerusalem and the architecture of the Temple, though utterly ignorant of the topography of Rome or London. . . . There was often a great deal of screaming and crying over the writing and arithmetic, and I never got on satisfactorily with the former till my Aunt Kitty or my grandmother took it in hand, sitting over me with a ruler, and by a succession of hearty bangs on the knuckles, forced my fingers to go the right way.

The idea that difficulty in understanding or unwillingness to learn can best be cured by hitting a child with a stick is one that has taken a very long time to show itself to be as stupid as it is degrading. When at the age of nine young Hare went to school for the first

ABOVE: John Pounds, the Bloomsbury cobbler, whose endeavours as a pioneer in education for the poor led to the founding of the Ragged Schools movement in 1847.

RIGHT: Under the Education Act of 1870, municipal School Boards were empowered to make education compulsory. Where facilities were provided, washing, if not compulsory too, was usually encouraged.

time, he knew more or less what to expect. The Rev. Robert Kilvert 'was deeply religious, but he was very hot-tempered, and slashed our hands with a ruler and our bodies with a cane most unmercifully for exceedingly slight offences . . . my recollection shrinks from the reign of terror under which we lived'. One is thankful to think that the Rev. Kilvert's vigorous sense of discipline was tempered perhaps by religious scruples.

A child of humbler birth than Augustus would probably have begun his education at the village dame school, the forerunner of the kindergarten, which was usually presided over by a woman as ignorant of educational theory as she was of life and learning. To her infant pupils she would impart such elements as she herself had grasped of reading, writing and doing sums, but beyond this had nothing to offer. And on the Sabbath there was Sunday school, where the curriculum was restricted to the solitary and impractical study of the scriptures.

In London there was one other type of school, the Ragged School. In April 1844, in a loft over a Bloomsbury cow-shed, a gathering of forty Christian souls formed themselves into the Ragged School Union. Between them, the Union and the London City Mission, which had been founded nine years earlier, took on the task of trying to teach the elements of reading, writing and arithmetic to destitute and homeless children in the poorer areas of London. In some parts of the East End, where hunger, filth, crime and brutality were in the natural order of things and where the police would only venture to go about in squads, Union teachers, many of them young women, sat in makeshift classrooms surrounded by verminous, stinking and often half naked children, patiently persuading them to learn their ABC and to do simple sums. In 1840 there were five hundred and seventy children attending the London City Mission's schools. By 1870 the Ragged Schools' four hundred and fifty paid teachers, helped by thousands of volunteers, were not only giving some form of daily instruction to twenty-five thousand children, but on Sundays were beseiged by their parents, clamouring for a little schooling for themselves. With the passing of the Board School Act in that year the work of the Union was gradually brought to an end and its functions merged with those of the schools established under the Act. In terms of learning the Ragged Schools' achievement may not have amounted to much; in terms of imaginative philanthropy it is one of the noblest ventures of the period.

The education of girls during most of the Victorian era was aimed at keeping them in a state of unsophisticated dependence on men. The resulting innocence of mind and emotion appealed strongly to the Victorian male's idealised picture of himself as a combined Sir Galahad and *paterfamilias*. An abundance of knowledge was therefore considered unladylike. It was enough if, besides reading, writing and doing simple arithmetic, a girl could speak a little French, knew a little general knowledge and the use of the globes, could paint timorously in water colours, sew, and dance the waltz and the quadrille. If she could also sing and play the pianoforte, so much the better, but a thirst for subjects more abstruse was generally regarded as a not very healthy predilection.

Instruction in these modest accomplishments came as a rule from that most pathetic specimen of Victorian womanhood, the governess, a young or sometimes middle-aged lady of genteel upbringing who, through some accident of circumstance had been forced into her poorly paid and unhappy situation. Her counterpart was the seedy and impoverished curate who was sometimes hired as a tutor to cram the dull, disinterested sons of rich parents. Resented by their pupils, despised by their employers for evidences of poverty they could not hide, patronised by servants, friendless and obscure, they often led lives as miserable and insecure as any of the multitudes of Victorian poor.

Such was the state of affairs during a good part of the nineteenth century. A long hard battle was to be fought against conscientious opposition and inertia before any substantial progress was made. Commissions of enquiry were to sit, some of them for years, investigating various aspects of educational policy; bills were to be introduced and argued over in Parliament; the basis and extent of state aid was to be reviewed in the light of changing circumstances; the training of teachers, the inspection of schools, and standards of examination, were all to be the subject of long and earnest study before it was admitted that the state had a responsibility to provide some form of free education for every child not attending either a public or a private school. Two Acts of Parliament, in 1876 and 1880, made school attendance compulsory. How necessary this compulsion was, distasteful though it may have been to those who took their stand on a parent's right to freedom of choice, is shown by the effect of these parliamentary acts on the numbers of children who benefited from them: in 1876 the average school attendance was estimated at two million; by 1881 it was four million.

Although standards of teaching began gradually to improve, for a long while they still left much to be desired. The swift expansion of the educational system not only increased the size of classes, but meant that in teacher-training quantity became a more important objective than quality. And paper qualifications are no substitute

OPPOSITE: Time off for students at Royal Holloway College for Women. The college, a residential extension of London University, was opened in 1886. Segregation of the sexes was still the watchword in higher education and in pursuit of this aim Royal Holloway was built some twenty miles outside London at Englefield Green in Surrey.
BELOW: The students' orchestra.

THE PEOPLES PALACE
FOR EAST LONDON

THE LIBRARY
AND READING ROOM

E.R. ROBSON, F.S.A
ARCHITECT.

BELOW AND OPPOSITE: Higher education for the lower classes was the worthy objective of Mr Barber Beaumont, who in 1841 left a sum of £13,000 with which to build a centre for the 'Intellectual Improvement and Rational Recreation and Amusement for people living in the East End of London'. More than forty years elapsed before Mr Beaumont's brain-child was born. In 1887 Queen Victoria opened the People's Palace in Stepney, providing East Enders with a technical and handicrafts school, a library (OPPOSITE), a winter garden, swimming baths, and an open-air gymnasium.

for the patience, psychological insight and dedication of purpose without which schoolmastering is apt to become a dangerous trade.

Inefficient teaching, however, was not the only defect in the system. The basis on which grants were allocated to schools was also unsatisfactory. Grants were given in accordance with the number of pupils who passed the inspectors' examinations; in other words, payment was based on results. Although this sounded fair enough, in practice it was not always so. All it meant was that some inspectors were better or luckier than others at getting the results they wanted; the examinations themselves, as examinations so often are, were of little use in assessing a child's real abilities or worth. But there was some slight improvement in the curriculum. It was no longer purely classical, though history, arithmetic and geography, which were among the subjects that had been added, were still regarded by many schoolmasters as less important than the classics.

The dispensation of 1847 had removed education from the sphere of clerical politics by freeing schools from their denominational shackles, but this was only one step in the long and fitful process of establishing a comprehensive educational system. Even as late as 1870, the year of the Elementary Education Act, there was still a good deal of reluctance to admit the need for such a system, though even those who opposed it on religious grounds were compelled to admit the force of the economic argument. E. W. Forster, a Liberal Member of Parliament, and son-in-law of Dr Arnold, speaking in the debate on the Act, told the House of Commons that:

On the speedy provision of elementary education depend our industrial prosperity, the safe working of our constitutional system, and our national power. . . . If we are to hold our position among men of our own race or among the nations of the world, we must make up for the smallness of our numbers by increasing the intellectual force of the individual.

Four years after this speech by Forster, 'a rather white-faced little boy in a holland pinafore and carrying a green baize satchel', was trotting up the High Street of Bromley in Kent to spend his first day at Mr Morley's Commercial Academy. He was not yet eight years old. Nearly sixty years later, and by then known to the world as H. G. Wells, he wrote, perhaps remembering the words Forster had used:

The new order of things that was appearing in the world when I was born was already arousing a consciousness of the need for universal elementary education. It was being realised by the ruling classes that a nation with a lower stratum of illiterates would compete at a disadvantage against the foreigner. A condition of things in which everyone would read and write and do sums, dawned on the startled imagination of mankind. . . . Bromley was served by a National School. That was all that the district possessed in the way of public education. It saw to the children up to the age of thirteen or even fourteen, and no further. Beyond that the locality had no public provision for technical education or the development of artistic or scientific ability whatever. Even that much of general education had been achieved against considerable resistance. There was a strong objection in those days to the use of public funds for the education of 'other people's children', and school pennies were exacted weekly from the offspring of everyone not legally indigent.

Learning to Write by Robert Martineau.

This objection did not stop ambitious plans from being made, and some from being fulfilled, for building new schools, though most of them were designed not so much for the convenience of pupils or staff as to gratify municipal pride or an architectural whim.

ABOVE AND RIGHT: Three views of the Oxford Museum for the study of Natural Sciences, a pet project of John Ruskin's. The ornate and unique capitals (RIGHT) imitating foliage were carved under his loving eye.

OPPOSITE: The Entrance Hall and the Staircase of the British Museum, 1845; two views painted by George Scharf, the elder. The Museum at that time occupied Montagu House, on the site of which the present building was erected. The giraffes at the top of the stairs were removed at the time of the rebuilding and are now in the Natural History Museum in South Kensington.

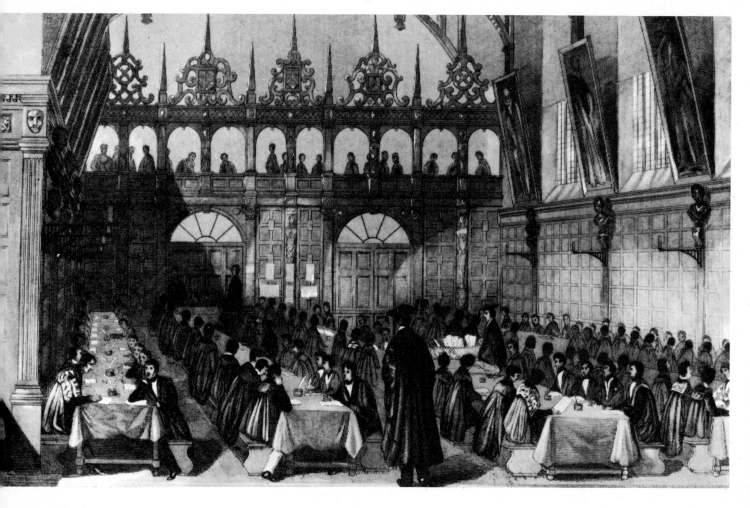

Examinations at Trinity College, Cambridge, 1842. Undergraduates then sat for their exams in the College Hall.

Many new schools were gaunt, gloomy and Gothic, admitting little light or air in summer and impossible to heat properly in winter. The best that could be said for them, as for the teaching, discipline, and expansion of the curriculum, was that they were an improvement on what had gone before.

So far as teaching and discipline were concerned, much of the improvement was due to the example set by Dr Arnold at Rugby. He was by far the most influential figure on the Victorian educational scene and long after his death in 1842, at the early age of forty-seven, his ideas still reverberated through the corridors of learning. His reputation rested on a conception of a schoolmaster's first duty which was then wholly original; it was that the development of a boy's character was more important than the training of his intellect. One of Arnold's pupils and a life-long disciple of his was Thomas Hughes, the author of the quasi-autobiographical story, *Tom Brown's Schooldays*. Arnold's concept is epitomised in the

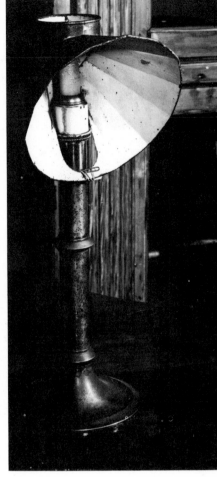

Rowing and reading were, as they still are, the chief preoccupations of a good many undergraduates.
ABOVE: Trinity College four at Cambridge, 1858.
FAR RIGHT: The candle lamps by whose cheap but efficient illumination earnest undergraduates pursued their studies after dark.

The midnight prowling of the University proctors and their aides, known as bulldogs, is ridiculed in this notice posted in mid-Victorian Cambridge.

NUISANCE.
£20
REWARD.

WHEREAS two persons, in official dresses of the University and styling themselves *Proctors*, (an office now *extinct* and *illegal*,) are in the habit of prowling about the streets at midnight, and disturbing the peace and comfort of the Undergraduates, by insisting on their wearing the Academical dress.

Notice

is hereby given, *that the above REWARD* will be given to any person or persons, producing such evidence as shall lead to the conviction and punishment of the offenders.

N.B. As several instances of madness in the Canine species have recently occurred, the Police have strict orders to take up and confine all dogs, *particularly BULL-DOGS*, which make their appearance in the streets of Cambridge, unprovided with muzzles.

By order of the Committee of the Resident Undergraduates,
THE SECRETARY.

words that he puts into the mouth of Tom Brown's father: 'What is he sent to school for? . . . If he'll only turn out a brave, helpful, truth-telling Englishman, and a Christian, that's all I want'.

This ambitious aim was not to be achieved without certain sacrifices. It imposed, for instance, a choice between scriptural belief and rationality. Dr Arnold, not surprisingly, was on the side of the angels. Speaking of his son's education he said: 'Rather than have physical science the principal thing in my son's mind, I would gladly have him think that the sun went round the earth, and that the stars were so many spangles set in the bright blue firmament'.

If this was the aim of scientific teaching at Rugby, a logical step might have been to send one's son either to Oxford or Cambridge. (Only Durham and London existed as alternatives, and both were unthinkable for the sons of gentlemen.) The chances are that he would have learnt very little at either university, unless he was intending to take holy orders, as many undergraduates aimed to do, and in that case he would have found plenty of instruction. Until about 1870 most dons were clergymen and any young man who enjoyed the odour of sanctity could usually sniff it in his college quadrangle. It was not until the late 'sixties, when the influence of Benjamin Jowett, the famous Master of Balliol, started to make itself felt, that the strength of this aroma began to fade away. Although Jowett was himself a clergyman and a theologian, he was also strongly in favour of revising the narrow and out-of-date curriculum of the University, and his success in this was shown by the high proportion of Balliol men who afterwards distinguished themselves in Parliament, the Law, and the Civil Service. But a lot of undergraduates were content with lowlier ambitions. Enjoyment of life, which meant hunting, whoring, gambling, racing, dining and drinking, amusements which were sometimes enlivened by cruel and elaborate practical jokes, was their principal aim.

This no doubt was another reason why Victorian parents were against education for their daughters. But luckily for the daughters there was an influential minority who were determined that this state of affairs must be brought to an end. Girton College for women undergraduates was established at Cambridge in 1869, and Newnham College in 1871. By 1879 Somerville College and Lady Margaret Hall were opened at Oxford.

The battle for higher education for women had been won. But not for the more advanced education of ordinary boys and girls. The primary school was still the only school to which most of them could go, and remained so till the end of the Victorian era. Not enough money was available to organise a comprehensive system of

ABOVE: Thomas Hughes, author of *Tom Brown's Schooldays* (1857), an autobiographical story of life at Rugby under Dr Arnold. Its moral tone and high-flown sentiments would hardly be likely to appeal to modern readers, but for many years it remained compulsive reading for Victorian schoolboys.

OPPOSITE: Throughout the Victorian era the presence of women students at universities was as strongly opposed by undergraduates as their existence is welcomed by them today. Women were allowed to sit for examinations, but not to take degrees. In 1897 a feminist campaign against this discrimination provoked a mass reaction among Cambridge undergraduates.

OPPOSITE: Miss Dorothea Beale, headmistress of Cheltenham Ladies' College, with the Empress Frederick of Germany (*seated*). Miss Beale's example as a pioneer in education profoundly influenced improvements in the methods and standards of teaching girls.

secondary education, and fourteen was the maximum age for a pupil at a higher grade elementary school. But things had certainly improved since the Act of 1870, which had provided more state aid and given school boards wider powers to compel attendance, as well as to acquire land for building schools. Yet there was still a long way to go before the educational system was to reach the standard that had already been achieved by other European countries. Why was this? Professor G. M. Trevelyan in his *English Social History* suggests an answer:

The main reason why English education lagged behind in the mid-Victorian period was that no government, Whig or Tory, could conceive a means of setting up a national system at the public expense that would not have given the bitterest offence either to the Dissenters or to the Established Church.

Was it perhaps of this that the atheistic Lenin was thinking when he described religion as 'the opiate of the people'?

FIRM BELIEFS

Chapter 6: Firm Beliefs ❡ The Oxford Movement ❡ God and Theology ❡ The Case of the Reverend Mr Gorham ❡ The Victorian Sunday ❡ *Origin of Species* ❡ Muscular Christianity ❡ Charity Begins in Church ❡ Spiritualism

The further we get from the nineteenth century and the deeper into our own age, in which both scepticism and disbelief have made such significant headway, the more difficult it becomes to appreciate the religious feelings of the Victorians. As a community they were on the whole a fairly hard-hearted lot, not over-endowed with spiritual imagination, nor noticeably more Christian in their general behaviour than their descendants. Why, then, were they so preoccupied with religion?

Intellectually the temper of the times was one of vigorous speculation and enquiry and it was natural therefore that the meaning and purpose of religion should be re-examined in the light of this new dawn, the beginning of which was symbolised by the enquiring and expectant image of a young, almost childish, sovereign.

The eighteenth century had been a period of eager activity among the innumerable sects of the dissenters – Methodists, Baptists, Congregationalists, Unitarians and the like, but for the Church of England it had been a period of gradually increasing sloth and neglect. It was reckoned in 1813 that out of nearly eleven thousand church livings, well over half were without benefit of regular clergy, some not even being afforded the ministrations of a curate. This was a sorry situation, but no more lamentable than that of which it was the result. Among the higher ranks of the clergy the rewards were often commensurate with those which a dutiful dean or a diligent bishop might have felt entitled to expect hereafter. But a large number of the lesser clergy were so poorly paid that they were little better off than their meanest parishioners. Then with the Reform Bill of 1832 there came a change in the religious atmosphere. A significant effect of the Bill was to place political power in the hands of a large body of Nonconformists and consequently to lessen the representative strength of those classes that traditionally gave their support to the established church. Such a situation was bound to produce discussion and reaction, which by the time Victoria came to the throne had assumed the character of a permanent public debate.

A year earlier, the Ecclesiastical Commission, which had already remedied some of the graver defects in the Church's organisation, had been established as a permanent body; but its duties were mainly administrative and rubric and ritual continued to be neglected. In effect, their observance was left to the clergy's own

OPPOSITE: The ritual of family prayers was an indulgence that the upper and middle classes, with time to spare, could afford more easily than the hard-pressed poor. The Lord's Day (ABOVE) 'from toil and trouble free', gave each and all an equal chance of supplication.

177

personal predilection; an open-ended invitation to all manner of subversive if not downright heretical practices. It was all most unsatisfactory. If the Commission could not, and the Bishops would not, attempt to put matters right, others must be allowed to do so. Some in fact had already started on the task.

The Oxford Movement was a loose association of like-minded men bent on reforming the Church's slipshod ways. The Movement had begun to take shape in 1833. By 1837 it was in full swing, and *Tracts for the Times*, issued periodically by its sponsors, were widely circulated and heatedly discussed. The founders of the Movement, John Keble, John Henry Newman and Hurrell Froude, were men of ability and deep sincerity and it was this that provoked the shrillest cries from their opponents; for it was the Tractarians' view that much of what was wrong sprang from forgetfulness of the fact that the Church of England was still in reality a satellite of the Holy Catholic Church, a doctrine deeply and instinctively repugnant to the Nonconformist conscience. It was a doctrine that reeked with the lethal vapour of incense, that suggested the sinful rustle of vestments, and pointed the way to a disgusting and improper use of candles.

Much store was set by the Tractarians on the value of symbolism as a reminder of the eternal verities, of which the image was in grave danger of becoming blurred in men's minds through the laxity and inertia of the Church. Even dissenters could not deny that there was a clear duty to keep such images brightly burnished. But to attempt this laudible aim with symbolical spit-and-polish seemed to many sheer anathema. Symbolism was for popish priests, for such deluded apostates as Pugin, who could write with relish of cope chests 'filled with orphreyed baudekins; and pix, and pax, and chrismatory are there: and thurible and cross'. Was it towards such Romish flummery that the Oxford Movement was leading?

Many feared that it might be so. But Keble, Newman and Froude pressed on undaunted by suspicions or criticism, firm in the belief, as Lytton Strachey puts it, that 'the Church of England bore everywhere upon it the signs of human imperfection', a state of affairs this hopeful triumvirate were determined to have a shot at putting right; 'it was the outcome of revolution and compromise, of the exigencies of politicians . . . and the necessities of the State'.

The attraction of the Movement was not so much to those who worshipped Christ as to those who worshipped theology. In spite of the sincerity of their convictions, not a great deal was done about putting into practise the advice offered, for instance, in the Sermon on the Mount. Care for the undernourished, the ill-housed, the

OPPOSITE: John Keble (*top*), John Henry (later Cardinal) Newman (*centre*) and Hurrell Froude, leaders of the Oxford Movement, among the aims of which was an increase in bigotry, gloom and superstition. Newman's withdrawal from the Movement in 1845 started its dissolution.

BELOW: The Pope's restoration of the Roman Catholic hierarchy in Britain, proclaimed in September 1850, aroused Protestants of all denominations to a frenzy of indignation. A mass meeting at the Guildhall denounced 'Papal aggression' in terms hardly likely to have won approval from the Prince of Peace.

uneducated, for the sweat-shop victim and the workhouse pauper, were indeed pressing problems; but to the followers of the Oxford Movement these things seemed less fundamental than those that concerned the nature of man's duties to God. Considerable thought and discussion were devoted to such questions as the number of males circumcised by Abraham and the vexed problem of Baptismal Regeneration. The Church's insistence on faith and repentance as prerequisites of baptism posed the difficult question of how such abstractions could be brought home to the infant mind. To some, the Reverend George Gorham among them, this was rather a poser. Mr Gorham went so far as publicly to express the view that the infant mind was unreceptive to dogma. But the Bishop of Exeter, a churchman of inflexible opinions, would have none of it. He refused a living to Mr Gorham on account of his views. Over this desperate situation a furious controversy raged in pulpit, chapter-house and drawing-room, as well as in the press. But it was not wholly barren; one tiny seed of common sense was watered by the tears of anguish

The real and the ideal.
OPPOSITE: St Augustine's Church, Kilburn (1877) a fine and enlightened example of late Victorian Gothic by J.L. Pearson.
ABOVE: St James the Less, Pimlico (1860), a laboured and less imposing effort by G.E. Street.
ABOVE RIGHT: Pugin's vision of the Gothic revival.

that rolled down the disputants' cheeks. In course of time they formed a globule large enough to be submitted for inspection by the Judicial Committee of the Privy Council, which after long deliberation pronounced a judgment in Mr Gorham's favour.

If proof were wanting of the instinctively religious feelings of the Victorians, it lies in the excitement aroused by the Gorham case. The issues at stake were as far removed from the realities of Victorian existence as the sentimental verses of Eliza Cook, queen of Victorian doggerel. To those – and there were many – who opposed Mr Gorham's views, no rational arguments, no practical evidence to the contrary made the slightest appeal. Mystical faith triumphed, not for the first time, over the reason of many moderately intelligent men.

It was the strength of this inner conviction that sustained such obdurate masochists as the Plymouth Brethren, the Calvinists, and others whose watchword was Darkness and for whom no path could lead to salvation unless it was a thoroughly uncomfortable one to follow. Nor was it only to such sects as these that religion appeared as something stern and sable-hued. The Papist Pugin was tainted with a like fondness for gloom. His *Apology for the Revival of Christian Architecture* is emphatic on the subject: 'MELANCHOLY,' he declared, 'and *therefore fit for religious buildings!!!*'. Newman too, in spite of outward kindliness and tranquillity, was the equal of these sterner sects in his insistence upon gloom as an essential part of the Christian religion. The grotesque notion that it might be represented as something joyful or uplifting he stamped upon with both feet. In his view, England would have been the better for a religion 'vastly more superstitious, more bigoted, more gloomy, more fierce'; an opinion that no doubt attracted some support for Carlyle's view that Newman 'had the intellect of a rabbit'. In spite of his rather intimidating theory, however, the Oxford Movement managed not only to survive but somehow to attract large numbers of eager and presumably bigoted, gloomy and fierce supporters.

It also attracted considerable opposition. Nonconformists of every hair-splitting degree were drawn together like iron filings to a magnet by their suspicion of Papist tendencies in the Movement; a suspicion not unjustified, as things turned out. For in 1845 Newman became a Roman Catholic, and was followed into the faith six years later by Archdeacon, later Cardinal, Manning, an ardent supporter of the Movement in its early days.

The defection of these two set an example that others were quick to follow and brought to an end the earnest efforts of the Movement to popularise the theological doctrines of its sponsors. The impetus that the Movement had given to church reform, to the proper observation of pastoral duties, and the responsibilities of the clergy was an ironic bequest to the church which the Movement's leaders had found wanting.

With the tightening of Church discipline came a reawakening to the singularity of Sunday and of the duty of consecrating it exclusively to the worship of God and examination of the soul. Not since the censorious conscience of Cromwell had forcibly imprinted itself on the community had Englishmen found themselves so circumscribed by the Sabbath. By common consent the more oppressive and inapt of ancient statutes had been gradually allowed to fall into disuse, though even as late as 1846, the year in which it was repealed, an act was still in force which made it an offence punishable by a fine of a shilling to abstain from going to church.

Sunday reading in the 1850s meant for most children either the Bible or improving literature such as *Familiar Dialogues*, which pointed to the mischief of failing to keep the Sabbath holy, as by riding donkeys or other heathenish practices.

ABOVE: In the country, as in town, Sunday Best was imperative for Church Parade.

RIGHT: Ascensiontide, or Holy Thursday, was the occasion of well-blessing in many villages where in the summer months water was often scarce. Hand's Well at Tissington in Derbyshire, like many others, was specially decorated for the ceremony.

The English Sunday is still a tedious experience for those without resources of their own, but compared with Sunday as it was in the Victorian era it seems like a fiesta. Recreation and amusement were assumed detestable in the sight of God. And mortification did not stop with the flesh, clad in uncomfortable clothes and forced to slump for long hours in hard pews; the mind also had to be purged of all but pious thoughts. Dickens in *Little Dorrit* paints a sad picture of the aimlessness that was forced upon the public by a thoughtless and hypocritical convention:

Everything was bolted and barred that could by possibility furnish relief to an overworked people. No pictures, no unfamiliar animals, no rare plants or flowers, no natural or artificial wonders of the ancient world – all taboo with that enlightened strictness, that the ugly South-Sea gods in the British Museum might have supposed themselves at home again. Nothing to see but streets, streets, streets. Nothing to breathe but streets, streets, streets. Nothing to change the brooding mind, or raise it up. Nothing for the spent toiler to do but to compare the monotony of his seventh day with the monotony of his six days, think what a weary life he led, and make the best of it – or the worst, according to the probabilities.

LEFT: God is Truth, God is Good, God is Holy, God is Just, God is Love; similarly the Lord is thy Shepherd, thou shalt not want, even in the workhouse. In the casual ward at Marylebone in 1867 it was perhaps hard to realise these comforting ideals.

OPPOSITE: Pre-Raphaelite piety was not an emotion understood by the masses. The secular realism of Millais' *Christ in the House of His Parents* (of which a detail is shown here) provoked a storm of protest sparked off by a vituperative and ill-conceived attack by Charles Dickens.

THE HAPPY HOME.

Happy the home, when God is there,
　And love fills every breast;
Where one their wish, and one their prayer,
　And one their heavenly rest.

Happy the home where Jesus' name
　Is sweet to every ear;
Where children early lisp His fame,
　And parents hold Him dear.

Happy the home where prayer is heard,
　And praise is wont to rise;
Where parents love the sacred Word,
　And live but for the skies.

Lord, let us in our homes agree,
　This blessed peace to gain;
Unite our hearts in love to Thee,
　And love to all will reign.

LONDON: RELIGIOUS TRACT SOCIETY.

No. 11.

Dickens was by no means irreligious, but was a hater of excesses which made even the reading of a book on Sunday, let alone a game of chess or croquet, seem a heinous sin. Sir Kenneth Clark in *The Gothic Revival* recalls that 'it was many years before Ruskin read any book but the Bible on that day . . . and every Sunday, for the fifty-two years that he lived with his parents, screens were put in front of all the pictures, lest their bright colours might distract the mind in its contemplation of man's sinful estate'.

Ruskin's religion, like that of most educated non-Catholics was based on the dual principle of veneration for the Established Church and detestation of all that smacked of Rome, and more especially of those who had been victimised by its pernicious wiles. In *The Stones of Venice* he speaks of those

. . . lured into the Romanist church by the glitter of it, like larks into a trap by broken glass; to be blown into a change of religion by the whine of an organ-pipe; stitched into a new creed by the gold threads on priests' petticoats; jangled into a change of conscience by the chimes of a belfry. I know nothing in the shape of error so dark as this, no imbecility so absolute, no treachery so contemptible.

There was only one point on which agreement could be found with the Roman Catholics: that was on the sacred duty of preserving the Sabbath. Similarly, whatever the causes of division between High and Low Church, or of schism within either fold, all were united in the preservation of this sacred trust. Freed at other times from this great conspiracy of gloom, High and Low scratched and fought among themselves.

That common cause could one day be found between opponents so shrill and so vociferous seemed almost impossible, but in 1859 that day dawned. Charles Darwin published *The Origin of Species*. The rational cat was among the mystical pigeons, but with beak and claw and with celestial vision dimmed by tears of outrage, the pigeons fought back. And they were not alone. So rapturous were some of those who advocated Darwin's views, so hectic in their zeal, that they did almost more harm than good. Professor Huxley, who was Darwin's most distinguished colleague, believed that for a time the theory of evolution was 'sadly damaged by some of its supporters'.

It was not the first time since the dawn of the scientific era that the conflicting claims of logical and spiritual belief had precipitated a crisis of conscience among intelligent people. Yet many of them found it possible to reject Darwin's theories without hesitation. He was attacked by churchmen of all dimensions, High, Low and Broad. But deep as was their hostility, and aggravated perhaps by

The outer and the inner man: clerical dignity and tradition demanded something distinctive in the way of hats; likewise a thirst for piety was not to be slaked with *vin ordinaire*.

OPPOSITE: The effluxions of the Religious Tract Society, spreading far and wide, gave balm to simple minds and brightened the walls of many a humble home.

The Rev. Charles Kingsley (TOP), theologian and novelist, and the Rev. F.D. Maurice, founders of Christian Socialism, the aim of which was to introduce Christian principles into industrial relations. The attempt was a failure.

a secret feeling that time might show itself to be not on the side of the angels but on the side of the monkeys, enough energy was still left to continue the fight among themselves over questions of scriptural interpretation, dogma, and ritual. For it was with questions such as these, with faith more than with works, that the early Victorians in particular nourished their feelings of religion.

Not all of them, though, were as deeply immersed in the higher realms of theological controversy. Charles Kingsley, a clergyman later to become well-known as the author of *Westward Ho!* and *The Water Babies*, was one who believed in the practical purpose as well as the divine inspiration of the Christian religion. He joined with Frederick Denison Maurice and Thomas Hughes, the author of *Tom Brown's Schooldays*, in founding the Christian Socialists (the originators of that unfortunate phrase 'muscular Christianity') whose aim was to apply Biblical standards to industrial relations – a vain hope then, as now – and to proclaim the virtues of co-operation over those of competition. They did not succeed in either aim. Both sides of industry remained as worldly as ever in their objectives and indifferent to appeals for brotherly love.

Was it perhaps that Maurice and his friends, though strong in muscle, were weak in oratory? For oratory was the driving force of the religious revival of the Victorian age. Men with sterner, more abstract views of Christianity than Maurice's band of hope, and others whose strength lay in simple vernacular fervour, were able to pack in huge audiences. It was an age of spell-binders. Canon Liddon at St Paul's, Dr Spurgeon in his Methodist Tabernacle at Southwark, Robert Candlish, the Free Church leader in Scotland, Lewis Edwards, the Calvinist in Wales, the Salvationist General Booth, preaching throughout the length and breadth of England, Henry Ward Beecher, the lustful Boanerges from New York, and Moody and Sankey, also from America, with their Gospel Hymns, as well as others of various denominations, exerted powers of attraction such as only a pop star could emulate in the 'sixties of the following century.

Preachers, with the possible exception of Billy Graham, can no longer be classed as popular entertainers, for it was more often the personality and performance of the preacher that attracted his audience than the matter of his discourse. But not all of them had powers of eloquence or compulsion equal to those of the leaders of the Oxford Movement, or of such men as Spurgeon and General Booth, and often listless flocks sat captive in their pews while some intricate theological argument wafted its way in at one ear and out at the other. Or, more especially in rural parishes, the theme might

The Feast of Tabernacles celebrated in the Great Synagogue at Duke's Place in the City, *c.*1850. This, the chief Jewish place of worship in London, built by James Spiller in 1790, was destroyed during the blitz 150 years later.

Life is real, life is earnest; so, it seems, was matrimony in 1895.

Holy Trinity – Dr Charles Spurgeon
(1834–92), Archbishop Tait (1811–82), and
Cardinal Wiseman (1802–65) – three of
the brightest stars in the religious
firmament of the Victorian era.

Dr C.H. Spurgeon, leader of the Baptist
community, was the most popular of all
nonconformist preachers. The
congregations at his Southwark
tabernacle numbered thousands, and
his sermons sold in tons.

Archbishop Tait, successor to Dr
Arnold as headmaster of Rugby, became
Primate of all England in 1868. As a
firm believer in the unity of Church and
State he was at the centre of many a
theological dispute.

Cardinal Wiseman, scholar, linguist
and administrator, appointed by the
Pope to the see of Westminster in
1850, was the first Roman Catholic
cardinal to be nominated in
England since the Reformation.

be contentment with one's lot, however humble, since the order of society, including in all probability the vicar's dependence on the goodwill of the squire, had been ordained by God.

The more intelligent preachers of course adapted their themes to the intellect of their congregations and were listened to attentively. In *Charles Dickens and Early Victorian England*, R.J. Cruikshank analyses the Victorian sermon:

Over the loaded Sunday dinner-table the morning's sermon was a main topic of conversation. Orthodoxy being taken for granted, the manner was usually more eagerly discussed than the matter. For the sermon was a Victorian art form, as it had been a seventeenth-century and eighteenth-century art form. Among strict Evangelical and Nonconformist families who regarded the playhouse as being under Satan's management and the novel as a corrupter of the young, the pulpit was in some part a moral substitute for both. It supplied dramatic interest, narrative power, analysis of character, passion and humour in addition to the vindication of sound doctrine. The connoisseurs of this ancient art expected, too, that a sermon should exhibit the same regard for form as a sonata. The text from the Bible on which it was built up was like a theme in music; and the firstly, secondly and thirdly of the preacher were the variations and fantasies upon the theme; and there was often a thundering finish to the sermon in which the text was heard, so to speak, in the triumphant key of C major.

OPPOSITE TOP: Surrey Congregational Chapel, Blackfriars, where from 1836 to 1854, James Sherman, one of the outstanding preachers of the day, held multitudes of the faithful spell-bound. Twenty years later, Brother Moody and Brother Sankey (OPPOSITE BOTTOM), barnstorming evangelists from America, were plucking at the religious heartstrings of huge audiences in the Agricultural Hall at Islington, an appropriate setting in which to sing of green pastures.

BELOW: A capacity for sustained oratory – and sustained listening – made the Victorians natural evangelists and natural disciples. Lectures such as Bro. Holding's were enjoyed as much by village communities as the sermons of famous preachers in the big cities.

I.O.G.T.
INDEPENDANT CHAPEL, BOURTON.
THIS TICKET WILL ADMIT BEARER TO A
LECTURE
IN THE ABOVE PLACE,
ON TUESDAY, MARCH 31, 1874,
BY
Bro. HOLDING, S.D.G.W.C.T.
SUBJECT:—
"WHY I AM A GOOD TEMPLAR,"
Being a REPLY to the ANONYMOUS PAMPHLET entitled—
"WHY I AM NOT A GOOD TEMPLAR."

CHAIR WILL BE TAKEN AT 7-30.
TICKETS TO BE HAD OF BRO. SMITH & OTHER FRIENDS AT BOURTON.

FAR LEFT: Salvation was preached by the soldiers of its army at mid-day meetings on the porch of the People's Mission Hall in Whitechapel. The mission opened its doors to receive repentant sinners in April 1870.
LEFT: General Booth, the peaceful warrior who founded the Salvation Army in 1878 to fight intemperance, prostitution, and exploitation of the working class. Booth, at first abused and derided, became one of the most powerful of Victorian demagogues.

Whether the theme was Redemption Through Suffering, Brotherly Love, Hell Fire, Faith, Hope or Charity, the preacher's interpretation of it was certain to provoke animated discussion. Charity in particular was a subject which preoccupied all classes, for most sectarian movements sponsored some form of charity. A huge army of volunteers belonging to all denominations collected and administered funds or helped to provide food, shelter, clothing or a modicum of education for those who needed it. It is always difficult for those who are well off and charitably minded to avoid being called patronising when trying to help people less fortunate than themselves. Dickens, Mrs Gaskell and others wrote about the resentment of the poor who felt that they were being patronised. But all the same, without such patronage the lives of many thousands of the poorest class of Victorian citizens would have been considerably harder and more hazardous than they were. Enormous sums were raised and spent, though often in haphazard and wasteful ways. 'There is no country in the world,' said Hugo Munsterberg, the psychologist, 'in which so large an amount is given in charity as in England and no country where less good is done with it'. In 1853 the first attempt was made to bring order out of chaos by the appointment by Parliament of the Charity Commissioners, who were vested with responsibility for seeing that the money that was being poured into innumerable charities was properly spent and accounted for.

Money rolled in from all directions, for never was there an age in which Englishmen were subjected to so many varieties of schismatic pressure, all applied with an unassailable conviction in their orthodoxy. The wonder is that under these conflicting influences so few succumbed to doubt. Perhaps it was easier then to accept the comfortable assumption of life everlasting than face the possibility of its being no more than a tale told by an idiot . . . signifying nothing. One who came reluctantly to the conclusion that his existence was likely to be confined to the terrestial world was Hurrell Froude's brother, the historian James Anthony Froude, who early in life had taken Holy Orders. Another was the poet Arthur Hugh Clough, whose muse with a touch of unkind irony had earlier inspired the hymn, *Say Not the Struggle Naught Availeth*.

Such men do not easily abandon the habit of faith, nor was their crisis simply one of conscience. In the climate of Victorian opinion to confess to being an agnostic was almost like admitting to having a veneral disease. Yet there was an even worse delinquency than agnosticism; there was atheism. Charles Bradlaugh, Member of Parliament for Northampton, was forcibly prevented for six years

MISSIONARY HYMN.

From Greenland's icy mountains,
  From India's coral strand,
Where Afric's sunny fountains
  Roll down their golden sand;

From many an ancient river,
  From many a balmy plain,
They call us to deliver
  Their land from error's chain.

What though the spicy breezes
  Blow soft on Ceylon's isle,
Though every prospect pleases,
  And only man is vile:

The hymns of Wesley, Heber and other earlier proselytizers were still immensely popular and were often included in those 'selections for juvenile readers' that were intended to combine amusement or instruction with moral uplift.

OPPOSITE: Lift Up Your Hearts, 1847. Thomas Webster's impression of a village choir (*detail*).

ABOVE: Every year, at the Foundling Hospital in Bloomsbury some five hundred unwanted children (the sexes segregated) were cared for, clothed and educated, and at lunchtime on Sundays were patronised by their elders and betters; a form of weekly penance for both the foundlings and the Hospital governors, who with friends or relations came to see that all was well.

RIGHT: When drunkenness cost no more than a few pennies and made the lives of a great many seem happier than when they were sober, the need to encourage temperance was vital. But in their zeal the reformers were sometimes inclined to overstate their case.

OPPOSITE: The evangelism of General Booth was rooted not in Biblical analysis, but in the practical application of Christ's teachings. Under his administration, the Salvation Army grew to be a well-organised agency for relief and rehabilitation. Pauperism and vice were to be reduced by the establishment of a system of 'colonies' where the needy or destitute could be given useful work, by the helping of discharged prisoners and the reclamation of fallen women, by the provision of legal aid for the poor, and other expedients. Against squalor, ignorance, and at first the violent hostility of opposing interests, the Army fought a continuous and heroic campaign.

'TONY,'
THE CHILD DRUNKARD.

No. 17.—Temperance Series. [See page 9.

from taking his seat in the House of Commons because he had refused to take the oath. The House declined to admit the alternative of affirmation, and so in effect from 1880 until 1886 the voters of Northampton, who repeatedly returned Bradlaugh in spite of his rejection by the Commons, were denied representation in Parliament. Detestable though Bradlaugh's opinions were to most Victorians, the tenacity with which he clung to them and the eloquence with which he defended them went some way towards absolving atheism from the taint of being a dirty word.

A word that most people found hardly less distasteful was 'spiritualism'. The emanations of this cult, imported from America, wreathed their way into the minds not only of naturally impressionable individuals, but also into those of some whose scientific integrity and rational instincts ensured a degree of interest in the subject which it might not otherwise have attained. There were rumours, too, that Queen Victoria's Highland servant, John Brown, had mediumistic powers by which the Queen kept in touch with the departed Albert. Certainly, this tiresome and presumptuous gillie had a singular hold over the Queen, but the possibility that this was an extra-sensory arm-lock seems doubtful. In spite of the exposure of a number of fakes and inconclusive scientific tests, spiritualism established itself as a faith not to be excluded from the synoptic pantheon of Victorian creeds.

Absorbed as the Victorians were with the possibility of life after death, death itself preoccupied them even more. Funerals have always been less a tribute to the dead than a status symbol for the living, and in Victorian times no symbol was more indicative of social ambitions. The dread of dying a pauper was not simply the dread of poverty, but of the social stigma attached to a pauper's grave, in which, as Mrs Gaskell describes in *Mary Barton*, 'bodies were piled up within a foot or two of the surface'. For those who could afford it, elaborate and expensive funerals were the thing. Sometimes the ceremony would cost as much as £1,500, though even so enormous a sum was no guarantee that the undertaker's men would be sober. Theirs was a notoriously drunken profession, and grave-diggers too were often drunk and would sometimes trail the funeral party from the graveside to the cemetery gates demanding more money.

Such proceedings were distressing enough, though hardly more undignified than much that went on throughout Victoria's reign in the name of religion. It was paradoxical that in an age so fervently religious, Christian zeal, that of Roman Catholics excepted, should have scattered the seeds of its own decline. Anglicans and

The outward forms of Christianity were often more important to the Victorians than its inner significance. Charles Bradlaugh, the atheist MP for Northampton, was for six years forcibly prevented from taking his seat in Parliament because he had refused to take the oath. The right of a man to his own opinions and to abide by his conscience was eventually conceded by the Christian community of the House of Commons, and in 1886 Bradlaugh took his seat.

Funerals were occasions for gloomy
ostentation. The obsequies of
Superintendent James Braidwood, chief
of the London Fire Brigade, who died
in the course of duty on 22 July 1861,
were more elaborate than most, though
extravagant display was an essential
sign of respect for the dead.

The forms of Victorian belief were
many and various. Spiritualism had
many detractors, none more effective
than 'Professor' J. H. Anderson, a
well-known conjuror, who used his
talents and his own weekly journal,
Psychomantic Reporter (ABOVE), to expose
the claims of certain so-called mediums.
The enigmas of Spiritualism included
D. D. Home (LEFT), the most famous of
all mediums, who practised his craft
without reward and, unlike many, free
from charges of chicanery.

Nonconformists, like Nonconformists themselves, were united by few common beliefs. Only in their abhorrence of Roman Catholicism were they firmly of one mind. A religion so fraught with internal conflicts could never be a match for a united church with a positive doctrine. The squabbles over doxy and dogmata, over rubric and ritual, in which so much time and energy was spent, gave the Catholic rivals of the disputants an advantage that they were not slow to grasp and have held on to ever since.

That eminent yet in some ways least typical of Victorians, Carlyle, who in his early days had dallied with the idea of becoming a minister, once stigmatised Dean Stanley, the Queen's favourite among her divines, as the personification of these self-destructive forces in English religion. With equal truth he might have said of the leaders of other sects, as he said of the Dean, 'There goes Dean Stanley, boring holes in the bottom of the Church of England'.

At this distance from the Victorian era it is difficult to follow, sometimes even to take quite seriously, a good deal of the theological controversy and ritualistic argument that went on. To many of us today, these things seem as remote as the dynastic squabbles of the Roman Empire. But it should be remembered, if we wish to understand the sources of the Victorians' self-confidence and achievement, that religion was as powerful and positive an influence in their lives as belief in the need for technological supremacy is in ours.

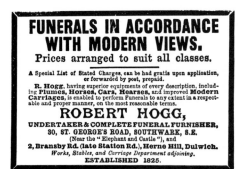

A HARD
DAY'S WORK

Chapter 7: A Hard Day's Work ¶ Employers and Employed
¶ Children Underground **¶** Climbing Boys **¶** The Factory Acts
¶ Casual Labour **¶** The Agricultural Worker **¶** Serving Behind
the Counter **¶** Domestic Service

History tends to show that on the whole human nature does not change. Even so, few employers of labour would not now be genuinely revolted by the scandalous and degrading conditions in which enormous numbers of Victorian men, women and children were forced to work. Trade unions, such as they were, had no political power and were more in the nature of friendly societies. Only three years before the Queen came to the throne, Melbourne, pushing his habitual indifference to the limit, had acquiesced in the brutal sentence of seven years' transportation passed on the six Tolpuddle workers from Dorset, whose crime had been to swear the ritual oaths of a friendly society which they had formed in the hope of raising their weekly wages from seven to ten shillings.

By the end of the era the lot of the working man and woman had greatly improved; not so far that they felt free to behave with contemptuous indifference towards their own unions or their employers whenever some petty dispute arose, but far enough to have raised the worst off from being no better than beasts of burden to the dignity of ordinary human beings. By comparison, the position of the employer and the professional man had changed far less. They had not had to endure poverty of the most disgusting kind or to work in foul and unhealthy conditions. They had not felt

'Stitch, stitch, stitch, in poverty, hunger and dirt,' wrote Thomas Hood – words that applied to conditions in many sweat-shops where clothing was mass produced and wages skimped. By comparison, conditions at the British Needle Mills (OPPOSITE), opened in the 1830s at Redditch, the centre of the needle and fishing hook industry, were considered very advanced.

their occupations to be threatened by perpetual uncertainty, nor lived in terror of the workhouse. It is therefore not with owners and employers, nor with the professional classes that we are concerned here, but with the bulk of the working population.

To picture all Victorian employers as tight-fisted parasites, though a good many of them undoubtedly were, would be an injustice to the more enlightened of them, such as Robert Owen, the practical and imaginative cotton spinner whose mills at New Lanark in Scotland were a model of their kind, and Sir Titus Salt, the Yorkshire wool manufacturer, remembered to this day by the district known as Saltaire near Bradford, the scene of his attempts to establish an ideal manufacturing community.

At the opposite end of the scale, and unfortunately more in evidence were mine, mill and factory owners whose treatment of their workers ranged from the negligent to the barbaric. In some industries, notably coal mining, the treatment of children was particularly revolting. In 1842 a report was issued by a commission on children's employment which had been set up by Parliament two years earlier. The commission's account of working conditions in the mines reads as though it might be the description of a painting by Hieronymus Bosch. In some mines, children were employed from the age of five. Occasionally, younger ones would be taken down not to work, but to sit and scare the rats away from their father's dinner. The passages through which the coal was shifted were sometimes too small for a man to squeeze into, so children were harnessed to the trucks like pit ponies and dragged them through the darkness on all fours. Others who worked the pumps sometimes had to stand ankle-deep in cold water for twelve hours at a stretch. Others again sat for long hours alone and in total darkness pulling the strings that worked the ventilator openings. The most that any of these pitiful little slaves earned was a few shillings a week. In parts of Lancashire and Yorkshire, the parish authorities bound workhouse boys, at the age of no more than eight or nine, to work in the mines for twelve years. They were found very useful for doing jobs that the miners, however impoverished, refused to let their own children do. As J. L. and Barbara Hammond remark in their biography of Lord Shaftesbury, whose life was dedicated to improving the lot of the working child, 'These children were called apprentices, but were as much slaves as any creature on two legs to be found on the plantations of the West Indies'.

The commission's report on the mines was the first one that it issued. In the years that followed, further reports were to appear that revealed conditions hardly less scandalous in other industries.

Mechanisation in the shipbuilding industry was slow and primitive for much of the nineteenth century. As W. Bell Scott's painting, *The Industry of the Tyne* indicates, in terms of human energy and man-hours the expenditure was enormous. Welfare and feeding arrangements were the concern of the workers, not of the managements. A man either took his dinner with him or had it brought from home.

BE UNITED · AND · INDUSTRIOUS

AMALGAMATED SOCIETY OF ENGINEERS, MACHINISTS, MILLWRIGHTS,
SMITHS, AND PATTERN MAKERS.

This is to Certify that _____ was admitted a Member of the
_____ Branch on the _____ day of _____ 18___
In witness whereof we have subscribed our names and affixed the Society's Seal.

PRESIDENT   SECRETARY

TOP: The New Lanark cotton mills in
Scotland, which Robert Owen, the
socialist, took over in 1800, may have
looked like a prison from the outside,
but in conception, management and
administration they were far in advance
of any other industrial establishment
of their size.

CENTRE: If Owen's enlightened policies
had found favour in other industries,
perhaps Leeds would have not have
looked like this eighty-five years later.

RIGHT: The Spitalfields hiring fair, 1850.
The employment of children in
iniquitous conditions, which persisted
in some quarters as late as the 'sixties,
made this fair seem agreeable by
comparison. Children, mostly girls of
about nine or ten, offered themselves
on Monday mornings as weekly cleaners,
cooks or baby-minders. Wages ranged
from a shilling to one and fourpence a
week, without food.

OPPOSITE: Many of the democratic ideals
with which most trade unions began
have gradually given way to the single
objective of solidarity. A century and
more ago there was nothing incongruous
in a union membership certificate
urging the holder to be industrious, nor
in its somewhat idealised conception
of union practice.

The employment of climbing boys by chimney sweeps, although forbidden by law in 1840, continued long afterwards. But not all sweeps were brutes. John Day, a reformed drunkard, became prosperous, respected and well known as the 'Temperance Sweep'.

OPPOSITE: Mining for Cornish tin, 1893. Except for the use of trucks, usually drawn by hand, mechanisation in the mining industry was almost unknown, and working conditions generally were scandalous. Safety precautions were primitive and there was a considerable risk to health from dust and bad ventilation. From 1842 onwards, reform, though bitterly resisted by the mine-owners, gradually improved the picture, but still left much to be desired.

In the 'sixties a report on child labour in the Potteries showed that eleven thousand children were being sweated, some of them for as long as sixteen hours a day and for as little as half a crown a week. Boys of between six and ten were lugging moulds from the potter's wheel into the furnace, where the temperature was about one hundred and twenty degrees. But even these little half-cooked unfortunates were better off than the 'climbing boys', the children who were sent up to sweep chimneys. In 1840, after years of opposition by the House of Lords, an act had been passed forbidding the employment of boys for this purpose. No appeals to conscience or humanity had previously had any effects on their lordships, who were more concerned with the state of their rooms and furniture (mechanical sweeping was said to make more mess) than with sweeps' boys being suffocated, burnt or injured, which sometimes happened if a boy got lost in a system of flues. Giving evidence before a Select Committee in 1862, when in spite of the Act of 1840 many climbing boys were still employed, a sweep, appropriately named Ruff, spoke of the sickening cruelty involved in toughening a boy for the job:

The flesh must be hardened. This is done by rubbing it, chiefly on the elbows and knees, with the strongest brine, close by a hot fire. You must stand over them with a cane, or coax them with the promise of a half-penny. . . . At first they will come back from their work with their arms and knees streaming with blood, and the knees looking as if the caps had been pulled off; then the brine must be rubbed in again.

In spite of this and other nauseating accounts of what went on, it was not until fifteen years later that an effective act was passed by Parliament and the scandal of the climbing boys came to an end.

For many years from the beginning of the Victorian era conditions of employment in industry and trade were often deplorable and usually uncertain, particularly for unskilled workers who were liable to be hired and fired with less discrimination then men who knew a trade or had had some sort of training. From the beginning of the century Parliament had almost always opposed attempts to improve the lot of the factory worker by legislation. Peel had tried in 1815 to introduce a bill limiting children's hours of work to ten instead of the twelve hours or even longer that some of them were made to work. He was not successful, nor was Lord Ashley, who made two attempts to bring in a ten-hours bill for the protection of all factory workers. It was not until 1847 that this was finally achieved, to the anger and dismay of many factory owners, who feared that shorter working hours would mean their ruin.

One of the first organised attempts to counteract the effects of the Industrial Revolution on the working man was the foundation of the Chartist Movement in 1838. In November 1839 an armed insurrection by Chartists took place at Newport in Wales, when an attempt was made to release their leader, Harry Vincent, from gaol. It was put down by troops who killed fourteen and wounded fifty of the demonstrators.

ABOVE: The IWMA, founded in 1864 to promote the drawing together of the working classes of all nations, had as its head in London, Karl Marx, who although he held no office in the Association, signed the membership card of every 'citizen'. The Association, as such, lasted only twelve years.
LEFT: The organised trade union conferences held annually at seaside towns originated in more informal gatherings such as this union meeting of farm workers, held at Yeovil, Somerset in 1877.

The ten-hours bill is a tribute to the humanitarian instincts and dogged zeal of Ashley and John Fielden, himself a cotton-mill owner, and also an MP, who after many months of delay and argument shamed a reluctant House into recognising the cruel and squalid truth about the lives of factory workers. Gradually it came to be realised that working and welfare conditions could not be left entirely to the judgment of employers, that the state had a responsibility for seeing that the safety and health of workers was not endangered through the indifference or opportunism of managements to whom output was more important than any other consideration.

Up to 1833 such Factory Acts as there were applied only to cotton mills, except the first Act of 1802, which limited children's working hours to twelve a day, but which was a dead letter from the start, as there were no means of enforcing it. The Factory Act of 1833 contained the seeds of a development that was to be of the greatest importance to the workers. It provided among other things for the appointment of factory inspectors armed not only with the right to enter factories at all hours, but also of sitting as justices to try those whom they believed to be evading the Act. Soon after this innovation mine inspectors were appointed too.

Manufacturers and industrialists as a whole were not much in favour of factory legislation, and Parliament, reflecting their opinions, was inclined to be equally unenthusiastic. Nevertheless, Factory Acts were passed from time to time, though these usually affected only certain sections of industry. It was not until well towards the end of the century that legislation of the comprehensive type now in existence began to take shape.

The growth of trade unionism was even slower. When this spectre first reared its ugly head it seemed to most people of the educated class to be synonymous with anarchy. Dr Arnold of Rugby, writing to a friend in 1834 remarked, 'You have heard, I doubt not, of Trades Unions; a fearful engine of mischief, ready to riot or to assassinate . . .'. Even to so fervent a believer in the desirability of education, it seemed impossible to imagine the existence of a working class sufficiently well educated to conduct negotiations with employers in a reasonable way. Yet trade unions did increase, although very slowly until the passing of two Acts, the first in 1871, the second five years later, which clarified the legal position of unions and the rights of their members. After the Act of 1871 unions began to multiply rapidly, but then declined with the trade depression that began in 1875 and thereafter showed little increase until about ten years later.

In country districts pedlars were familiar figures even after the turn of the century. By 1890 the ballad seller had disappeared from city streets, but was still to be seen going from village to village.

But no acts of parliament or union rules could safeguard workers against the seasonal unemployment that affected many jobs, or the periodic slumps, such as that of the mid-seventies, or of 1886, when it was estimated that more than nine per cent of the population were out of work. As W.G. Reader remarks in *Life in Victorian England*:

Many of the Victorian poor were people who had no hope of ever doing more than picking up a few days' or a few weeks' money here and there, existing in the intervals as best they could. . . . And so they jolted down an uneven road of poverty to old age in the workhouse, if they lived so long.

In London and other large cities there was a huge force of itinerant workers who scratched a bare living from the streets as hawkers, traders, porters, lightermen, cabbies and entertainers, or by doing whatever the season or the locality had to offer. In this last category came the innumerable dung-collectors, nightmen or cess-pool

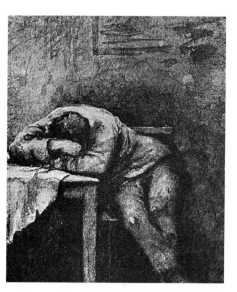

Out of work.

212

BELOW: Charitable organisations did much to relieve both the Exchequer and the conscience of Parliament. In 1858 – a bad winter – the Bethnal Green Employment and Relief Association found work, at nine shillings a week, for hundreds of East Enders, breaking stones for road-making. But out of a local population of 120,000 many more had no means of support.

Street cleaners, first known as 'orderlies', made their appearance in London in 1843, not as council workers, but as employees of the National Philanthropic Association. Among its aims was 'the promotion of social and salutiferous improvements . . . the employment of the poor, so that able-bodied men may be prevented from burdening the parish'. It was the beginning of the end for the crossing sweeper (BELOW), who worked in all weathers, keeping busy crossings free of mud, horse dung, and refuse.

In every city numbers scraped a living in the streets, some as hawkers, or traders, some as bootblacks, some selling matches, in boxes crudely but attractively designed, at a halfpenny each.

cleaners, rubbish-carters, crossing-sweepers, rat-catchers, chimney-sweeps, ballast men and mudlarks – those who fished in the slime of the Thames foreshore for anything that might fetch the price of a night's lodging. A good many who were reduced to this kind of employment had no homes and slept in doss houses, when they could afford to; for not every day yielded the twopence or threepence a night that was charged for a lice-ridden shake-down in one of these establishments.

In the streets hawkers and traders offered for sale an enormous variety of articles, ranging from food and drink, both hot and cold, to clothing, umbrellas, haberdashery, hardware, furniture, cutlery, clocks and watches, toys, pets, song-sheets and ballads. From early morning until late at night London echoed with the sound of street cries. Many of the poorer class bought almost all they needed in the street, seldom venturing into a shop, unless it was the gin shop.

Bad as conditions were for the urban poor and the unskilled worker during most of the Victorian era, few of them in its first decade would willingly have exchanged their jobs for that of a farm labourer.

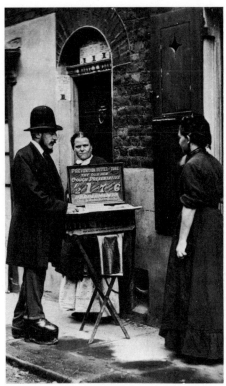
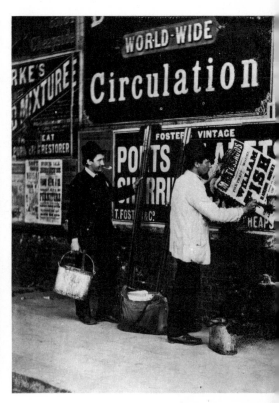

TOP: Other familiars among the family of street traders were the milkman, selling milk that went directly from cow to can – the knife-grinder, whose wheel hummed at the door of every butcher, fishmonger or housewife who needed a sharp-edged knife – the lemonade-seller, with his polished urn and air of respectable poverty – the medicine man, whose mysterious elixirs were compounded of balsams and faith – and the bill-poster seeking space for his announcements.

No less familiar in the country, and often more essential, were those who kept down rural pests, such as this snake-catcher (OPPOSITE) of the New Forest. He also sold the vipers' fat, which was reputed to cure rheumatism and brass poisoning as well as bites from rats or adders.

RIGHT: A survival from the Middle Ages, still to be seen in some parts of Britain as late as the 'nineties, was the man with a dancing bear, no longer accompanied by pipe and tabor, but more often by a mouth-organ or a tambourine.

The flower-girl at Piccadilly Circus and
the blind busker outside the music hall
were familiar London figures. Less often
seen at work were the letter-taker and
the female pickpocket.

Although in good weather the conditions of his work in the open air were preferable to the dust and fumes and the unceasing din of many works and factories, the farm labourer's wages were even lower than those of the working class in urban areas and his housing conditions often as bad, if not worse. In the early 1850s agricultural wages in some districts were only about seven shillings a week. To supplement this pittance, the labourer was usually allowed a certain amount in kind, some milk perhaps, or possibly half a ton of potatoes during the year, with some beer or cider and a bit of food at harvest time. The rent of his cottage would be low, or possibly there would be no rent at all; a reasonable concession where the 'cottage' consisted, as it often did, of a wretched shack or a broken-down lean-to in which a family of eight or ten might have to live.

With such a family to feed and clothe, seven shillings a week did not go very far and often the labourer's wife and children would have to work in the fields as well, sometimes walking five or six miles to get there and then home again at night.

Wages were usually a little better near the towns where factory workers' higher rates of pay tended to push up those of the farm hand, but for many years his housing conditions remained a scandal. Some landlords, among them the Prince of Wales, who in 1861 had bought the seven thousand acre estate of Sandringham in Norfolk, set an example by rehousing their farm workers in new or rebuilt cottages. But in more isolated regions, where there were fewer critical eyes to see and less chance for workers to compare their living conditions with those of others, there was less compulsion upon the farmer-landlord to ensure that his tenants were properly housed.

In the matter of education, too, the farm worker was at a disadvantage. Until the Education Act of 1870, which theoretically brought some form of schooling within the reach of every child, those of the farm labourer, possibly living in some remote hamlet, often grew up more or less illiterate, and inevitably the stupider for having no such incentives as the town-bred child had to sharpen its wits. Since Shakespeare's day the traditional stupidity of the yokel had been a joke with tragic undertones, and in that it often made the farm hand a prisoner of his environment, it long remained so.

The boom years of the Victorian era, from the 'fifties to the 'seventies, brought growing prosperity to agriculture and for the time being better wages for the farm labourer. But by the end of this period of expansion the Utopian doctrine of Free Trade was beginning to show itself unequal to the changing demands of the economy. As trade and industry began to decline, so did agriculture.

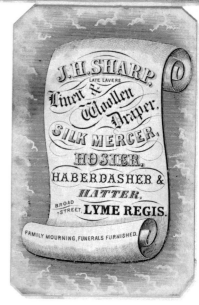

The engraved trade card has been superseded, often to our loss, by fashionable typography and ambiguous wording. The municipal ass who thinks of a rat-catcher as a rodent operative would surely have found fault with Messrs Oakley, Hall & Sharp's direct evidence of their callings.

Legislation and enlightenment contributed throughout the Victorian era to a gradual improvement in working conditions generally. In offices the austerity and discomfort of places like Mr Scrooge's counting house, or the musty establishment of Spenlow and Jorkins, to whom David Copperfield was articled, gave way to offices better planned and considerably more cheerful. In 1888, when the makers of Pears' Soap opened new premises in Oxford Street, these were considered the last word in office accommodation.

LEFT AND ABOVE: In agriculture mechanisation was virtually unknown. Almost every process of farming and husbandry was performed by hand. In Ireland, however, those hands were too few, even if the capital had been forthcoming, to carry out a plan put forward in the 'seventies for draining and reclaiming the bogs. Instead of providing a new and necessary means of food production, the bogs continued to yield only peat, which the impoverished cottagers gathered to use as fuel.
OPPOSITE: Birket Foster's painting, *The Milkmaid* (1860), from which this detail is taken, suggests the almost medieval simplicity that agriculture retained till after the turn of the century.

The output of the textile industry was supplemented by cottage-woven materials, for which a cumbersome Jacquard loom was often used.

Farmers all over England were badly affected, prices of sheep and cattle and corn fell and farm hands began to drift away from the land. By 1881 there were a hundred thousand fewer than there had been ten years earlier, and the movement towards other spheres of employment at home and abroad was gathering momentum.

In 1884 the vote was given to agricultural workers, putting them on a level with the bulk of the working population, but it was too late for this new-found implement to be used as a means of stopping the decline. 'It was an irony of fate,' says Professor G. M. Trevelyan,

... that the farm hand was given the Parliamentary and local franchise only after the destruction of English agricultural life had set in. . . . The agricultural labourers, if they stayed in the countryside, could now take part in its government, but in fact they were trooping off to the towns.

But with little education and only the brawn and limited experience of a farm labourer, what was there for most of them to do? They could become builder's labourers perhaps, or navvies working on the roads, or could learn to drive a brewer's dray or an omnibus. But they could hardly aspire even to the lowest ranks of trade or commerce, where a personable appearance and some semblance of education were essential.

Even in early Victorian days a shop assistant in a fashionable milliner's would have fancied himself as something of an exquisite, however meagre his wages and threadbare his background. Lower down the scale and a little later in time, the life of a provincial draper's assistant, as H. G. Wells knew it in his adolescence, and which was fairly typical of employment in other types of retail trade, was a sad one for all but the cleverest or most resilient. The assistant would be expected to be clean, tidy and alert on a salary as wretched

OPPOSITE: F. J. Linnell, *Kensington Sand Quarries*, 1856. These quarries, little more than a mile from Marble Arch, were a main source of supply for the building industry in the early Victorian period.

Although the village postman is still with us, the village blacksmith exists only as a rare and quaint survival from a past dimly remembered by a diminishing generation.

as the conditions in which he lived, unless he happened to be unusually lucky in his 'crib'. Assistants were mostly boarded on the premises. They slept in attic dormitories, were inadequately fed in dingy dining-rooms, began their day's work at seven-thirty in the morning, and ended it at the same time in the evening. Besides the poverty, the exhaustion and the tedium, the threat of getting the sack hung permanently over many an employee or apprentice, and if it descended there was no unemployment pay to fall back on and almost certainly there would be no savings. It was a dreary and precarious existence, the pattern of which is familiar as the background to most types of employment in the lower ranks of Victorian trade and commerce.

A Christmas Carol, published in 1843, epitomises Bob Cratchit as the down-trodden early-Victorian clerk, who 'had but fifteen "Bob" a week', and five dependent children. But the picture gradually improves. By the late 1880s a senior clerk like Charles Pooter, the tragi-comic hero of *The Diary of a Nobody*, was getting a salary ten times larger than Bob Cratchit's. But by then the counting-house clerk, though not presuming to social equality with his boss, had so far advanced himself as to have acquired a well-defined status in society. The Pooters not only kept a maid, but had a charwoman in to do the rough work, and also did a fair amount of entertaining, all on a salary that was probably in the neighbourhood of four hundred pounds a year.

Servants were plentiful and cheap. No longer were they treated as they were some twenty years earlier, when, says Augustus Hare:

No servant would have thought of giving up a place which was essentially a good one because they were a little roughly handled by their mistress. In those days servants were as little liable to personal chastisement as the children of the house, and would as little have thought of resenting it.

The chronic poverty of the agricultural labourer's household and the low wages paid to unskilled factory workers, combined with their conditions of employment, induced many young boys and girls to try and escape from the threat of such drudgery as early as possible. Domestic service, which must have seemed bliss by comparison, was the aim of most of them. For boys there was the prospect of eventually graduating from the scullery or kitchen to become a footman or a butler. A butler could earn more, but a footman's responsibilities were fewer and his livery more dashing, though an occupational hazard was derision by street urchins, to whom a pair of white silk calves on the hind splash board of any elegant equipage was an irresistible target for mud.

To the hard-pressed housewife of the twentieth century the parlour maid seems as remote a figure as the medieval serf. In the Victorians' domestic hierarchy she ranked second only to that demi-goddess, the cook.

In the 1860s a young girl going into service for the first time, probably starting as a kitchen-maid, would have been lucky to get ten pounds a year. If after a long apprenticeship and good service she were to become a still-room maid, a decided cut above a mere housemaid, she might get as much as sixteen or even eighteen pounds. Her duties would include looking after the best china, and making not only tea, coffee and chocolate, but also biscuits, jams, preserves and cordials, in which the early and mid-Victorians were so fond of indulging. Her next step would be to become a cook, a dazzling prospect at a starting salary of twenty pounds a year and a position of almost unlimited autocracy. Riches beyond the dreams of avarice were the sort of wages paid to a first-class chef in a noble household, which might be several hundred pounds a year.

Maids were recruited by domestic agencies, certified by testimonials, summoned by bells. They were expected to begin the day's work early and end it late, to look neat and behave deferentially, and to thank their lucky stars for a situation where their wages might rise to as much as £25 a year.

If the fireman's uniform was less elegant than that of a regiment of the line, it was a calling whose dash and daring gave it a glamour second to none.

When I first put this uniform on,
I said, as I looked in the glass,
'It's one to a million
That any civilian
My figure and form will surpass.'
                                    W. S. Gilbert

The anonymity of khaki was reserved for the field of battle. Those who 'took the Queen's shilling' could count not only on an active career, probably with service abroad, but also on the appeal of a smart uniform.

By the 1890s the Pooters would have had to pay Sarah, their maid-of-all-work, probably even more than a still-room maid got in the 'sixties, perhaps as much as twenty-five pounds a year. Sarah would have been expected to rise at six o'clock in the morning and be lucky if she got to bed much before ten at night. On Sunday her labours might be lightened by her getting up half an hour later and going to bed half an hour earlier; and there would have been one half-day off a week. Instead of sitting with vacuous gaze in the launderette for half an hour or so, a day would have been set aside for her to do the household washing, first boiling it in a copper, then doing the starching and ironing with a flat-iron heated on a coal-burning kitchen range. Instead of the spin-dryer and the hoover, there was the dish cloth and the dustpan and brush. There were coals to be carried up two or three flights of stairs, and hot water, and trays of food. There were ornaments to be dusted, silver to be cleaned and furniture to be polished. All the same, it was decidedly better than sleeping seven in a room on a straw mattress in a damp cottage, rising at dawn and working for eleven hours, gleaning or hoeing turnips.

At no period in English history, either in time of war or peace, have the British worked so hard as they did for the greater part of the Victorian era. Their strongest incentive was economic necessity. Yet it is difficult to believe that the Victorian working man, artisan or craftsman, with a sense of pride in his job and responsibility towards his workmates, would not have felt some contempt for the ideas and attitudes of many of their kind today.

FROM PLACE TO PLACE

Chapter 8: From Place to Place ¶ Travelling by Coach ¶ Metropolitan Locomotion ¶ Omnibuses ¶ Hazards of the Railway ¶ Cheap Excursions ¶ Mr Train's Tram ¶ The Underground Railway ¶ Bicycles ¶ A Glimpse of the Future

On 14 June 1842 Queen Victoria wrote to her Uncle Leopold from Buckingham Palace: 'We arrived here yesterday morning, having come by the railroad, from Windsor, in half an hour, free from dust and crowd and heat, and I am quite charmed with it.' A washerwoman or a maidservant would not have been quite so charmed, assuming either of them could have afforded the fare of 1s 6d. Instead of travelling in a comfortable saloon furnished like a drawing-room, 'with the sides and roof thickly padded with quilted silk, to deaden the noise and vibration', they would have been crowded with other travellers into a third-class 'department' (which, if they were lucky, would have had wooden seats) with sides so low that passengers often fell off as the train went along. Third-class departments were usually open to the elements, though some had wooden awnings, so that in wet weather most of the passengers were drenched, and wet or dry, were showered with cinders from the high-funnelled engine or stifled with smoke and fumes when the train went into a tunnel.

The surprising thing was that in spite of these conditions, by the time Victoria came to the throne the railways were already well on the way to putting the coaching system out of business. Speed was not the only reason for this. Although the accident rate was high and the idea of travelling at thirty miles an hour or more decidedly alarming, the combined appeal of convenience and novelty was beginning to tell and coaching receipts were dropping, though the coach companies in their efforts to compete for passenger traffic had slashed their fares.

On the whole, the coaching system, while it lasted, had been quick and efficient. This was not simply because it was well organised, or because of the skill of the crack stage-coach drivers, who were as well-known to the public as sporting champions are today. It was mainly because of the building and improvement of turnpike roads under the influence of two of the nineteenth century's greatest civil engineers, Thomas Telford and John McAdam. Before their time, British roads were notoriously bad, but by 1836, when both Telford and McAdam died, most of them were well-drained and soundly constructed. Unfortunately this improvement did not last. With the expansion of the railway system came a decline in the number of coaches using the turnpikes and consequently a reduction in

Londoners were lamenting their traffic problems as long ago as the 1860s. Today they are at least spared such hazards as wandering sheep and are compelled by law to observe the rule of the road.
OPPOSITE: Gustave Doré's impression of Ludgate Circus in the 'sixties.
ABOVE: The Circus as it was in 1895.

Long after the railway train had superseded the stage coach, the private four-in-hand remained popular as a status symbol. Until the 1890s equipages such as the one above, usually driven by the owner, were used for taking parties on excursions or to the races.

turnpike tolls. Many of the turnpike trusts by which the roads were maintained collapsed and the cost of keeping up the roads fell back once more on the parishes, which in earlier times had been largely responsible for keeping them in repair, a duty that was often neglected.

In the period that followed, travelling by road was often as uncomfortable and inconvenient as it had been before the turnpike era. Not until well into the 'seventies did Parliament show much interest in the state of the roads and it was only by degrees that their administration and upkeep came to be properly organised.

At the beginning of the Queen's reign the chief form of long-distance travel was either the mail coach or the stage coach. The more well-to-do would use a posting chariot driven by postillions, or a heavy and less elegant barouche driven from the box. Every night from the General Post Office at St Martins-le-Grand twenty-seven mail coaches set out from London to cover some 5,500 miles of road. Every day about a hundred and fifty stages left from various parts

ABOVE: The stage-coach breakfast, a welcome conclusion to a long night's journey, was often eaten to an impatient obligato on the guard's post horn. RIGHT: The Bull and Mouth, a famous coaching inn, since demolished, in Aldersgate Street in the City.

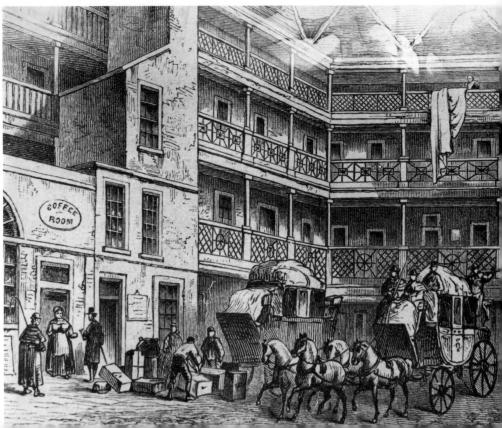

of the city and another three hundred or so were running in other parts of the country. Each coach had its own name and many of them were well known, such as Isis, Mazeppa, Flower of Kent, Hirondelle, Emerald, Zephyr, Star of Brunswick and Quicksilver.

Coaches were the pride of their guards and drivers. In R.J. Cruikshank's survey of the period, *Charles Dickens and Early Victorian England*, there is a lively description of the stage coach starting out on its journey:

The smart coach, the crack coach, rolled out in a glitter of new paint; there were scrolls on its sides carrying in golden letters the name of famous cities – that handsome, grave lettering of the period which makes even JNO, JONES, POULTERER TO THE NOBILITY AND GENTRY look like the beginning of an ode, or the inscription of a military victory. The brasses were so beautifully polished that they flashed like looking glasses, the ornaments on the harness rippled and tinkled, and there were coloured ribbons and streamers floating out, as though every day was from now on to be proclaimed a holiday.

The mail coach, running at an average speed of about ten miles an hour, was the most reliable way of travelling because the responsibility of carrying Her Majesty's mails meant keeping an eye on the time-table. Stage coaches were more or less free of this tiresome necessity. Occasionally the passengers might take it upon themselves to rearrange the schedule, stopping an hour or so longer at some beauty spot to admire the view or a couple of hours to look over a

Before the hackney, and later the hansom cab appeared, a number of strange vehicles were for hire, among them this cabriolet, described by Dickens in *Sketches by Boz* and drawn by Phiz.

236

Road versus Rail, 1845 – one of Fores'
Coaching Incidents. Messrs Fores, as
the best-known sellers of coaching
prints, had a vested interest in
depicting not only the comfort and
efficiency of travelling by coach, but
also the perils of entrusting oneself to
the railway.

The hansom cab, which first appeared
on the streets in the 1850s, was to
Victorian Londoners what the taxi is
to those of today. It remained in use
for more than sixty years and a few
were still to be seen clopping and
jingling their way about the West End
as late as the 1930s.

237

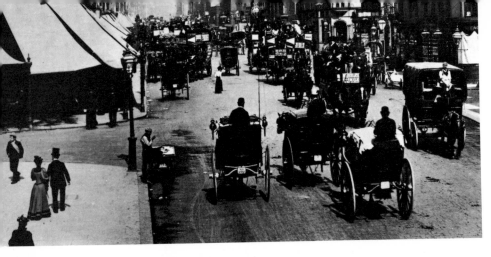

Oxford Street (LEFT), and The Strand
(OPPOSITE) in the 1890s. With the Underground railway still in its infancy,
and cab fares high, buses were the means
by which most people made their way
about town.

ABOVE LEFT: 1859 saw the introduction of
a new type of bus. It had no brakes or
bell; its accident rate is not known, but
was no doubt commensurate with their
omission. The knifeboard of 1891 (LEFT),
with room for twenty-three passengers,
showed several improvements, including
a staircase at the back in place of bare
rungs. ABOVE: It Pays to Advertise is a
theory in which the Victorians were
firm believers.

castle or a cathedral. It was not unknown for an extra day to be added to the journey if the town where the coach had stopped seemed worth exploring. Then there was always the possibility that a young blood, or a party of them, would be on board and might persuade the coachman to let them handle the ribbons for a mile or so. According to the skill or the inexperience of these amateur jehus, passengers were likely to find themselves either leaving the coach ahead of time at their proper destination or involuntarily over the top of a hedge.

Yet on the whole there is something very agreeable about the idea of travelling by coach. Hazlitt, Nimrod, Surtees, Dickens and Ruskin all wrote about its exhilarating effects, about the delight of posting through the countryside behind a brisk, jingling team, about the pleasant, easy motion, the sense of speed, and the satisfaction of arriving eventually at a snug inn. But was it always so pleasant? Dickens also gives another side of the picture. In the chapter on Early Coaches in *Sketches by Boz* he describes what might be inflicted as a punishment on 'an especially obstinate miscreant':

... we would have booked him for an inside place in a small coach, which travelled day and night: and securing the remainder of the places for stout men with a slight tendency to coughing and spitting, we would have started him forth on his last travels: leaving him mercilessly to all the tortures which the waiters, landlords, coachmen, guards, boots, chambermaids and other familiars on his line of road, might think proper to inflict.

Stage coaches were only for long-distance travellers. The British were still by and large a pedestrian race and the usual form of locomotion in town was a pair of legs. As most of London's working population lived on the outskirts and usually walked to work, a trudge of five or six miles each way was nothing out of the ordinary. For those who could afford it, there was the hackney cab or coach. The hackney was at first a kind of hooded gig in which the driver sat inside with two passengers. Then came a curious contraption with only room for one, the driver being perched outside on the same level. Next was a cab for two with the driver's seat on the roof and a door at the back; and finally in 1850 there came the hansom cab, of which two or three, with clopping hooves and jingling harness-bells, continued to rattle their way round the West End of London until the 1930s.

The hackney cab was almost as expensive as a taxi is today; for a short journey, such as from Westminster Bridge to Piccadilly, the charge in 1837 was 1s 6d for a coach or a shilling for a cab, and unless a tip of at least fourpence was added to a shilling fare the

THE MISERIES OF AN OMNIBUS.

Lithog.d & Printed by G.E. Madeley, Wellington St.

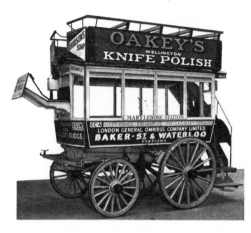

LEFT: Although in general the bus was a boon, it had its disadvantages during the rush hour. A popular song of the 'forties, *The Miseries of an Omnibus*, probably seemed a good deal less comic than it was meant to be if you travelled by bus every day.

In 1859 another type of bus (ABOVE) appeared. Instead of the knifeboard, it had 'garden seats', one behind the other; but seating both inside and out was still cramped. However, by 1895 (BELOW), as this painting by George Joy shows, standards of comfort and convenience were beginning to approach those of the present day.

OPPOSITE: William Maw Egley, *Omnibus Life in London*, 1859.

W. MAW EGLEY.

SOUTH EASTERN & CHATHAM RAILWAY
NOTICE
TO
CABDRIVERS.

Any Cabman skylarking or otherwise misconducting himself while on the Managing Committee's premises or Smoking whilst his Cab is standing alongside the Platform will be required to leave the Station immediately *By Order.*

In contrast to the traditional familiarity of the omnibus conductor (commonly known, and often with good reason, as the 'cad'), a proper sense of decorum was expected of the hackney cab driver.

OPPOSITE: Differences between First and Third Class railway travel were sharply defined in the early days. The First Class compartment of the 1850s, as Abraham Solomon indicates (TOP) was not unlike that of today. Charles Rossiter's painting (BOTTOM) of Third Class travel shows there was not much distinction between this and cattle accommodation.

passenger was likely to be showered with a stream of fanciful obscenities. Dickens' advice was that 'it is very bad policy attempting to save the fourpence. You are very much in the power of the cabman, and he considers it a kind of fee not to do you any wilful damage'. Not that damage, if any was done, was always wilful. 'We are not aware,' Dickens adds, 'of any instance on record in which a cab-horse has performed three consecutive miles without going down once.' Added to such risks as this, there was also the pleasure that hackney drivers took, traffic permitting, in racing each other through the cobbled streets.

They were a strangely assorted, foul-mouthed lot, the hackney drivers. Many of them, it seems, became cab drivers as a last resort, having failed in other jobs. In *London Labour and the London Poor*, Mayhew gives a list of occupations said to have been followed by a number of London cab drivers in the 'sixties. Some had been clerks, some greengrocers, and some jewellers. Others were broken-down gentlemen, or had been grooms, shopkeepers or musicians. Among the rest were footmen, housebreakers, scholars, ex-policemen, scene-shifters, barmen, and that ubiquitous Victorian character, the swell-mobsman, or gentleman swindler.

Hackney coaches, as distinct from hackney cabs, although less dangerous to life and limb, were no less uncomfortable. In his *Reminiscences* Sergeant Ballantine, a well-known lawyer of the period, describes the hackney coach as 'a machine . . . licensed to carry six people, redolent of damp straw, driven by a still damper coachman. . . . The driver was called a Jarvey, a compliment paid to the class in consequence of one of them named Jarvis having been hanged'.

For those who could not afford either a hackney cab or coach, or looked for a more tranquil means of progress, there was the horse-drawn omnibus. Since the first bus had appeared in London in 1829, transport companies had sprung up everywhere, cramming the streets with brightly-coloured buses – yellow and red from Paddington to Liverpool Street, pale blue from Fulham to Kilburn. The 'Atlas' from Camberwell to St John's Wood was light green, and the Chelsea-to-Hoxton bus chocolate-coloured. Those on the Camden Town-to-Victoria route were pale yellow, and the 'Favourite', running between London Bridge and Hornsey, dark green. The glaring uniformity of London Transport buses or the drabness of New York's would make a poor show beside the kaleidoscope of Victorian traffic.

Until 1850, London's buses, like those of most other capitals to this day, were single-deckers. Then, with the Great Exhibition approaching, some enterprising companies, in defiance of the law which limited the number of passengers a bus might carry, put seats on the roof, knifeboard fashion, where the passengers sat back to back along the length of the bus. There was, however, a snag about this arrangement. It was one thing for an honest working girl to travel by herself *inside* a bus – though only strict necessity would have induced a girl of genteel family to do so – but travelling *outside* was another matter. Those reprobate females who, in defiance of this taboo, insisted on travelling upstairs, presented the bus companies at first with a ticklish problem. Human nature, much the same under Queen Victoria as under Queen Boadicea, impelled the Victorian male to look aloft from the pavement at ladies sitting on the top deck. The companies' solution to this problem was to put 'decency boards' along the sides of the roof; a move that palliated the prevailing sense of sin and at the same time showed commercial profit, for instead of an intriguing glimpse of ankles or underwear, the eye met with an advertisement for Okey's Knife Polish, Fry's Cocoa or Bryant and May's matches.

Externally, the omnibus was a thing of glowing colours and tasteful appeal to the appetites, the senses, or the pocket. Inside, it was another matter. A correspondent of *The Illustrated London News* wrote in 1856:

No one who has ever travelled in a Paris omnibus can question its superiority to the narrow, low-roofed, ill-ventilated and overcrowded conveyance which constitutes the principle nuisance in the streets of London. . . . We all know, by sad experience, the discomforts attendant upon a ride in a bus. The crushing of hats, the trampling upon toes, the poking of the eye or in the ribs as the clumsy gentleman or timid lady flounders in the van. Nor does the adventurous youth who climbs hand over hand to a seat on the knifeboard fail to repent of his rashness, when at each spasmodic jerk he is flung upon his right shoulder or his left. . . . There is yet one other point – the impertinence or rather the insolence of conductors has passed into a proverb.

The cad, as the conductor was called, stood outside on a step at the back of the bus, from which it was easy to jump down and whip in anyone who looked as though he might be intending to go somewhere. Again, to quote Dickens:

He could tell at a glance where a passenger wanted to go to, and would shout the name of the place accordingly, without the slightest reference to the real destination of the vehicle. He knew exactly the kind of old lady that would be too much flurried by the process of pushing in, and pulling out of the caravan, to discover where she had been put down, until too

John C. Bourne's lithographs of early railways are an important source of information about their construction and development. The four miniatures above show the construction of the London and Birmingham Railway, from the first survey in 1830 to its opening on 21 September 1838.

Mail coaches, once the fastest and most efficient of long distance travel, were brought to an ignominious standstill by the railways. In 1845 the coach from Louth, in Lincolnshire, to London, its days already numbered, travelled from Peterborough to Blisworth, a distance of some 48 miles, by rail.
BELOW: Commemorative mugs were manufactured to suit all occasions, and the opening of a new railway (in this case the Sheffield and Rotherham line, on 31 October 1838) was always one of importance.

late ... and never failed to make himself agreeable to female servants, whom he would place next the door, and talk to all the way.

The swift, haphazard proliferation of bus companies between the 'thirties and the 'fifties, to say nothing of the competitive methods of cads, resulted in a considerable waste of time, money, facilities and public patience. What was needed was a properly organised and efficient system. The genius whom time and circumstance called upon to provide this was a Frenchman, M. Léopold Foucaud, who had successfully reorganised public transport in Paris. To reduce the chaotic situation in London to something like order took Monsieur Foucaud some seven years, but by careful planning, gradual amalgamation and the introduction of up-to-date equipment, it was eventually achieved.

In much the same way, and at much the same time as bus traffic began to increase in the towns, by piecemeal and unorganised growth, railway traffic was increasing all over the country. So, too, was speculation in railway shares. But it was not till 1845 that the real boom began. In the space of a single month 357 new railway projects were advertised in the newspapers. The cost of one scheme alone was estimated at forty million pounds. In spite of the obvious impossibility of all, or anything like all, these schemes getting up enough steam to make any headway, fantastic sums of money were

ABOVE: Building the retaining walls of the Camden Town cutting, still in use, on the London and Birmingham Railway, from a drawing by John C. Bourne in 1839. Except for the use of horse-drawn trucks for removing the thousands of tons of earth excavated from the site, and for bringing materials to it, every operation of this massive project was performed by hand.

LEFT: George Hudson, the Yorkshire Midas who made and lost both his fortune and his reputation in laying the foundations of the English railway system; from a painting by Francis Grant.

OPPOSITE TOP: Digging up Marylebone Road to make London's first tunnel for the Metropolitan Railway, known as the 'Sewer'. It was by this laborious method of construction that the earliest sections of London's underground system were built.

BELOW: On the day the 'Sewer' opened in 1863, some 30,000 passengers were carried, only a few on official business, the rest to see what it was like.

poured into them, not only from the pockets of the rich, but from the threadbare purses of tens of thousands of people living on tiny or uncertain incomes.

Many of the schemes were fraudulent; some were genuine but still failed to make the grade; a few were hugely successful. Most of those that prospered were controlled by a crooked Yorkshire Midas, George Hudson, three times Mayor of York, Deputy-Lieutenant of the County of Durham, and Member of Parliament for Sunderland. In 1848 Hudson was chairman of three railway companies and controlled something like two-thirds of the five thousand miles of railway that then existed. He was a clever, shoving parvenu who made and lost a gigantic fortune and died disgraced. But he was also something considerably more than a financial crook. Just as Monsieur Foucard had rationalised the chaos that threatened London's bus traffic, Hudson brought order into the development of the railway system by sensible planning and sound administration. While shadier promoters than himself were scrambling to build railways anywhere anyhow, he stuck to the policy of building them only where they were genuinely needed or would obviously be wanted in course of time. It was not Hudson's ideas that were spurious, it was his character.

Railways as Hudson planned and built them were never merely novelties, though the appeal of novelty was strong at first. Charles Greville, that gregarious and observant diarist, made his first trip by train a few weeks after Queen Victoria's accession:

Nothing could be more comfortable than the vehicle in which I was put, a sort of chariot with two places; and there is nothing disagreeable about it but the occasional whiffs of stinking air, which it is impossible to exclude altogether. The first sensation is a slight degree of nervousness, but a sense of security soon supervenes and the velocity is delightful. Town after town, one park and château after another, are left behind with the rapid variety of a moving panorama, and the continual bustle and animation of the changes and stoppages make the journey very entertaining. . . . It certainly renders all other travelling irksome and tedious by comparison.

In spite of a number of drawbacks, this on the whole was true, even of the primitive railways of Greville's day. Before long they had become a boon to thousands of travellers. Those who had no

A royal railway coach, one of the first to be brought into service, built in 1842 for the use of the Queen's aunt, Queen Adelaide.

OPPOSITE: The interior of Queen Victoria's private saloon, built in 1869. The furnishings were of yellow satinwood upholstered in royal blue moiré silk, the metal work was of gilt brass, and the walls and ceiling were padded to deaden noise and vibration. BELOW: The Queen's bedroom.

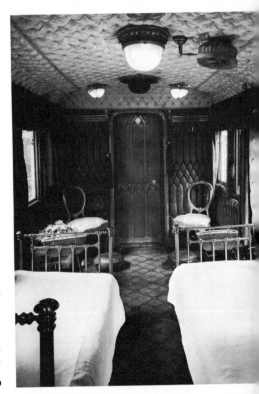

An early innovation on the Metropolitan Railway was the workman's train, which offered cheap fares; a drawing made by Gustave Doré in the small hours of the working man's day.

Cheap fares were also offered to excursionists. From Ludgate Hill Station day trips ran to the seaside at Margate and Ramsgate, to the Crystal Palace (removed to Sydenham in 1854), and elsewhere. The station, built in 1846, stood on the site of the notorious Fleet Prison, beyond whose ruined walls stood the booking office.

An excursion in miniature, popular with visitors to Brighton, was the run by Volk's Marine Railway (gauge 2 ft 8½ in) alongside the beach from the Chain Pier to Paston Place, a distance of about a mile and a half.

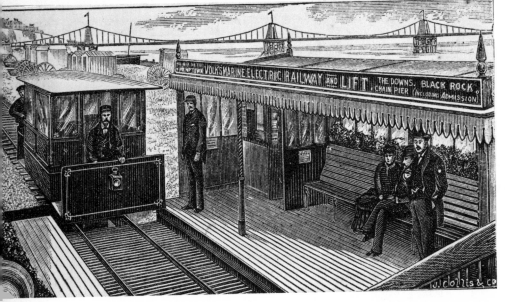

OPPOSITE: Is there any need why travel tickets should look as monotonous as those of today? The Victorians did not think so. Tickets for their journeys by coach and train were pleasantly varied in appearance.

Oxford, Worcester, and Wolverhampton Railway.

No. 84   No.

FREE TICKET.—FIRST CLASS.

Goods DEPARTMENT.

Any Train January Year 1853

From any Station to any Station

Name Mr. Underwood

Why granted On Service

for T. Adcock

Alfred Elwes Head of Department.

N.B. Free Tickets are granted to Persons employed on the Company's Business only, and must be given up when demanded.

BRADFORD TURNPIKE TRUST.

CUMBERWELL GATE.

This Ticket will clear any one of the undermentioned Gates on this Trust (except Limepit.)
1. Winsley and Side-Gate, Dean Bottom, Turley, and Cumberwell Bars.
2. Cumberwell and Bar, and Frankleigh Bar.
3. Forewood's Common.   4. Staverton.
5. Bradford Leigh. 6. Widbrook. & 7. Elms Cross.

Day of April 1866

	TOLL.	
	s.	d.
Carriage		
Gig		
Waggon		
Cart		
Horse		/
Beast		
Cattle		
Sheep, Pigs......		

London & North Western Railway.

Nº 152   DOWN   Nº 152

FREE TICKET,   FIRST CLASS.

FOR ONE JOURNEY ONLY.

Goods DEPARTMENT.

Any Train November 6th 1859

From Birmingham to Salop

Name Mr. Page

When granted Rhymney Rly Co

Head of Dep!

N.B. Free Tickets are granted to Persons employed on the Company's Business only, and must be given up when demanded.

BRADFORD TURNPIKE TRUST.

LIMEPIT GATE.

Day of Mar 1866

	TOLL.	
	s.	d.
Carriage		
Gig		
Waggon		
Cart		
Horse		/
Beast		
Cattle		
Sheep, Pigs........		

No._____   Expires on _____

DUNDEE & NEWTYLE AND SCOTTISH NORTH-EASTERN RAILWAYS.

SECOND CLASS
COMPOSITION TICKET,

_____ and _____

From _____

_____ inclusive.

NOT TRANSFERABLE.

For the Companies, _____

L & S
RAILWAY
LONG LANE
Nº 4

Reigate Junction
TO
Clapham Junction
THIRD CLASS
Passengers should ascertain if they have to

London & North Western Ry.
Issued subject to the conditions & regulations in the Co's Time Tables Books Bills & Notices & unless stated therein be NOT available by Irish Mail.

SCORTON TO
GARSTANG & CATTERALL

THIRD CLASS   610 (S)   [Parly
GARSTANG   FARE -/3

5848

---

22 AT 92

0.JL.99

LANCASHIRE & YORKSHIRE RLY.
SECOND CLASS
PRESTON (E.L.)
TO
SOUTHPORT (LZY)
Available on day of issue only
240
TURN OVER Southport LZY   Fare 1s4d

7578

SOUTH EASTERN RAILWAY
CATERHAM to
CATERHAM JUN.
Third Class
Caterham Jn   Caterham Jn

2523

T. V. R.
PENRHIWCEIBER
TO
PONTYPRIDD JUNCTION
Parly Third Class 6d.
This ticket is issued subject to the Company's Bye Laws and conditions stated on Time Bills.

7914

8.JY.98

N.S.R. PARLIAMENTARY.
HANLEY To
ETRURIA
AVAILABLE FOR ONE JOURNEY ON DAY OF ISSUE ONLY.

0 15
Turn over   Etruria 35   Fare 1d

8181

CALEDONIAN RAILWAY.
This Ticket is issued subject to the Regulations & Conditions stated in the Co.'s Time Tables & Bills
THIRD CLASS. FARE 4s. 8d.
PERTH
TO
COATBRIDGE
Via Dunblane & Gartsherrie

6443

Highland Railway.
THIRD CLASS
Inverness
TO
NOTTINGHAM
via Dunkeld from Perth West by & Mar

Fare
37/2½

(Over.)   (Nottingham)

98P99
N
104

need to use them were inclined to dismiss them as mechanical nuisances – unless they had chanced to sell their lands to railway promoters or bought shares in a successful company. Ruskin repeated what many had felt when he declared in *Fors Clavigera*, 'Now, every fool in Buxton can be in Bakewell in half an hour and every fool in Bakewell at Buxton', and it is still a common fallacy of simple minds to equate speed with progress. But to the industrious Victorians time was a precious commodity. Ruskin was a man of leisure and had no need to save time, and it was here that the railway scored over the leisurely coach that he preferred. Still more must he have disliked the compromise that was often adopted at first, of lashing a coach on to an open truck attached to the end of a train. The coach's outside passengers were even worse off than those in third-class compartments, who sometimes had a roof of sorts over their heads to protect them from the wind and weather and from the smoke, dust and fumes.

These were not the only disadvantages, however, of travelling by train. There were also periodic stoppages, not so that passengers could get out (on some trains they were locked in, so that in case of

253

accident they were imprisoned) but for the purpose of oiling and examining the machinery. Passengers travelling between Liverpool and Manchester were told in the Company's advertisements that on these occasions, 'as the Directors are determined, by every means in their power, to prevent the practise of supplying liquor &c on the Road, Passengers are particularly requested not to alight'. Appeals such as this to obedience and temperance were not always successful, nor was the strict prohibition on smoking, which could usually be overcome by tipping the guard.

Trains were often late. One of the earliest railway jokes was about a youth of sixteen found to be travelling at half-fare, who pleaded that he had been under twelve when the train started. Another source of merriment, which has stayed with us, but is no longer quite so funny, was the deplorable standard of railway catering. But in spite of the jokes, the delays, the accidents, the inconveniences, in spite of prognostications of failure and the opposition of agricultural and other interests, the railways within a very few years had established themselves as the main means of transport and, as freight traffic increased, a major influence in British industry.

The rigid class consciousness of Victorian society made it necessary from the beginning to segregate passengers on the railways. First, second, third and sometimes even fourth class beings were differentiated. Each had their own standards of comfort and convenience, their own waiting rooms, and their own fares. Although the slow encroachment of democracy, that phantom of Victorian nightmares, has now whittled down these class distinctions to first and second, Pullman passengers have increased in number. These voluptuaries, unknown until the 1870s, when Pullman cars were first introduced, were the antithesis of the 'excursionist'. The Pullman was for the traveller who wanted comfort and seclusion. The excursion train was for a more gregarious type to whom the row and bustle of railway travel was half its fun. Michael Robbins, in *The Railway Age*, gives some idea of what it was like to go on one of these sprees:

The early excursions must have been astonishing affairs; it seems to have been usual for them to have been welcomed at their destination by bands of music, and they were often enormously long. . . . The following report from Leicester is dated 24 August 1840: About half past twelve o'clock this day a train, perhaps the longest ever known, came along the Midland Counties Railway from Nottingham. It had four engines to drag it forward, and to the beholder appeared like a moving street, the houses of which were filled with human beings. . . . The number of carriages was sixty-seven, and the number of passengers nearly 3,000, most of whom were well and respectably attired.

Thomas Cook's first tour, advertised in 1841. Cook, a Baptist lay preacher, organised the outing in an attempt to whip up support for a temperance meeting.

There is not much to be said, even today, for British Railways' catering arrangements, but first come, first served, even in a dismal cafeteria, is probably fairer than the sort of scramble depicted by Richard Doyle in the 1840s.

The English have always been especially fond of jamborees and the railway excursion of those days, with its ever-present possibilities of unscheduled halts, accident, fire or derailment, must have added considerably to the fun. The first excursions were run chiefly in the North and Midlands, where new industrial towns had sprung up and older ones had expanded. The rapid growth of such areas meant that before long a good many railway termini became engulfed in bricks and mortar, and instead of standing on the outskirts, were soon halfway towards the centre of the town they had originally been built to serve.

The newly-created industrial suburbs created in their turn a need for public transport into the towns, which from the 'forties to the 'sixties was provided by the horse omnibus. And then in 1861 there appeared in Bayswater Road in London a single-deck horse-drawn car, faintly Gothic in design, which ran on miniature railway lines. This was the invention of an American, George Francis Train. It was in fact Mr Train's tram, the first vehicle of its kind to be seen in England. It was not popular, nor financially successful and was soon withdrawn. Nine years later it appeared again (in the provinces, where it was also given a trial, it was powered this time by steam) but with wheels that ran in sunken grooves. The novelty of this arrangement seemed to appeal instantly to Londoners. They now

THE IMPROVED STREET RAILWAY CARRIAGE.
PATENTED BY GEORGE FRANCIS TRAIN.

took to trams as readily as they had dismissed them on their first appearance, and by 1885, when the tramway system became electrified, they were as much a part of the London street scene as hansom cabs and costermongers' barrows.

The tram was, and always remained, a more plebeian vehicle than the bus, which in later life acquired a certain *ton* that the tram, which ran mostly through working-class districts, never achieved. The late Victorian tram was huge, draughty and cumbersome and had its own peculiar smell, a compound of metal, grease and hot rubber. Yet in spite of the bulk and inconvenience of their trams, Londoners clung to them with obstinate affection. Not until 1952 did the last of these clanging leviathans cease to zoom its way along the Embankment and away into the limbo of South London.

Two years after Mr Train's unsuccessful experiment in Bayswater, another new and strange – and no doubt faintly alarming – experience was to be had by Londoners: in 1863 the first section – Paddington to the City – of London's underground Metropolitan Railway was opened. It was commonly known as 'The Sewer', and its passengers, as they rumbled along – the carriages were simply open trucks – were deafened by the noise, or if they were standing on

Mr Train's tram at Marble Arch. This, the first vehicle of its kind, appeared in the London streets in 1861. As a means of transport it was less popular than this picture suggests and it soon ceased to run.

256

the platform, choked by smoke as the engine belched its way out of the tunnel. Railway travel by now was no longer the novelty it used to be, but The Sewer was rather different. It ran not through green fields, but through the bowels of the earth and on its opening day some thirty thousand travellers went simply for the ride.

The bus, the tram, and now, for Londoners, the Metropolitan Railway, provided cheap collective transport. For such as could afford to travel more exclusively there was still the private carriage, the brougham, or the public hackney or hansom cab. A method even more exclusive, and decidedly more uncomfortable, was the velocipede. Within a few years of the opening of the Metropolitan Railway a craze for velocipedes developed. Most of these were freak inventions of eccentric pioneers and it was not until 1868, when a French velocipede, the Michaux, began to be made in England, that the boom really started. There is no discomfort to which the machine-crazed Englishman will not submit in search of some new mechanistic experience. The Michaux, shakiest of all boneshakers, assured the maximum of effort with the minimum of ease. It was a heavy crank-driven iron-tyred machine that shook the daylights out of its rider on anything less smooth than a brand-new macadamised road.

Hammersmith Bridge (1884–5), a monument to Victorian pretentiousness, formed part of a road improvement scheme that involved the demolition of a simpler and more elegant structure built in 1827.

257

ABOVE: An early ancestor of the modern bicycle was Michaux's crank-driven boneshaker (1868). Heavy, cumbersome and unsprung, it was a challenge both to the rider's endurance and the nimbleness of the pedestrian. Many a strange contraption preceded it, among them (LEFT) Sawyer's velocipede (c.1860). Its popularity was no doubt limited by the difficulty of steering it and the superhuman effort needed to start or stop it.

OPPOSITE: Starley's Royal Salvo tricycle set new standards of discomfort and inconvenience in self-propelled vehicles.

Any pair of riders sufficiently foolhardy could make the Duplex (1876) for themselves simply by removing the rear wheels from their penny-farthing bicycles and joining the front wheels with a specially made connecting iron and a blind faith in providence.

LEFT: Charles Spencer's *The Modern Bicycle* (1876) contained many useful hints for the beginner, such as how to get on and off 'in a respectable manner.... Another capital way of alighting ... while in motion is to throw the right leg over the handles' – and trust to luck.

By the 'nineties bicycling had become a craze with both sexes and all classes. The tour de Camberwell, Blackheath or Romford was an important fixture in the working-man's calendar of recreations.

Mixed bicycling in Hyde Park, though a popular pastime, was apt to attract more onlookers than cyclists.

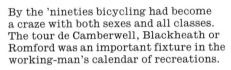

Propulsion for young and old.
LEFT: The Stanhope, a de luxe model for de luxe babies.
ABOVE: Bath chairs were designed to accommodate all figures and to suit all weathers.

TO THE NOBILITY & GENTRY
MAY 1896

THE GREAT HORSELESS CARRIAGE Co. Ltd

HAS THE HONOUR TO PRESENT

This NOVEL vehicle is propelled by an

INTERNAL COMBUSTION ENGINE

OF **2** CYLINDERS AND **6** HORSE POWER

relying on petroleum for its motive force

THE MECHANICAL carriage
will attain the comfortable speed of

TWELVE MILES PER HOUR
on the level, while hills can be ascended
and descended in safety

The Daimler Wagonette
is admirably suited to the needs of the

◦SPORTSMAN◦

AND LOVER OF THE COUNTRYSIDE,
giving as it does full facilities for
the enjoyment of
FRESH AIR AND AN
UNINTERRUPTED VIEW OF THE *Scenery*

'A new mode of transport that has undoubtedly come to stay'
— VIDE DAILY PRESS

THE TWIN-CYLINDER 6 H.P. WAGONETTE {See Engraving}

Of all that the twentieth century was to inherit for good or evil from the Victorian era, nothing was to be more influential than the internal combustion engine. The hideous and complicated vehicles propelled by the earliest types of engine emphasised the dichotomy that was growing between industry and art, contrary to what the Prince Consort had ardently wished and worked for.

Improved versions of this punishing contraption led by degrees to the lighter but ludicrous 'ordinary', or 'penny-farthing', with a wheel at the back twelve inches in diameter and another of sixty-four inches in front; not a machine for sufferers from vertigo. For them there was the tricycle, until in 1876 that great benefactor of the human race, H. J. Lawson came up with the so-called safety bicycle, prototype of the machine that is ridden today.

The Victorians, with their acute yet arbitrary sense of propriety, which made it all right for a woman in evening dress to show a tantalising amount of bust, but made the showing of her shin almost an act of indecency, decided that bicycles were not the thing for ladies. But by the 'nineties (bicycling was then a well-established male activity) ladies were beginning to show a startling desire to reach equality with men. The bicycle seemed just the thing to help them get where they were going. It might be said, in fact, that indirectly H. J. Lawson did as much for the cause of female emancipation as Amelia Bloomer, Elisabeth Garrett Anderson, or Emmeline Pankhurst.

An encyclopaedia would be needed to give a proper idea of all the varieties of transport that carried the Victorians about their business and on their social jaunts. Here nothing has been said about steam

261

The shape of things to come.

carriages, nor about ships, river ferries, canal barges, balloons, bath chairs, or any of those strange mechanical contrivances that the ingenious minds of Victorian inventors delighted in. Nothing has been said about the traffic problems that harassed the Victorians almost as much as we are harassed by our own. Narrow streets strewn with refuse and horse dung were often packed from end to end with traffic moving in all directions. Drays, vans, waggons, omnibuses, carriages, cabs, donkey carts, street traders with hand barrows, and crossing sweepers darting among the traffic, made it a long, slow haul to get through the City or the West End. A noisy and uncomfortable journey, wet or fine. As R. H. Mottram says of Town Life in *Early Victorian England*: 'We must think of Central London in those days as an endless roar of traffic, under an opaque sky and a steady drift of smuts, sending up, according to season, fountains of mud or whirlwinds of dust, straw, and paper.'

Before the Victorian era ended, the shape of things to come began to look like something seen through a glass darkly, uncertain in outline, obscure in significance. Along the roads of Britain there began to rumble and splutter a new type of vehicle: it was called a motor-car. From time to time steam-driven carriages or wagons had been given a trial, but as an alternative to horse-power such mechanical contrivances had never seemed to have much future. Now the ambiguous powers of the motor-car began to put new ideas into Victorian heads. There could be no doubt that in speed and convenience there was a lot to be said for it, but not everyone regarded it as an unmixed blessing. One is tempted to wonder whether the ghost of some departed Victorians, surveying Britain from the infinite seventy years later, would feel inclined to be less equivocal.

Hours of Leisure

Chapter 9: Hours of Leisure ¶ All Work and No Play ¶ Tea Gardens ¶ Astley's Circus ¶ The Studious Mechanic ¶ Lectures to Suit all Tastes ¶ The Great Exhibition ¶ Sporting Ventures ¶ Dancing, Cards, and Kill-Joys ¶ Theatres and Music-Halls ¶ The Holiday Spirit

The year 1886 was a year of special significance for junior shop assistants. It was the year of the Shop Hours Act, which restricted the employment of young persons under the age of eighteen to not more than seventy-four hours a week. With what delight must this concession have been greeted by Victorian teenagers, secure in the knowledge that their working day would be restricted henceforth to thirteen and a half hours and six and a half hours on Saturday. No doubt there were those who wondered gloomily how this group of privileged adolescents would spend the long hours of leisure that would now be theirs, just as there are today some who wonder what sort of use will be made of the leisure that will come with a universal forty-hour week. The Victorians, we must not forget, were without the boon of television, the solace of the cinema, the bowling alley or the amusement arcade, without the intellectual preoccupation offered by the filling in of pools coupons, without betting shops or bingo halls. Their opportunities to participate in organised sports, or to watch them, were far more limited than are ours. How in God's name, then, did the Victorians amuse themselves? Why did not great numbers of them go mad with boredom?

OPPOSITE: Sunday Best. Ready for an East End outing, c.1890.
RIGHT: Sunday in Victoria Park, Bethnal Green.

The reason why this did not happen was because most people had far less leisure than they have now, so that free time was in itself a luxury, even if it was put to no better use than lying in bed or hanging about the streets. The leisured class were, of course, in a different predicament. Their problem was to know what to do with their time. In the country, agricultural and sporting interests were a help, but such occupations were confined to men. Ladies of genteel birth had not much with which they could occupy themselves, apart from charitable works such as distributing soup and woollen comforters, or visiting friends and relations, or reading or sewing. But genteel ladies were in a minority; most women worked hard and many had large families to look after. Among the working classes, therefore, leisure was seldom a problem for either sex, nor boredom the menace that it so often is today. To this state of affairs there was one unhappy exception. On Sundays the moral pressure of churchmen, High and Low, made it almost impossible for anyone to spend the day in wholesome and sensible pursuits, and left the vast majority with little to do and few places to go to, except church or Sunday school. Gideon Mantell, the surgeon and geologist, writing in 1842, described the scene in Battersea Fields on a Sunday, when:

Tens of thousands of mechanics, little tradesmen and apprentices, and their wives and sweethearts were strolling about the fields; and the beer shops and inns were filled with them! . . . Smoking and drinking were the only amusements – not even a fiddle or a hurdy-gurdy – but music would be a profanation of the Englishman's Sabbath! It was a lamentable sight. . . .

ABOVE: The barrel-organ brought delight to children who seldom, if ever, left the back streets.
RIGHT: 'In the chill waters of some Northern clime. . . .' The English passion for paddling is always proof against the English climate.

The pre-bikini age. The sands at
Yarmouth (ABOVE) and at Southsea
(RIGHT) in the 'nineties. Over-exposure
to the sun was not a risk that bothered
holiday-makers in the Victorian age.

The poorest of the poor, among whom, ironically, were many of the most hard-working, probably had less leisure than the rest of the community; a dispensation perhaps fortunate for themselves, for a good deal of their spare time, such as it was, would be spent in the gin shop or the tavern, not so much for the enjoyment of companionship as for that of blessed oblivion.

For the office worker, the counter clerk, the warehouseman and others of a similar occupational status, leisure was often restricted by the time it took to travel to and from work on foot. But, in the summer months especially, the City clerk or shop assistant would probably arrive home in time to spend part of the evening in one of the various tea gardens that were popular places to go to. Here families could be taken without risk to their respectability, and at moderate cost. Or a young man, if he were unmarried, might spend his evening in a tavern with male friends, or at one of those forerunners of the cabaret where refreshment and entertainment, not always of the most refined type, were combined. Typical of such establishments for Men Only, were the Cyder Cellars in Maiden Lane, where Percival Leigh's Mr Pips went after a visit to Astley's Circus and had 'Kidneys and Stout, then a small glass of *Aqua-Vitae*

Cremorne Gardens in Chelsea, 1858. This, the most popular of London's outdoor places of amusement, offered dancing, concerts, theatrical entertainments and a circus, as well as food and drink.

and water, and thereto a Cigar,' listening meanwhile to glees and comical ditties, of which 'the song of Sam Hall the chimney sweep going to be hanged' was voted the most enjoyable. And all for a modest outlay of two shillings and sixpence, including fourpence for the waiter.

The tea garden, as distinct from the coffee house, which was a purely metropolitan institution, used largely as an unofficial place of business and hence patronised almost exclusively by men, was often the offshoot of a surburban public house. Behind the premises in the open air, beer, wine and spirits were to be had, as well as tea and a variety of plebeian snacks. Some tea gardens were quite small, with only a few chairs and tables and perhaps not more than a couple of waiters. Others were large bustling establishments with boxes or rustic shelters to accommodate the more affluent patrons, the *hoi polloi* being left to sort themselves out at communal tables. Boz's description of one such garden gives a very lively impression of the atmosphere and the clientèle:

The heat is intense . . . and the people, of whom there are additional parties arriving every moment, look as warm as the tables which have been recently painted, and have the appearance of being red-hot. What a dust and noise! Men and women – boys and girls – sweethearts and married people – babies in arms, and children in chaises – pipes and shrimps – cigars and periwinkles – tea and tobacco. Gentlemen, in alarming waistcoats . . . promenading about, three abreast . . . ladies with great, long white pocket-handkerchiefs like small table-cloths, in their hands, chasing one another on the grass in the most playful and interesting manner, with the view of attracting the attention of the aforesaid gentlemen – husbands in perspective ordering bottles of ginger-beer for the objects of their affections, with a lavish disregard of expense; and the said objects washing down huge quantities of 'shrimps' and 'winkles', with an equal disregard of their bodily health and subsequent comfort – boys, with great silk hats just balanced on the top of their heads, smoking cigars, and trying to look as though they liked them – gentlemen in pink shirts and blue waistcoats, occasionally upsetting either themselves or somebody else, with their own canes.

At some of the larger tea gardens the proceedings were enlivened by music, dancing and fireworks, and occasionally by balloonists ascending from the grounds. Entertainments of a more elaborate kind were provided at Cremorne Gardens in Chelsea, the largest and most famous of all the London tea gardens. Here from time to time visitors could watch a tight-rope crossing of the Thames, and among other attractions were the reconstruction of a medieval tournament, an illuminated pagoda, a ballroom with accommodation for four thousand dancers, two theatres and a circus.

The poor in search of recreation usually found it at the pub.

St Giles's Fair, still held every year in the main street at Oxford, was a great occasion in Victorian days, when it still retained something of the atmosphere of the original Tudor festivities.

CIRCUS

GRAND SELECTION OF NOVELTY
DAY PERFORMANCE
On SATURDAY, March 21, 1840.

Doors will be Opened at ONE, and Commence at TWO precisely.

Under the Immediate and

DISTINGUISHED PATRONAGE
OF THE RIGHT HONOURABLE THE

Earl & Countess of MORTON
THE RIGHT HONOURABLE THE

Earl & Countess of BUCHAN,
AND THE HONOURABLE

BOUVERIE F. PRIMROSE.

Mr COOKE, begs, in the most friendly manner, to assure all the Directors and Masters of

PUBLIC CHARITY SCHOOLS,
And other Useful Institutions, that on a Children and Servants connected with the Charities, and attended by the Directors,

MAY WITNESS THE DAY PERFORMANCE ENTIRELY FREE OF EXPENSE.

FETE OF PEKIN.

AFRICAN COCOA NUT DANCE !
SURPRISING AND PECULIAR FEATS OF HORSEMANSHIP.

ACT OF DOUBLE LEAPING !!

I'D BE A BUTTERFLY.
THE DANCING STEED,

COOKE'S CIRCUS.   NICOLSON STREET.

The TOAD in a HOLE.
WONDERS OF THE OLYMPIANS
Messrs JAMES and GEORGE COOKE.

A FAVOURITE PAS SUEL ON THE ELASTIC CORDE BY MISS EMMA JANE COOKE.

SOMERSET ROPE-DANCER

THESSALIAN GAMES AND TRIAL OF SKILL

Mr COOKE, Jun.
Mr SPRAKE.

MASQUERADE BALL ON HORSEBACK !
The Dance of Follies on their Gay Steeds.

FRONT BOXES, 3s. SIDE BOXES, 2s. PIT, 1s. GAL. 6d.

The EARL of WEMYSS and MARCH, and
the Hon. HENRY COVENTRY.

THE FARMERS OF MIDLOTHIAN

OPPOSITE: The travelling showman was a familiar figure all over England, a type of seedy impresario who presented freaks, variety turns or crude melodrama at fairgrounds. Dickens in *Sketches by Boz* (Greenwich Fair) describes the most famous of these entertainments, Richardson's Show.
LEFT: Then, as now, the Zoo in Regent's Park was a big attraction and a ride on the elephant a long-remembered childhood thrill.

OVERLEAF: The popularity of the Prince of Wales (later Edward VII), though liable to fluctuation, was considerably boosted by his marriage in March 1863 to Alexandra, Princess of Denmark. London gave itself over to a junketing such as it had not enjoyed since the opening of the Great Exhibition in '51. Holman Hunt's painting, *London Bridge at Night*, shows the festivities in full swing.

Cooke's travelling circus was famous throughout the country. Traditional circus acts were combined with elaborate spectacles and pantomime.

The Egyptian Hall in Piccadilly attracted a variety of audiences. Here the original Siamese Twins appeared, General Tom Thumb was 'at home',

Albert Smith lectured on his ascent of Mont Blanc, spiritualist séances were held, and Maskelyne and Cook gave their famous displays of legerdemain.

THE SHOWMAN.

Concanen lith.

Stannard & Son, imp.t

WRITTEN BY

COMPOSED BY

CHAS. LINDA,   J. WOOLLEY,

SUNG WITH THE GREATEST SUCCESS
BY

HYRAM TRAVERS.

LONDON, HOPWOOD & CREW, 42 NEW BOND ST.

Pr 3/-

OPPOSITE: The most famous theatrical partnership in the history of the English theatre, that of Gilbert and Sullivan, began in 1871 and lasted for more than twenty years. A first night at the Savoy Theatre, where eight of their fourteen operas were produced, was an outstanding social event.

Circuses, until well into the Victorian era, were a standard form of popular entertainment, as distinct from the amusements of the nobility and gentry, and were frequently patronised by family parties. The acts, however tawdry they may have seemed, showed considerably more variety and imagination than the circus acts of today, with their stereotyped routines and predictable thrills. The enterprising Mr William Cooke, one of the most famous of itinerant showmen, included among his turns a Fête of Pekin, 'got up with the strictest correctness of costume, emblematic accessories, etc., characteristic of the Tartar Chinese', and Thessalian Games and Trials of Skill, 'showing various exercises of the Conisterium or Ancient Gymnasium', performed by a quartette with the singularly un-Hellenic names of Tomkinson, Twist, Baker and Steward; these and other spectacular divertissements being followed by a 'Comic

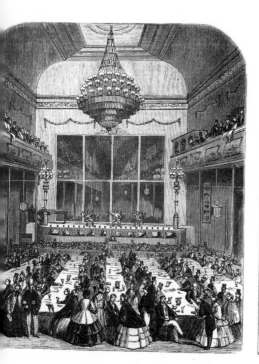

A popular place of mid-Victorian entertainment was the tavern music hall. Not all were as luxurious or as well conducted as the Lord Raglan in Bloomsbury, where there was less risk than at some such establishments of bringing a blush to the cheek of a young person.

A garden party at Holland House, 1875. The tradition of Holland House, established early in the era under the autocratic aegis of the celebrated Lady Holland as a stamping ground for political society, was carried on for many years by her successor, Mary Augusta, Lady Holland.

277

Equestrian Scena, with mechanical changes, metamorphoses, etc., etc., called The Toad in the Hole'.

For many years the most popular circus in London was Astley's in Westminster Bridge Road, where Ducrow, the famous horseman appeared in what were known as equestrian dramas. From being an ordinary circus, Astley's gradually expanded into something that combined the usual circus turns with music hall and melodrama, though the emphasis was still on horse-flesh. In the 'fifties and 'sixties the great attraction was *Mazeppa*, which was revived again and again. Its most sensational star was the American actress, Adah Isaacs Menken, who, in a state of decorous *déshabillé*, and tied to the back of a horse enacting the part of a fiery steed, thrilled audiences with her performance as the unfortunate Page of the Polish legend.

As means of public transport began to improve, the popularity of the circus and the tea garden started to decline. People were able to go further afield and so needed to rely no longer on local entertainments. They could now go for excursions by train and river steamers, or easily get from one part of town to another by omnibus.

This improvement in the mobility of the public was a reflection of improvements in social and economic conditions generally. Not only was there more leisure, there was more money – if only a very little more – in the pockets of the artisan, the small tradesman and their like, to spend on getting about and on entertainments, social occasions and holidays.

But entertainment was not the sole objective of a good many; leisure was increasingly devoted to self-improvement, and Mechanics' Institutes, of which there was one in almost every large town, and similar semi-educational establishments had no difficulty in filling their lecture halls and class rooms; for nowhere else could the working man, if studiously inclined, go to improve his education. Not until 1845 was a bill introduced in Parliament – and then against stiff opposition – to enable local authorities to establish free libraries. And it was not until seven years later that Manchester, the first city to do so, took advantage of the provisions of the act.

Not all the young men who spent their evenings at Mechanics' Institutes were mechanics, or indeed members of the working class. In fact, it was the exception rather than the rule to find a majority of working-class men at any Institute. The members of most of them were much more likely to be ambitious young men in trade, or else clerks, manufacturers, or skilled craftsmen.

This thirst for knowledge was reflected also in an enormous vogue for public lectures, at which, quite often, as many ladies were to be seen as gentlemen. In the 'forties and 'fifties lecturers of all kinds,

No figure in the Victorian scene was more widely or more consistently popular than Charles Dickens. The portrait (ABOVE) by his friend Ary Scheffer was painted when Dickens was forty-one and at the height of his fame. The sensational success of Dickens' readings from his own works, by causing him to tax himself beyond his strength, contributed to his death at the age of fifty-eight.

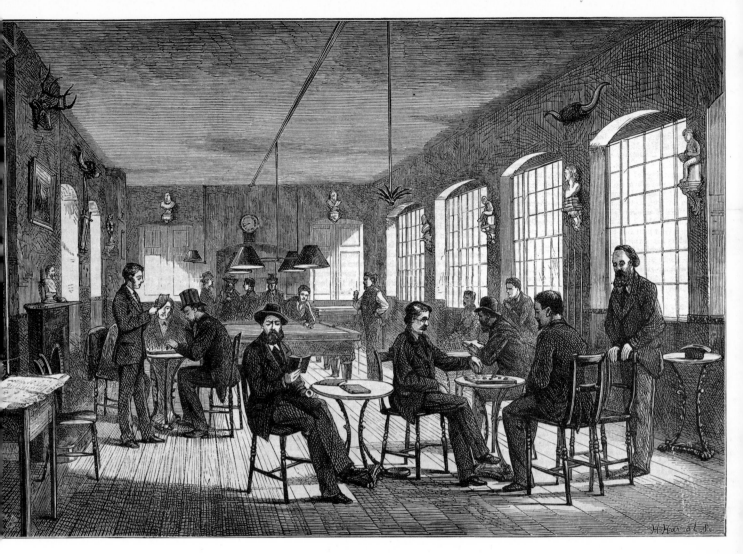

A spontaneous desire among the more
enlightened type of working man for an
alternative to the pub as a place in
which to spend the evening, led in the
'fifties and 'sixties to the formation
of working men's clubs, which sprang
up everywhere, offering opportunities
for self-improvement and rational
recreation in quiet surroundings.

Scientific curiosity was as keen among
the Victorians as it is today, though
fewer were sufficiently well-educated to
appreciate the possibilities or
understand the problems of science.
Lectures by well-known scientists, such
as Faraday, seen here addressing an
audience at the Royal Society in 1846,
were usually crowded to capacity.

some of them with decidedly dubious credentials, expounded their views or theories or recounted their experiences to packed audiences. In London alone the spate of lectures given within the space of a few weeks in 1855 included Mr T.H.Huxley discoursing on The Natural History of Man, Signor Monti on Ancient and Modern Sculpture, Mr W.Knight on Turkey and the Turks, Mr W.M. Thackeray on Humour and Charity, and Mr E.Jekyll on Siege Operations in connection with Sebastopol. Besides these, there were during the same period innumerable lectures on other subjects, including lectures in series that were given at various learned and scientific societies.

The spoken word seems to have had an irresistible fascination for the Victorians. It was an era not only of marathon talkers, but of instinctive listeners. Gladstone could, and unfortunately did on occasions, speak for three or four hours at a stretch, and other politicians, equally long-winded, were often listened to with grave attention as they held forth on matters of little or no importance. Preachers, especially in early Victorian days, went on and on and on. A Sunday sermon seldom lasted less than an hour, and a zealot such as Spurgeon could keep his congregation wrapt for a whole evening with none of the promotional gimmicks or unctuous earnestness of the modern evangelist.

Though earnestness was in the air, it would be wrong to suppose that the Victorians took their pleasures sadly. The Great Exhibition of 1851, the apogee of their earnest intentions and still more earnest endeavours, was for the great majority merely the occasion for a spree. In the one hundred and forty days that the Exhibition was open to the public, there were just over six million visitors, and during the final week nearly 110,000 people paid for admission in a single day.

The main purpose of the Great Exhibition was, of course, to benefit trade and industry, but it is doubtful whether trade or industry got more out of it in increased business than did the public in the way of innocent pleasure. The attraction of the Exhibition, both to the imagination and the eye, can be gauged by the impression it made on a little girl who noted in her diary:

I declare when the organs are playing and you hear them and look down from the gallery it is beautiful, exquisite . . . the nave is so fairy-paradisy-like a looking place that when you gaze from the top to the bottom down the immense length it seems surely this cannot be built by men. . . . Oh, it was Eden itself. I wished all the people away no one to jostle against and I should have thought among those beautiful works of art that I had dropped from the earth onto the abode of fairies and Peries,

The band enclosure in Kensington Gardens was a favourite summertime resort of mid-Victorian crowds.

oh, that silver and ebony inkstand with a deer and a fawn and the ink-stands formed of stumps of trees all in chaste silver – it did not look at all like what it was, it was lovely.

The luxuriant style and observant eye of the young diarist were later turned to good account in the novels that she wrote under the pseudonym of Ouida.

Most of those who visited the Exhibition went not so much for instruction, nor even out of curiosity, but simply to enjoy themselves; and if statistics of what was consumed in the refreshment courts is anything to go by, enjoy themselves they certainly did. Even by Victorian standards the collective appetite of the visitors seems prodigious. Between them they managed to get through 113 tons of meat, 33 tons of ham, sandwiches and patties beyond computation, nearly a million Bath buns, more than 870,000 buns of other sorts, 32,000 quarts of cream, and pastries, fruit and cheese galore. All this was washed down with well over a million bottles of soft drinks, the Commissioners of the Exhibition having decided, perhaps wisely in view of the number of visitors expected and the cheapness of beer and spirits, that no alcohol should be served.

Crowds far larger and drawn from all corners of the world thronged Hyde Park in 1851 to see the Great Exhibition, whose magnetic force George Cruikshank epitomised in his frontispiece to Mayhew's *The World's Show*.

Getting drunk was an easy and traditional way for the poor to occupy their leisure, particularly in the great industrial towns, and for a considerable part of the Victorian era there was not much else for them to do. In the country there were various kinds of sports to watch or take part in, such as whippet-racing or the flying of pigeons, which were, as they still are, popular amusements among miners. But not all sports were by any means so innocent and a good many were brutal in the extreme. Bull- and bear-baiting by ferocious dogs was still going on in parts of the West Country till well after 1840. Bare-knuckle prize-fighting, in which savage injuries were often inflicted, was not at all uncommon. In Lancashire a popular sport was 'purring', in which two contestants kicked each other with clogs until one or the other was too badly battered to continue. Cock-fighting, often with spurs attached to the birds' legs, went on until well into the 'sixties, despite the fact that it had been prohibited by law in 1849. Rat-catching by terriers was also widely enjoyed, and enormous bets were laid on both cocks and dogs. The Marquis of Hastings, a typical profligate ass of the period, thought nothing of wagering five hundred or a thousand pounds on the number of rats a favoured terrier could kill in an hour, the dog and its victims being penned up in a space some eight feet by ten

ABOVE: Gambling, although not yet so widespread, highly organised, and insidious as it is today, already impoverished the lives and families of many who could ill afford the sacrifices it demanded. It also enriched a few, among them indolent swells such as Millais portrayed in his drawing, *The Race Meeting*.

LEFT: The most notorious as well as the most recherché brothel of the 'fifties was Kate Hamilton's, off Leicester Square. The proprietress, a fat, swarthy and officious bawd, included among her patrons the Siamese Ambassador and, on the occasion of his visit to London in 1872, the Shah of Persia.

OPPOSITE: Ratting by trained terriers – some could kill more than seventy rats in an hour – was a so-called sport on which huge bets were made.

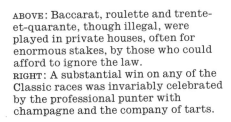

ABOVE: Baccarat, roulette and trente-et-quarante, though illegal, were played in private houses, often for enormous stakes, by those who could afford to ignore the law.
RIGHT: A substantial win on any of the Classic races was invariably celebrated by the professional punter with champagne and the company of tarts.

from which there was no means of escape. Morally strait-laced though the Victorian middle class liked to think itself, it was a long while before public opinion caught up with the law and some of the more brutal and already illegal forms of entertainment were finally stamped out.

In contrast with such pursuits were the innocent pleasures of the Victorian bourgeoisie, the At Homes, the musical evenings (then far more popular than they are now), the ladies sewing bees, the meetings of Friendly Societies, and sports such as cricket, rowing, billiards and especially archery, which, except for croquet, and until the craze for bicycling spread among ladies in the 'nineties, was almost the only sport that public opinion would allow women to indulge in.

OPPOSITE TOP: A favourite sport of the
'sixties was croquet, to which the
crinoline added a hazard not allowed
for in the rules.

RIGHT: In the 'seventies a sport much
in vogue was bicycle racing. The
'ordinary' or 'penny-farthing', though
a cumbersome and ill-balanced
contraption, could travel at twenty
miles an hour.

OPPOSITE BOTTOM: Without the boon of
Batman and other innocent delights of
TV, the Victorian juvenile was left
largely to its own devices on the
occasion of a party.

BELOW: A meeting of the Ladies
Archery Club at Kensington Gardens,
1900. Archery, one of the few sports
permitted to ladies, first became
popular in the 'sixties.

In London one of the most popular amusements was going to Hyde Park, either to stare or be stared at. Much innocuous delight was given to both parties. The East Carriage drive, nowadays crowded with buses and cars, would be jammed on a fine afternoon with the phaetons and barouches of the *haut monde*, attended by flunkeys 'up behind' in plush and powdered wigs, or a diminutive 'tiger' would appear in a cockaded top-hat and striped waistcoat, perched with stiffly folded arms on the rumble seat of some elegant curricle.

Expense is nowadays virtually the only factor that prevents the middle classes and the poor from enjoying the same amusements as the rich. It was not so in Victorian times. The economic factor was there, of course, but even if by some peculiar turn of fate the fun and games of the rich had been available to the whole community, ethical and religious scruples would still have led enormous numbers of people to condemn them and to try to prevent others from enjoying themselves as the upper classes did. An evening spent in playing whist, or dancing even so innocuous a measure as the quadrille, was looked upon in a great many households, especially in the nonconformist manufacturing towns, as worldly and therefore sinful. No difference was perceived, perhaps because it was deliberately not looked for, between a young girl taking a hand at loo with her brothers and sisters and the reckless idiot who, in a single night's play at Almacks, might throw away a fortune. Leisure was thought to be better employed in conversation, no matter how trivial, in needlework, no matter how superfluous, or in listening to a reading from some improving book, no matter how dull, than in the sort of occupations with which well-brought-up young people of the upper classes amused themselves. The stoical endurance of boredom and discontent were rated more beneficial to the character than the enjoyment of innocent pastimes.

Dancing especially was frowned upon, but such is the perversity of human nature that, strange to say, it gradually became more and more popular. The waltz, first introduced in the days of the Regency, remained throughout Victoria's reign the favourite ballroom dance. The quadrille and later the polka and the lancers each enjoyed in their turn considerable popularity and were danced as vigorously at fashionable balls as they were at suburban hops. Evening parties at which there was no dancing might be described as Drums, Routs, Crushes, Soirées or Assemblies, according to their size and formality. At all of them there would be food and drink, sometimes provided on a truly lavish scale, although at musical parties, where presumably it was hoped that a more decorous atmosphere might prevail, it was more usual to serve tea.

May Day in an Oxfordshire village, *c.*1900. The tradition, dating from medieval times, of keeping the First of May as a day of festivity and dancing, persisted in many villages long after the Maypole had disappeared from towns and cities.

Punch and Judy were throughout the summer months the delight of every urban child, and if the origins of Guy Fawkes day were lost on most of them, the slogan 'Penny for the Guy!' certainly had a tangible sound about it. Adults as well as children cashed in on the annual observance, often parading Guys of fierce and fanciful appearance.

Those who held cards and dancing to be the Devil's handiwork naturally looked with revulsion upon the theatre. In thus averting their gaze they were not alone. For other and perhaps better reasons, a good many less prejudiced people looked upon the theatre with revulsion too. The trouble was that until comparatively late in the Victorian era there was hardly a single dramatist then alive, except for T. W. Robertson, author of *Caste*, the first so-called realistic drama, whose plays were worth intelligent consideration. Not only in the provinces, but in London too, the boards creaked beneath loads of trash by authors whose names have since sunk into well-merited oblivion. And yet there were many more theatres in England then than there are now, and touring companies, of which Mr Vincent Crummles's was no exaggeration of the type, packed in attentive, if wholly uncritical audiences.

Times change, but audiences, it seems, do not. Night after night in their own homes audiences now gaze with as little exercise of their critical faculties at entertainments as false and vacuous as anything written by Sheridan Knowles or H. J. Byron, two of the most popular of mid-Victorian dramatists. However, the alchemy of public taste is strange, and while such dramatists still flourished, a sudden renaissance began in the English theatre and before the era ended fashionable audiences had become as appreciative of Pinero, Wilde and Shaw as they had been of their mildewed predecessors a few years earlier.

Less change was noticeable in the traditions of that theatrical megalith of Victorian times, the music hall. It was much the same at the end of the era as it had been at the beginning – boisterous, elementary, stereotyped, and now and then overshadowed by moments of excruciating sentimentality. It remained throughout the whole of the era a cheap and easy way of filling in the leisure hours of evening. It touched few of the emotions with anything like genuine feeling and gave everybody a good measure of laughter.

An off-shoot of the music hall, of which a fatuous and tactless parody exists in the so-called Black and White Minstrels of today, were the troupes of 'nigger minstrels' whose exploitation of the accident of birth that produces Negroes was enjoyed by simple-minded audiences. Curiosity drew Gideon Mantell to one such entertainment. He records in his journal for 1847 a visit to St James's Theatre 'to hear the Ethiopian Serenaders – six fellows painted black . . . singing a few pretty ditties, and playing the buffoon! And this night after night to crowded houses. A very melancholy characteristic of the Times'.

To those who abhorred the theatre, the music hall was perhaps the

The appeal of the Victorian music hall was either to sentiment or vulgarity, or to jingoistic patriotism – and the gallery was packed every night.

ABOVE: The immense pleasure that Oscar Wilde gave to Victorian audiences was forgotten overnight when it was discovered that he, like many of themselves, led a private life that was not above reproach. A master of paradox, he created none more absurd than that of his own appearance. His love of self-advertisement betrayed him into adopting a vulgar eccentricity in dress that he would have abhorred in literature.
OPPOSITE: The most luminous star of the Victorian theatre, Ellen Terry, with her daughter Edith Craig, in Irving's production of *Henry VIII* at the Lyceum Theatre, 1892.

vilest form of Thespian iniquity, for it was the most uninhibited. It not only dealt with such painful realities as lust, marital relations, insobriety and greed, but dealt with them as subjects for jesting. Worse still, it often made, like the circus, a wanton display of the female form divine, than which nothing could be more affronting to the nonconformist conscience and therefore ripe for condemnation. And so, taking it by and large, a good time was had by all.

Opera, like the theatre, was for some time strongly disapproved of by the Victorian kill-joys and with the more adamant remained forever suspect. Professor Kellett, speaking of Victorian ethics, pointed out that 'it was not until Jenny Lind conquered the prejudice that anything but oratorio was considered safe,' for Jenny Lind's exemplary behaviour, both in public and private, was well known and no doubt contributed to her stupendous popularity, which was in its day of Beatle-like immensity.

There was, however, no one of Jenny Lind's spotless integrity and universal fame to give respectability to women's sports, and it was not until forty years after she had retired from the operatic stage, at the age of twenty-nine, that anything more vigorous than shuttlecock and battledore was approved of for women – except, of course, riding to hounds, but that had always been a perquisite of the rich and had needed no imprimatur.

Towards the end of the century came ominous signs that women were beginning seriously to consider ways and means of achieving their emancipation from the strangleholds of masculine supremacy. These signs included their assertion of the right to spend their leisure in amusements decidedly unladylike. It was not a pleasant prospect, though fortunately such futile feminine fancies were entertained mainly by a minority of uninfluential cranks. All the same, it was disconcerting to see the number of women who at this period began to take up such sports as hockey, tennis and cycling. Where such unsexing might take them, there was no knowing, and certainly no suspicion that ultimately it would be onto the Centre Court at Wimbledon or across the Channel from Dover to Cap Griz Nez. Ladies wishing to get to France at the beginning of Victoria's reign went not under their own steam, but under that of the cross-Channel packet. They went mostly as diplomats' wives or as distinguished visitors. It was not until the 'sixties that the middle classes also began to go abroad, having established by common custom their right to an annual holiday in the summer. That the working classes might also be entitled to holidays was still regarded in the 'fifties as a subversive doctrine, calculated, like education, to breed discontent and thoughts of independence.

Throughout the Victorian age amateur sport remained a cottage industry, its commercial possibilities scarcely realised. Sport for sport's sake was the unimaginative axiom of those who enjoyed athletic pastimes. 'Fish' Smart (TOP LEFT), a famous Norfolk skating star, acquired little but glory for his feats, like the champions of putting (TOP RIGHT) and in Scotland of curling (CENTRE), who won only the pleasure of recognition.

Cricket, through the MCC (established in 1788), was better organised than any other sport. Outstanding members of the All England eleven in 1864–5, when the team toured Australia, were Thomas Heyward (LEFT) and Robert Carpenter (RIGHT).

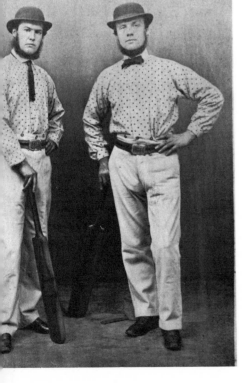

This annual migration of the urban middle classes, to which the expansion of the railway system had given impetus, had begun some ten years earlier. In 1841, a Baptist lay-preacher and temperance addict, living at Market Harborough in Leicestershire, arranged for the Midland Counties Railway Company to run a special train from Leicester to Loughborough, where a temperance meeting was to be held. The distance all told was twenty-six miles and the return fare a shilling a head. This trip was followed by others, on which the enterprising Baptist was paid a percentage on the number of tickets sold. Some twenty years later he began to organise excursions on a more ambitious scale, transporting parties to the Continent and back. This move was an immediate success and consolidated the fame and fortunes of his agency, still known throughout the world as that of Thomas Cook and Son.

In *All the Year Round*, then edited by Dickens, Edmund Yates wrote of the benefits that Cook's excursions brought to many humble, hardworking citizens, whose parents would have thought a journey to the moon no more improbable for themselves than a holiday in the Lake District or the Highlands:

The shorter excursions in England attract tradesmen and their wives, merchants, clerks away for a week's holiday, roughing it with a knapsack, and getting over an immense number of miles before they return; swart mechanics, who never seem to be able entirely to free themselves from the traces of their life-long labour, but who . . . are by no means the worse informed, and are generally the most interested about the places they visit.

Not everyone was as enterprising as Cook's swart mechanics. Many of the genteel middle class preferred the more refined atmosphere of one or other of the various watering places, such as Cheltenham, Matlock, Buxton or Torquay, which became fashionable or increased in popularity at about the middle of the century. Swart mechanics and their like would hardly have been welcome at such resorts, where day trippers were strongly discouraged and their behaviour frowned upon. Nor did their conduct always recommend them to foreigners. Cook's Whitsun trips to the Continent were reported by Yates as being

. . . mostly composed of very high-spirited people, whose greatest delight is 'having a fling', and who do Paris, and rush through France, and through Switzerland . . . carry London everywhere about them in dress, habits and conversation, and rush back, convinced that they are great travellers.

291

It is to be hoped that the impression they must have left was modified by visitors later in the year:

From these roysterers the July and September excursionists differ greatly; ushers and governesses, practical people from the provinces, and representatives of the better style of the London mercantile community . . . all travel as if impressed with the notion that they are engaged in fulfilling the wishes of a life-time, in a pleasant duty never to be repeated.

As the working man's right to an annual summer holiday came more and more to be accepted, however reluctantly by some employers, so did seaside towns and watering places begin to expand and flourish. Towns such as Blackpool, still the favourite holiday resort of Lancastrians, grew rapidly, as did Scarborough and Bridlington in Yorkshire, and Margate and Ramsgate to meet the needs of working-class holiday makers from London. The English are a ritual-loving people and once the ritual of two weeks' annual leisure had been established, it also became a ritual to return year after year to the same place.

For most people throughout the Victorian era, leisure was seen as a reward only to be expected in return for a fair day's work. Time has not wholly disproved the validity of this proposition, but that it has been modified is beyond dispute, though the values by which we measure that which is fair in such cases differ considerably from the values of the Victorians. Considerations of humanity and health play a greater part in industrial relations. Economic disparities are less pronounced, the penalties of poverty less severe, and some degree of social security has been established. Yet the fact remains that more leisure is now expected for less work. Looking back on the Victorians' achievements, and on all that we have inherited from their energy, resource and diligence, it would seem that there is still something to be said for the meaning which they attached to leisure.

The infancy of Ariel, 1901. The electrophone, a 'picturesque and entertaining adjunct' of the London telephone system and a forerunner of sound broadcasting, was listened to with rapt mystification by audiences who made a night of it at Soho's 'electrophone salon'.

Sources of illustrations

The illustrations on pages 11, 20 *top*, 36 and 68 are reproduced by courtesy of Her Majesty the Queen.

The author and publishers wish to thank all those who have given permission for objects, documents and books from their collections to be photographed and reproduced in this book:
Thomas Agnew and Sons, 66 *top*. Amalgamated Engineering Union, 206. Ashmolean Museum, Oxford, 274–5, 282 *top*. Gordon Barnes Esq., 62 *top*. Barnes Museum of Cinematography, 47. Bettman Archive, 60, 239. Birmingham Public Libraries, 183 *bottom*. British Museum, (by courtesy of the Trustees), 52 *bottom*, 111 *right*, 133 *bottom*, 137 *right*, 168 *top and bottom*, 186, 272 *bottom*. British Railways Board, 251. Cambridge Folk Museum, 49, 91 *bottom*, 171 *top right and bottom*, 215 *top right*, 228 *centre*, 291 *top left and bottom*. Cheltenham Ladies' College, 173 *bottom*. City Museum and Art Gallery, Birmingham, 81 *bottom*, 242 *bottom*. Country Life, 126 *top*, 216 *bottom*. Courtauld Institute of Art, 65 *bottom*, 65 *top*. Sir Robin Darwin, 56. Fitzwilliam Museum (Glaisher Collection), Cambridge, 81 *centre left*, 110, 111 *left*, 245 *bottom*. James Forbes Esq., 41 *left*. General Post Office (by courtesy of H.M. Postmaster General), 245 *top*. William Gordon Davis, 81 *centre right*, 97 *top*, 139 *bottom*, 171 *top left*, 229 *top*, 233, 235 *bottom*, 254, 272 *top right*, 277 *right*, 285 *bottom*, 287 *top*. Guildhall Museum and Library, 64 *bottom*, 82, 100, 104, 120, 193 *top*, 199 *top*, 214 *top*, 215 *top left and bottom*, 216 *top left and right*, 218, 237 *bottom*, 247 *top and bottom*, 248 *top*, 256, 260 *centre*, 268, 277 *left*, 283 *bottom*. James Hall, Greenock, 207 *top*. Mrs J.B. Haywood, 228 *top*. Hereford City Library, 138 *bottom*, 211, 217 *bottom*, 222 *top*. Keystone Press, 97 *bottom*. Leeds Museum of Education, 152 *bottom left and right*, 153 *bottom*, 155 *top and bottom*. Liberty & Co., 131 *top*. London Museum (by courtesy of the Trustees), 22–3 *top*, 240 *bottom*, 252. London Transport Executive, 238 *centre left and right, and bottom*. Manchester City Art Gallery, 54. Mander and Mitchenson Collection, 28, 273, 276, 278 *top*, 288 *bottom*, 289. Mansell Collection, 61 *top*, 62 *bottom*, 88 *top*, 94, 95 *top and bottom*, 112, 146, 156 *top*, 160 *top*, 172, 176, 188 *bottom*, 193 *bottom*, 203, 207 *bottom*, 210 *top and right*, 212 *top*, 213 *top*, 214 *bottom*, 225, 240 *top left*, 279 *top and bottom*, 283 *top right*. Edward Marno Esq., 72 *top*. Ministry of Works (Crown copyright), 21 *bottom*. Morris Collection, Greenwich Public Libraries, 219 *top*. Morris Museum, Borough of Waltham Forest, 76, 77. Museum of British Transport, 240 *top right*, 242 *top*, 243, 248 *bottom*, 249. Museum of English Rural Life, Reading, 90 *bottom*, 126 *top and bottom*, 127 *top and bottom*, 138 *bottom*, 156 *bottom*, 183 *bottom*, 189 *bottom*, 210 *bottom*, 211, 216 *bottom*, 217 *bottom*, 222 *top*, 226 *bottom*, 286. National Monuments Record, 34, 61 *bottom*, 62 *top*, 65 *left*, 71 *top right*, 75 *top*, 81 *bottom*, 83, 99 *bottom*, 164, 165, 180, 181 *left*, 221, 238 *top*, 253, 257, 270–1. National Portrait Gallery, 15, 20 *bottom right*, 21 *top right*, 27, 29, 39/1–4, 43 *top*, 69 *top*, 148 *top*, 178 *top, centre and bottom*, 188 *top*, 278 *bottom*. National Union of Agricultural Workers, 210 *bottom*. Oxford Public Libraries,

270–1. Radio Times Hulton Picture Library, 20 *bottom left*, 21 *top left and centre*, 25, 26 *top and bottom*, 39/5–9, 40, 43 *bottom*, 66 *bottom*, 71 *top left*, 73 *top*, 98 *top left*, 128 *top*, 134, 138 *top*, 142 *top left and bottom*, 148 *bottom*, 150 *bottom*, 160 *bottom*, 163 *top and bottom*, 170, 173 *top*, 183 *top*, 184, 199 *bottom*, 207 *centre*, 228 *bottom*, 246 *bottom*, 261, 264, 265, 267 *top and bottom*. Dora Raeburn, 37, 116, 139 *top*, 140 *top right and bottom left*, 141 *top and bottom*. Royal Institute of British Architects, 151 *top*. Rugby School, 149. Salvation Army, 192 *left and centre*. Science Museum, 74, 234, 250 *bottom*, 258 *left and top right*, 259 *top*, 262 *top, centre and bottom*. M.Georges Sirot, 41 *right*. Edwin Smith, 47, 80, 248 *bottom*, 249, 260 *top and bottom*. G.Stedman Jones Esq., 23 *bottom*. Tate Gallery, 17, 55, 109, 157, 167, 185, 224, 241. Taunt Collection, Oxford City Libraries, 286. Thankful Sturdee Collection, Lewisham Local History Department, 152 *top*. Penny Tweedie, 169 *left top and bottom and right*. Victoria and Albert Museum (Crown copyright), 24 *left*, 31 *bottom*, 58, 70 *top*, 75 *bottom left*, 117, 140 *top left and bottom right*, 195, 205, 215 *top left*, 223, 226 *top*, 236–7 *top*, 266 *left and right*. Sir Oliver C.E.Welby Bart., 65 *bottom*. Messrs William Wimms, 109. Mrs Francis Winham, 103.

The following are from the author's collection: 10, 12, 13 *top and bottom left*, 18, 35 *top and bottom left and right*, 42, 46, 48, 118–9, 142 *top right*, 144, 190–1, 192 *right*, 220, 272 *left*, 284 *top*.

The following illustrations were taken from books, periodicals and catalogues in the collections of the author, A.Hayter, Dora Raeburn, Michael Raeburn, Gareth Stedman Jones, the early children's book collection in the London Borough of Hammersmith Public Libraries, and from the libraries of the British Museum, the Science Museum and the Victoria and Albert Museum:
Album Lingua Floris, 38. *The Alphabet of Flowers* (1877), 158, 159. Ada Ballin, *The Science of Dress* (1885), 130 *top*, 135 *bottom*. William Bardwell, *What a House Should Be* (1873), 72 *bottom*. Robert Hall Baynes, *The Illustrated Book of Sacred Poems* (1867), 177. 'Cuthbert Bede BA', *The Adventures of Mr Verdant Green* (1853–7), 174. Mrs Isabella Beeton, *The Englishwoman's Cookery Book*, 89 *top*. William Booth, *In Darkest England* (1890), 196. John C.Bourne, *Drawings of the London and Birmingham Railway* (1839), 244, 246 *top*. J.C. Burrow, *'Mongst Mines and Miners* (1893), 208. *Cassell's Household Guide*, 94. Mrs Charles Clarke, *High-Class Cookery Recipes* (1892), 106 *right*. D. Croal Thomson, *Fifty Years of Art, 1849–99* (1900), 45 *top and bottom*. George Cruickshank, *The Bachelor's Own Book* (1844), 93. Charles Dickens, *Nicholas Nickleby* (1838), 154. Charles Dickens, *Sketches by Boz* (1837), 236 *bottom*. Gustave Doré and Blanchard Jerrold, *London* (1872), 65 *top*, 101 *top*, 32, 250 *top*. Richard Doyle, *Bird's Eye View of Society* (1864), 284 *bottom*. Richard Doyle, *Manners and Customs of ye Englyshe* (1849), 123, 255, 280. A.C.Ewald, *Earl of Beaconsfield KG, and his Times* (1882), 26 *centre*. Charles E.Francatelli, *The Modern Cook* (1862), 86/2, 4–10. E.Geldart,

The Art of Garnishing Churches (1884) 187. E.C. Grenville Murray, *Under the Lens* (1885), 283 *top left*. F.Hottenroth, *Le Costume chez les peuples anciens et modernes* (1896), 132–3 *top*. London *Interiors* (1841), 189 *top*. E.McHardie, '*Tony*', *the Child Drunkard*, 197 *bottom*. Sir Theodore Martin, *The Early Years of the Prince Consort* (1867), 24 *right*. Henry Mayhew, *The Great World of London* (1856), 282 *bottom*. Henry Mayhew, *The World's Show* (1851), 30 *top*, 31 *top*, 281. *Moral Poems* (1837), 194. James Owen, *Natural History for Beginners*, 153 *top*. Augustus W.N.Pugin, *Apology for the Revival of Christian Architecture* (1843), 181 *right*. *The Queen and Her Empire* (1900), 52 *top*. G.Herbert Rodwell, *The Pic-Nic* (1842), 90 *top*. George R.Sims, *Living London* (1902), 67 *top and bottom*, 84, 219 *bottom left and right*, 288 *top*, 292. Adolphe Smith and J.Thompson, *Street Life in London* (1877), 64 *top*, 69 *bottom*, 99 *top*, 129, 209, 217 *top centre and right*, 229 *bottom*, 269, 287 *bottom*. Alexis Soyer, *The Gastronomic Regenerator* (1852), 86/1, 3, 11–2, 88 *bottom*. Alexis Soyer, *The Modern Housewife* (1849), 98 *top right*, 108 *top and bottom*. Charles Spencer, *The Modern Bicycle* (1876), 258–9 *bottom*. Mrs H.M.Stanley (Dorothy Tennant), *London Street Arabs* (1890), 105 *top left*, 212 *bottom*. 'A Teacher', *Familiar Dialogues for Sunday-Schools* (1850), 182. Walter Thornbury, *Old and New London* (1889), 19, 105 *top right*, 128 *bottom*, 250 *centre*.

Art Union Journal (1851), 75 *bottom right*. *The Builder* (1848), 59. *The Graphic* (1869), 291 *top right and centre;* (1870), 132 *bottom*, 222 *bottom;* (1873), 89 *bottom*, 98 *top left;* (1875), 193 *bottom*, 285 *top;* (1883), 122; (1885), 71 *top left;* (1889), 70 *bottom*. *Illustrated London News* (1846), 22 *bottom;* (1850), 105 *bottom*, 179; (1851), 32–3 *bottom;* (1852), 91 *top;* (1862), 150 *top;* (1867), 98 *bottom;* (1868), 213 *bottom;* (1881), 198; (1892), 197 *top*. *Moonshine* (1884), 13 *bottom left*. Professor Anderson's Psychomantic Reporter (1864), 199 *centre*. *Punch* (1877), 107 *bottom;* (1888), 114. Spurgeon's Almanack (1887), 87; (1889), 131 *bottom*, 200. *Vanity Fair* (1892), 136 *left*.

Catalogue of the Great Exhibition of 1851, 30 *bottom*, 32 *top left and right*, 33 *top left*, 73 *bottom*, 106 *left*. Catalogue of the 1862 Exhibition, 33 *top right*, 202. Catalogues of the Army & Navy Stores (1884), 121 *bottom*, 135 *top*, 136 *right;* (1897), 137 *left top;* (1900), 71 *bottom left*, 130 *bottom*, 137 *left bottom*, 227 Catalogues of Doulton and Co. (1882), 78, 81 *top;* (1883), 51; (1894), 79; (1895), 71 *bottom right*. Catalogue of Samuel Bros (c.1869), 121 *top*.

The majority of photographs in this book were taken by J.R.Freeman & Co. and Derrick Witty.

Index